W9-AFB-343

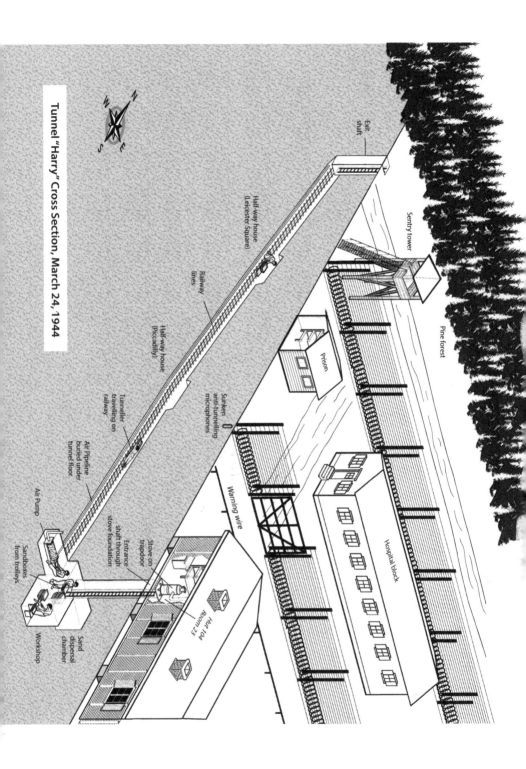

Tunnel "Harry" Cross Section, March 24, 1944

N W E S

Exit shaft

Sentry tower

Pine forest

Half-way house (Leicester Square)

Railway lines

Half-way house (Piccadilly)

Prison

Tunneller travelling on railway

Sunken anti-tunnelling microphones

Air Pipeline buried under tunnel floor

Air Pump

Sandboxes from trolleys

Warning wire

Stove on trapdoor

Entrance shaft through stove foundation

Hut 104 Room 23

Hospital block

Workshop

Sand dispersal chamber

Ted Barris is an award-winning author, journalist, and broadcaster. In addition to his on-air work for radio and television in the U.S. (NPR) and Canada (CBC, CTV, and TVOntario), he is a regular contributor to the *National Post* newspaper and such periodicals as *Esprit de Corps*, *Air Force*, *Legion*, and *Zoomer* (where his feature story on The Great Escape was short-listed for a National Magazine Award). Barris has authored seventeen non-fiction books. In 2011 he received the Canadian Minister of Veterans Affairs Commendation and in 2012 the Queen Elizabeth II Diamond Jubilee Medal. In 2014 *The Great Escape* received the Libris Award for Non-Fiction Book of the Year, and the U.S. Stalag Luft III Prisoners of War Association awarded Barris its civilian "Certificate of Honor." He is based in Toronto.

ALSO BY TED BARRIS

MILITARY HISTORY

*Behind the Glory: Canada's Role in the Allied Air War*

*Days of Victory: Canadians Remember, 1939–1945*
(with Alex Barris, 1st edition, 1995)

*Deadlock in Korea: Canadians at War, 1950–1953*

*Canada and Korea: Perspectives 2000* (contributor)

*Juno: Canadians at D-Day, June 6, 1944*

*Days of Victory: Canadians Remember, 1939–1945*
(Sixtieth Anniversary edition, 2005)

*Victory at Vimy: Canada Comes of Age, April 9–12, 1917*

*Breaking the Silence: Veterans' Untold Stories from the Great War
to Afghanistan*

OTHER NON-FICTION

*Fire Canoe: Prairie Steamboat Days Revisited*

*Rodeo Cowboys: The Last Heroes*

*Positive Power: The Story of the Edmonton Oilers Hockey Club*

*Spirit of the West: The Beginnings, the Land, the Life*

*Playing Overtime: A Celebration of Oldtimers' Hockey*

*Carved in Granite: 125 Years of Granite Club History*

*Making Music: Profiles from a Century of Canadian Music*
(with Alex Barris)

*101 Things Canadians Should Know About Canada* (contributor)

# THE GREAT ESCAPE

## THE UNTOLD STORY

## TED BARRIS

## DUNDURN
### TORONTO

**Library and Archives Canada Cataloguing in Publication**

Barris, Ted, author
The great escape : the untold story / Ted Barris.

Originally published: Toronto : Thomas Allen Publishers, [2013].
Includes bibliographical references and index.
ISBN 978-1-4597-2844-8 (pbk.)

1. Stalag Luft III. 2. World War, 1939-1945--Prisoners and
prisons, German. 3. Prisoners of war--Canada--Biography.
4. Prisoners of war--Germany--Biography. 5. Prisoner-of-war
escapes--Poland--Zaga´n. 6. World War, 1939-1945--Personal
narratives, Canadian. I. Title.

D805.5.S73B37 2014      940.54'72430922      C2014-905858-6

Cover design: Gordon Robertson
Cover image: Tony Pengelly Collection
Back cover image: US Air Force Academy, McDermott Library, Stalag Luft III Collections
Maps: Lightfoot Art & Design Inc.

2  3  4  5      18  17  16  15  14

Conseil des Arts du Canada  Canada Council for the Arts  Canadä  ONTARIO ARTS COUNCIL / CONSEIL DES ARTS DE L'ONTARIO / an Ontario government agency / un organisme du gouvernement de l'Ontario

We acknowledge the support of the **Canada Council for the Arts** and the **Ontario
Arts Council** for our publishing program. We also acknowledge the financial support
of the **Government of Canada** through the **Canada Book Fund** and **Livres Canada
Books**, and the **Government of Ontario** through the **Ontario Book Publishing Tax
Credit** and the **Ontario Media Development Corporation**.

Care has been taken to trace the ownership of copyright material used in this book.
The author and the publisher welcome any information enabling them to rectify
any references or credits in subsequent editions.

*J. Kirk Howard, President*

The publisher is not responsible for websites or their content unless they are
owned by the publisher.

Printed and bound in Canada.

Visit us at
Dundurn.com  |  @dundurnpress  |  Facebook.com/dundurnpress  |
Pinterest.com/dundurnpress

Dundurn
3 Church Street, Suite 500
Toronto, Ontario, Canada
M5E 1M2

To air force veteran Charley Fox and military history buff Dave Zink—both gone now—who challenged me to properly retell this great, great story.

# CONTENTS

The author and publisher gratefully acknowledge the permission granted to reproduce the copyright material in this book. Every effort has been made to trace copyright holders and to obtain their permission for the use of copyright material. The publisher apologizes for any errors or omissions and would be grateful if notified of any corrections that should be incorporated in future reprints or editions of this book.

The author would like to acknowledge the following for the use of published and unpublished works as follows:

*A Gallant Company*, Jonathan F. W. Vance, permission from copyright holder.

Air Force Association video interviews, 1970s and 1989, permission from rights holders National Air Force Museum of Canada, Trenton.

*Bonds of Wire*, Kingsley Brown, permission from copyright holder Ethel Alle.

*Forced March to Freedom*, Robert Buckham, permission from copyright holder Nancy Buckham.

Frank Sorensen collection, permission from Glenn, Stephen, and Vicki Sorensen.

*Goon in the Block*, Don Edy, permission from copyright holder.

*In Enemy Hands*, Daniel G. Dancocks, permission sought through Hurtig, Random House.

*It's All Pensionable Time*, George Sweanor, permission from copyright holder.

John Colwell diary, permission from copyright holder Harold Johnstone.

John Weir letters, permission from Mrs. Frances Weir.

*Lonesome Road*, George Harsh, permission from publisher W. W. Norton, New York.

*One Man's War: Sub Lieutenant R. E. Bartlett, RN Fleet Air Arm Pilot*, Stuart E. Soward, permission from copyright holder Sheila Soward.

*Serving and Surviving: An Airman's Memoirs*, John R. Harris, permission from copyright holder.

*The Great Escape*, Paul Brickhill, permission from rights holders David Higham Associates, UK.

*The Great Escape, Stalag Luft III (from the original drawings made by Ley Kenyon 1943)*, permission from copyright holders RAF Museum, Hendon, UK.

*The Tunnel King: The True Story of Wally Floody and the Great Escape*, Barbara Hehner, permission from copyright holder.

*They Were So Young*, Patricia Burns, permission from copyright holder.

"Tom, Dick and Harry of Stalag Luft III," Bob Nelson, unpublished manuscript, permission from Sally Hutchison.

# Acknowledgements

THE CONTEMPORARY ROAD to Zagan is nearly as inhospitable and neglected as it must have been in 1942, when the town became neighbour to a prisoner-of-war camp. Even when I travelled on it in 2010, most of the one hundred miles of road southeast of Berlin, primarily in western Poland, didn't seem to have ever enjoyed priority status. The post-Soviet-era asphalt was still as patchy, the lanes still as poorly marked, and the rough countryside terrain still encroaching the roadside shoulders right to the road surface as it likely had when the Nazis occupied Poland during the Second World War.

Likewise, the Zagan (the Polish spelling of Sagan) train station at the edge of town looked as if it hadn't enjoyed any remodelling since it was built in the early 1900s. When I walked inside, I could almost see the first wave of Great Escape fugitives hurrying through ticket queues and platform document checks by guards in the morning gloom on March 25, 1944, to get aboard the Breslau-to-Berlin express train without raising suspicion. And the trees—the omnipotent pine forest to the south—between the railway platforms and the prison camp looked as dense and claustrophobic as they must have been to the air force officers trying to escape a generation ago.

When I approached the actual North Compound site at Stalag Luft III, now overgrown with mature trees, dense underbrush, and weeds, I could see scattered bricks and concrete pads where the barracks huts had stood on blocks. None of the buildings remained. I could see the foundations of the infirmary, the cooler, and the coal store. Beyond it, farther south, I could see the fire pool, the cement floors of the kitchens (with scorched circles where huge soup cauldrons had boiled every day). Beyond them lay the brick foundation of the North Compound theatre (where a fourth tunnel, "George," has just recently been unearthed). And finally, on the surface of the still very sandy soil, I walked along a walkway of crushed stone with wooden borders, just twenty inches wide (the same width of the tunnel), showing above ground where tunnel "Harry" had stretched underground—some 336 feet—from the concrete pad beneath Hut 104 to beyond the Stalag Luft III fence, but just short of the woods.

I imagined about eighty POWs who had all served in one capacity or another in the manufacture of the tunnel excavation and its ancillary requirements (sand dispersal, security, intelligence, forgery, document production, tailoring, language study, compass manufacture, ration supplies, et cetera) making their way from inside the North Compound. I visualized one POW disappearing into "Harry" every three minutes through the night of March 24–25, travelling along the trolley way northbound (beneath where I stood in 2010), and then popping up from the other vertical shaft beyond the prison camp wire. This was the home of the Great Escape, or at least an attempt to cause enough havoc behind German enemy lines to suck away valuable manpower in the search and recapture of the escapers.

A few thousand feet away, I came to the cemetery of those who'd died in captivity during their existence at Stalag Luft III. Next to the individual tombstones, I found the stone memorial to the fifty Commonwealth air force officers murdered by the Gestapo after the breakout. Here, too, I sensed the blood of six Canadians, or at least the ashes in urns buried there during a ceremony on December 4, 1944 (the ashes later exhumed and reburied in the military cemetery at Poznan, Poland). This was the home of the Great Escape. This was the place where myth and reality had inspired books, documentaries, and Hollywood movies. Arriving there, walking there, remembering there in 2010, moved me emotionally, and moved me professionally to fulfill a longtime promise to my veteran friend, RCAF fighter pilot Charley Fox, to tell the story of the Great Escape the way it could and should be told—as a Canadian story.

Not only have I chosen to write this story as an homage to Charley Fox, who died in 2008, but here also I want to offer my gratitude to others who have assisted this labour of love both recently and over many years of preparation and research:

Among other veterans and their families, I want to thank George and Joan Sweanor, and their daughter Barbara; Albert Wallace and his daughter Barbara Trendos; Don Edy and his daughters Barb Edy and Jane Hughes; John R. Harris; Vicki, Stephen, and Glenn Sorensen, who gave the gift of their father Frank Sorensen's correspondence; David (and Cathy) Pengelly for remembering brother Tony Pengelly; Chris Pengelly, Tony's son, for the treasure trove of his father's personal records of Stalag Luft III; and friends Mary and David Ross (and their trusty Facebook account), who helped track down the Pengellys; Fran Weir for letters written home by her husband John Weir; Margaret Bartlett, and her daughter Anne Dumonceaux and grandson Nick Dumonceaux, for remembering Dick Bartlett; Don McKim, with the assistance of son Al McKim, daughter Wendy Johnson, and friend Bernice Marsland; Catherine Heron, sister of Wally Floody, for the scrapbook and photo files of her brother Wally Floody's career, and son Brian (and Lorraine) Floody for their interview collections of Wally; Ethel Alle and Kingsley Brown Jr. for access to their father Kingsley Brown Sr.'s memoirs; Barry Davidson Jr. for access to his father Barry Davidson Sr.'s logs; Fred and Susan Bendell, as well as daughter Katie Bendell, for material from Gordon Venables' experience in the prison camp; Nancy Buckham for access to her husband Robert Buckham's diaries and sketches; Marjorie Acheson (with help from Kitchener Public librarian Karen Ball-Pyatt) for access to John Acheson's memoirs; Kim and Kelley Crozier for access to their father John Crozier's diaries; Sally and John Hutchinson for the gift of her father Bob Nelson's writings; Harold Johnstone for granting access to John Colwell's precise images and diary; Keith Ogilvie Jr. and Jean Ogilvie for photos of their father Keith "Skeets" Ogilvie; Ted Nurse for permission to refer to his account of his father Edward Nurse's experience at Stalag Luft III; Marilyn Walton for assistance in obtainiing US Air Force Academy photos; and Don and Linda Jarrell for stories about Don's father, John MacKinnon "Mac" Jarrell as a kriegie.

Thanks to support and data (files and photographs) provided by Marek Lazarz and the volunteers at the Museum of Allied Forces Prisoners of War Martyrdom at Zagan, Poland.

As well, a debt of gratitude to James Taylor, Parveen Kaur Sodhi, and Sally Richards at the Imperial War Museums in the UK for assistance in gaining access and rights to their Stalag Luft III photo archives. Also in the UK, my thanks to Andrew Dennis and Vinit Mehta at the Royal Air Force Museum at Hendon for their help securing the rights to the Ley Kenyon sketches of The Great Escape.

No one writes who doesn't also read and recognize the previous work of fellow authors (specific references and permissions are contained in the endnotes). Among those key to my interpretation of this story are Paul Brickhill (*The Great Escape*), Kingsley Brown (*Bonds of Wire*), Robert Buckham (*Forced March to Freedom*), Patricia Burns (*They Were So Young*), Andrew Carswell (*Over the Wire*), H.P. Clark (*Wire Bound World*), Art Crighton (*Memories of a Prisoner of War*), Daniel G. Dancocks (*In Enemy Hands*), Ian Darling (*Amazing Airmen*), Don Edy (*Goon in the Block*), Hugh Godefroy (*Lucky Thirteen*), Philip Gray (*Ghosts of Targets Past*), John R. Harris (*Serving and Surviving*), George Harsh (*Lonesome Road*), John Hartnell-Beavis (*Final Flight*), Barbara Hehner (*The Tunnel King*), Stuart G. Hunt (*Twice Surreal*), Harold Johnstone (*John Colwell*), Phil Marchildon (*Ace*), Wayne Ralph (*Aces, Warriors and Wingmen*), Stuart E. Soward (*One Man's War*), George Sweanor (*It's All Penshionable Time*), Tyler Trafford (*Almost a Great Escape*), and Jonathan Vance (*A Gallant Company*).

In various ways, but drawing on their unique expertise, I wish to thank Susan Hall for her wisdom about music; Dave Zink (who died in 2012) for his encyclopedic knowledge of war history and militaria; Barb and Stuart Blower for their assistance in restoring old photographs; Don Young for his sense of Canadian storytelling; and Marian Hebb for her legal acumen and commonsense approach to getting books from writers to readers.

In terms of the special assistance of colleagues and friends in journalism, creative non-fiction writing, and publishing, I owe much to authors Malcolm Kelly and Byron Christopher, journalism professors Lindy Oughtred, Stephen Cogan, and Ellin Bessner, broadcaster Rick Cluff, publisher Marc Coté, and editor Don Loney. Special thanks to my neighbour, Navy veteran Ronnie Egan, for her homemade sandwiches that helped me maintain my daily writing quota. I thank my team of transcribers, Octavian Lacatusu and Michael Laing-Fraser. At Thomas Allen Publishers, I'm grateful to editors Janice Zawerbny and Linda Pruessen, to proofreader Ruth Chernia, to marketing team Krista Lynch and Catherine Whiteside, and to my favourite TAP triumvirate of David Glover, Bonita Mok, and Heather Goldberg. Special thanks to Beth Crane for making our photos sparkle. And as he has done for all of my TAP books, Gordon Robertson has contributed his exquisite visual sense to the design of this project.

And the first shall be last: I thank my wife, Jayne MacAulay, who edits by profession, and thinks clearly by nature.

—Ted Barris 2013

# "HEROES RESURFACE"

---

A HEAD OF HIM in the distance, lie the Alps. Disguised in a German dispatch rider's battledress and *stahlhelm* helmet, a fugitive hero brings his motorcycle to a sudden halt in the middle of this back road in wartime Germany. Nervously jerking the bike's throttle, he wheels his body around in the saddle, searching for his pursuers. A close-up catches his face as his eyes settle on the mountains ahead.

"Switzerland," he says under his breath.

He throttles up, pops the bike back into gear, and roars off. Minutes later, his disguise revealed, the motorcyclist bashes through a checkpoint, peels off the now useless German uniform, and blasts cross-country toward the distant mountains and, he hopes, freedom. Behind him, military trucks, motorcycles with sidecars, and what seems to be half the German Army are in hot pursuit. All the while, Elmer Bernstein's stirring film score accelerates in tempo and rises with crescendo. Then, in his character's final moments on the run, actor Steve McQueen launches himself and his 650 Triumph over the first of two barriers of sharp pickets and barbed wire. Unable to make it over the second barrier, US Army Air Force Captain Virgil Hilts crashes into the fence, entangles himself in the wire, tries to break free, then realizes the futility of his struggle and surrenders to the hordes of German troops who've now overtaken him.

These few minutes of flight and pursuit, caught on 35-millimetre colour Panavision film, remain among the most thrilling in the canon of Hollywood war moviemaking and viewing. Indeed, this climactic sequence, among many crowd-pleasing, escalating jolts of action and drama in *The Great Escape*, earned Hollywood film editor Ferris Webster an Academy Award nomination.* Based on Paul Brickhill's non-fiction book *The Great Escape*, published in 1950, the movie became an immediate hit when it was released in North American theatres in the summer of 1963. On the whole, it also garnered upbeat critical reviews.

"With accurate casting, a swift screenplay, and authentic German settings," *Time* magazine raved, "producer-director John Sturges has created a classic..."[1]

Was it a classic? Yes. In 2006, more than forty years after the film's release, a poll asked TV watchers and moviegoers in the United Kingdom which flick they would most want to view over Christmas. *The Great Escape* came in third among families, first among male viewers. Was it authentic? In part it was. A group of veterans returning to the site of the escape on the occasion of the sixty-fifth anniversary, in 2009, told journalists reporting the event that Hollywood had depicted much of the life in the infamous Stalag Luft III prisoner-of-war camp accurately.

On the other hand, there was no Captain Virgil Hilts, "The Cooler King," in the actual Great Escape. Nor were there a lot of Americans in the prison's North Compound when the breakout occurred. Nor was there a motorcycle chase. When writers James Clavell, W. R. Burnett, and Walter Newman originally scripted the fictitious USAAF Captain Hilts into the screenplay, they had him attempting to escape aboard a train among other fleeing Allied POWs. However, Steve McQueen, contracted by Sturges and the Mirisch Company to

---

* During the Academy Awards ceremony at the Santa Monica Civic Auditorium on April 13, 1964, actor Sidney Poitier awarded the best editing Oscar to Harold F. Cress for his work on *How the West Was Won*. While it was eligible for best picture in 1963, *The Great Escape* earned no other Oscar nominations.

co-star in the film, had such a passion for motorcycle racing that he insisted on having the chase scene built into the film.

Did the movie present authentic settings? Apparently, it didn't matter to the producers that the actual Great Escape occurred near the town of Sagan in southern Poland, not in southern Germany, near the Swiss Alps. Nor was it relevant to McQueen or the movie's creators that the escape happened on March 24, 1944, when a metre of snow still lay on the ground, where no motorcycle could easily travel, let alone leap barbed-wire fences.

Here are the facts of the escape. On the night of March 24, 1944, eighty Commonwealth air officers crawled through a 360-foot-long tunnel and slipped into the darkness of a pine forest beyond the wire of the North Compound at Stalag Luft III near Sagan. The intricate breakout, more than a year in the making, involved as many as two thousand POWs, extraordinary coordination, and a battle of wits inconceivable for the time. As dawn broke on March 25, however, German guards outside the compound spotted prisoners emerging from the exit hole, set off an alarm, and over the next few days managed to recapture all but three of the escapers. In a rage over the incident, Adolf Hitler called for the execution of all the escapers; instead, the death list was adjusted downward and fifty Commonwealth air officers were executed, with perpetrators claiming the prisoners were shot while attempting to escape Gestapo custody. Their bodies were cremated and buried in a remote corner of the Stalag Luft III grounds to hide the truth.

A hint about the accuracy of Hollywood's version of the story is evident in one of the movie's final scenes. It shows the fifty officers gunned down en masse by a German machine-gun crew in an open field somewhere in Germany. In truth, after their recapture, imprisonment, and interrogation, the officers were taken out and shot in twos and threes by Gestapo death squads hand-picked and given licence to execute the officers in cold blood by a German High Command edict known as the Sagan Order. The little-known origins of the order add much intrigue to this story.

But was the casting as accurate as the rave reviews said? True, the hiring of Steve McQueen, Richard Attenborough, James Garner, Charles Bronson, Donald Pleasence, and James Coburn among a cast of hundreds made a lot of sense. The on-screen ensemble of principal actors represented the cream of Hollywood idols in the early 1960s. They ensured *The Great Escape* would become among the best box-office draws of the year. But did the movie escape committee accurately represent the real escape committee?

In an effort to make the movie plot and its characters more inviting and palatable to an American audience, the writers invented Flight Lieutenant (F/L) Bob Hendley, an American in the RAF, as the scrounger inside Stalag Luft III. Sturges cast US screen and TV star James Garner to play the part. In fact, the scrounger was a twenty-eight-year-old Blenheim bomber pilot from Calgary, Alberta, named Barry Davidson.

For the key roles of the tunnel designers and diggers, Sturges's creative team invented RAF F/L Danny Velinski and RAF F/L Willie Dickes and cast American actor Charles Bronson and British actor/singer John Leyton in the roles. The actual tunnel king was a downed Spitfire pilot, twenty-five-year-old Wally Floody, originally from Chatham, Ontario. His tunnel digging partners were fellow RCAF fighter pilots: twenty-four-year-old John Weir from Toronto, Ontario, and twenty-six-year-old Hank Birkland, from Spearhill, Manitoba.

When it came to portraying the chief forger—the POW who designed many of the fake documents used by the air officers during the escape—the screenplay writers manufactured another British flyer named Colin Blythe and cast seasoned British film and TV actor Donald Pleasence (who had actually been a POW during the war) in the role. The actual forger behind much of the document fabrication, however, was twenty-four-year-old Whitley bomber pilot Tony Pengelly, from Truro, Nova Scotia.

Next, the Hollywood production team imagined one of the intelligence chiefs in the camp and parachuted into the script a British air officer named Andy MacDonald, casting Scottish-born actor Gordon Jackson to play him. In fact, among the officers conducting much of the intelligence activities was thirty-two-year-old Kingsley Brown, a journalist and father of four from the Toronto area.

To portray an officer in charge of the security of the three tunnels—"Tom," "Dick," and "Harry"—the movie producers conceived an RAF F/L Sorren and cast British actor William Russell in the role. In fact, the security team inside the wire at the North Compound included thirty-three-year-old RCAF air gunner George Harsh, originally from Milwaukee, Wisconsin, and twenty-four-year-old RCAF bomb-aimer George Sweanor, from Port Hope, Ontario. And that doesn't include the air officer in charge of security at the entrance of the main tunnels, the so-called *trapführer*, twenty-six-year-old Patrick Langford from Edmonton, Alberta.

For organizing what were called "diversions" inside the compound, the movie producers invented RAF F/L Dai Nimmo and then hired English horror and mystery film actor Tom Adams to play him. Among the actual diversionary geniuses, however, was twenty-five-year-old George McGill, an RCAF navigator from Toronto; McGill helped orchestrate boxing matches and other sporting attractions to distract German guards during some of the earliest escape attempts at Stalag Luft III. As well, the escape committee inside the North Compound had organized diversionary "culture appreciation sessions" in the prison library, where twenty-nine-year-old RCAF navigator Gordon Kidder from St. Catharines, Ontario, actually taught conversational German to the soon-to-be escapers. Adding to the real diversionary linguistics staff was another Canadian, twenty-one-year-old Spitfire pilot Frank Sorensen, who taught the head of the escape committee, Roger Bushell, basic conversational Danish as the two men exercised on the walking path inside the warning wire at the compound.

In a delicious irony of casting and accuracy, *The Great Escape* screenplay writers chose to change Roger Bushell's name to Roger Bartlett. Coincidentally, the man responsible for servicing and hiding an inside-the-camp short-wave radio that delivered nightly newscasts from the BBC was yet another unheralded Canadian, twenty-four-year-old dive-bomber pilot Richard Bartlett, from Fort Qu'Appelle, Saskatchewan.

In other words, contrary to Hollywood's Anglo-American version of the Great Escape story, the actual mass breakout owed much of its design, execution, and tactical success to an extraordinarily talented crew of air force officers from Canada. Again, the producers' rationale for stacking the script with US and UK character names and stars was clear: to help the audience connect to the story and to give the marketing and promotional team plenty of recognizable talent to build box office. And it worked. A film that cost roughly four million dollars to produce grossed more than eleven million dollars in ticket revenue during the summer of 1963.

Motorcycles and the Hollywood dream factory aside, recognizing that the actual Great Escape brain trust was largely Canadian is not the only reason for revisiting this unique war story. The wider picture, occupied by other Canadian air officers shot down during the war and sent to Stalag Luft III, illustrates just how remarkable this escape feat really was. As *Kriegsgefangenen* (prisoners of war)—or, as they called themselves, "kriegies"—the air officers were not required to work inside the wire. They had to report for appell (roll call) several times a day and abide by all the other rules administered by their Luftwaffe (German Air Force) jailers. But beyond that, they were spared the forced labour, wrath, and deprivation of concentration camps or non-commissioned officer (NCO) compounds.

Consequently, the Commonwealth air officers were left to their own devices day and night—feeding themselves, clothing themselves, educating themselves, entertaining themselves, keeping themselves fit, and conspiring among themselves. For the months and years that they were imprisoned at Stalag Luft III, the POWs—many of them Canadian—built, seemingly from thin air, an extraordinarily orderly world inside the wire. There was "the Tin Man," John Colwell, who built a pot, or chair, or escape tool nearly every day of his imprisonment. There were the extroverted officers, such as James Wernham, Don Edy, Arthur Crighton, and Tony Pengelly, whose penchant for performing led them to become regulars in the musicals, concerts, revues, and full classical productions staged weekly at the North

Compound theatre. And since plenty of the officers had played international or professional sports—including big league pitchers Phil Marchildon and Bill Paton—the sports grounds at the North Compound buzzed with tournaments on the baseball diamond, football pitch, or ice-hockey rink, no matter the season. There was even an inside-the-wire press corps to publish results and colour commentary. But beneath that veneer remained a secret society of officers—about a third of whom were Canadians—intent on breaking out of the camp, or at least disrupting the German war machine sufficiently before being recaptured, sent to solitary confinement for a time, and finally returned to the barracks huts inside Stalag Luft III.

In addition to a review of the existing accounts, telling the Canadian story of the Great Escape has yielded new and disturbing information about some little-known aspects of the breakout and its aftermath. For one, the struggle for power between the Luftwaffe and the Gestapo may have doomed the escape plot and escapers long before the breakout on March 24–25, 1944. For another, it appears that no intervention by Red Cross, Luftwaffe prison administrators, or articles of the Geneva Conventions, could have prevented the murders of the fifty Commonwealth officers, including six Canadians. Conditions of the Sagan Order, and the inbred hostility of those hired to carry it out, meant certain death. Ultimately, as resilient and innovative as the kriegies proved to be throughout their incarceration, the forced march during the last months of the winter in 1945 and on the eve of their liberation proved a final test of mind and body some could not endure.

If there remains any doubt that the Great Escape myth and reality continue to resonate and demand Canadians' attention, consider the appetite for the story on the eve of the seventieth anniversary of the historic breakout. Across the country today, the legacy of the kriegie experience lives on in local, regional, and national reunions (albeit in ever decreasing size and frequency). Fascination for the story persists because the surviving wives, sisters, and brothers kept letters and news clippings. It lingers because daughters and sons and grandchildren never stop seeking the answers to unresolved questions about their kriegie parent's experience. Meanwhile, the Great Escape tale grows exponentially; every year, fresh stories emerge in newly discovered postcards and letters, never before published photos, unearthed tunnel archaeology at the site near Zagan, Poland, and remembrances that are finally shared by kriegie offspring and dedicated collectors with the rest of us. Documentarians and authors continue to expand the library of discoveries and views. Canadians and others never stop asking why this kriegie lived or that one died. And then, on Christmas break, near the anniversary, or online, there always seems to be a constituency—young and old—eager to watch Hollywood's version, right down to Steve McQueen's mythical motorcycle attempt to beat the odds.

About the longevity and indelibility of The Great Escape story at Stalag Luft III, US Air Force veteran and historian Arthur A. Durand may have assessed it best.

"In a day when we don't have many heroes, it's kind of nice to see some heroes resurface," he wrote. "And while there's a part of it that says instinctively, 'Yeah, but that's Hollywood,' there's the other part that says if even a fraction of that was true . . . then here's something to [make us] take notice and find inspiration."[2]

# THE KING'S
# REGULATIONS

T HE ESCAPE SEQUENCE from a Whitley bomber about to crash
seemed pretty straightforward in the procedure manual. Pilot
Tony Pengelly had practised it often enough with the other
four members of his crew, although they had only done it when the
Whitley was stationary and sitting on the ground. When the bail-out
order comes and the Whitley is flying straight and level, the Royal Air
Force (RAF) manual said, Pengelly's co-pilot, seated behind him in
the cockpit, had to move quickly down a couple of steps to the cabin
escape hatch below and to the right of the pilot. By the time he got
there, the observer-bombardier, positioned below the pilot in the
nose of the Whitley, would have opened the escape hatch door on
the floor next to him, and the door would have dropped open with
gravity. That would allow Pengelly's co-pilot to be the first to crouch,
fall backwards through the escape hatch and free of the aircraft, open
his parachute, and descend safely to the ground. He would be followed by the observer-bombardier, next by the wireless radio oper-
ator-gunner, and finally by the pilot himself. The manual stipulated
that the tail gunner had to extricate himself from the rear turret, fit
on his parachute, and climb to the escape hatch in the roof of the rear
of the fuselage. The rear-gunner was always pretty much on his own.

The problem remained, however, that a Whitley wouldn't necessarily be flying straight and level in such an emergency. It could be side-slipping, diving, spinning out of control, or upside down in its unscheduled descent. It could be stricken by icing on its wings, hit by lightning, or buffeted by upward or downward turbulence. Nor did the procedure manual take into account such variables as a power failure, fire in the fuel tanks, explosions in a bomb bay, blocked passageways, or any other unexpected impediments to an orderly escape. Finally, the official RAF instructions for bailing out of a Whitley bomber in its death throes did little to account for the final variable in such an event—the nighttime skies over enemy-occupied territory.

When Armstrong Whitworth Aircraft introduced its state-of-the-art prototype Whitley bomber aircraft in 1934, the Royal Air Force adopted it as its first heavy night bomber. Among its unique characteristics, to offset the absence of flaps, the Whitley's main wings were set permanently at a high angle to potentially improve its takeoff and landing capabilities. Aircrews recognized right away, however, that the Whitley seemed to fly with a pronounced nose-down attitude, and its pilots sensed this added to the aircraft's considerable drag in flight. By the time he began piloting them in 1938, Flight Lieutenant (F/L) Pengelly was flying a version of the Whitley bomber that included higher performance Rolls-Royce Merlin engines, modified fins, de-icing on the wings' leading edge, manually operated turrets armed with .303 Browning machine guns, and an extended tail section for a better field of fire for the tail gunner. But all that made his Whitley considerably heavier and less manoeuverable. Pengelly and his comrades considered the Whitley—with a crew of five, capacity for a seven-thousand-pound payload of bombs, and a maximum speed of 230 miles per hour at sixteen thousand feet—vulnerably slow, notoriously cold, and, if forced to shut down an engine, unable to maintain altitude. Whitley crews came to refer to their bomber as "the flying coffin."

To offset the Whitley's alleged shortcomings and intimidating nickname F/L Pengelly—being a stickler for detail—ensured that his aircrew was fully trained to cope with them. But as meticulously as he prepared his crew, Pengelly prepared himself even more so. Whenever new navigational aids appeared at his home aerodrome, the Canadian bomber pilot learned to use them as well as his navigator could. He paid close attention to the way meteorological officers read cloud formations and wind velocities so that he could read them equally well. And because the airworthiness and efficiency of his Whitley bomber depended so directly on the skills of his Erks, the ground crew, Pengelly developed tight working relationships with the mechanics, artificers, armourers, and riggers at RAF Topcliffe, where 102 Squadron was based in Yorkshire, England.

When his Whitley Mk V arrived at Topcliffe, Pengelly studied all its attributes and idiosyncrasies—engine revolutions, gun armament, bomb loads, petrol capacity, and the location of everything from the wireless radio to the evacuation dinghy. On days the squadron wasn't briefed and dispatched to bomb targets in German-occupied Holland or France, he even took to blindfolding himself and his aircrew, simulating nighttime conditions inside the Whitley in an emergency. Pengelly insisted that if their aircraft were hit by flak or night fighters, all members of his crew had to be able to find any piece of equipment or reach an escape hatch by touch alone. As much as he could, he wanted to inspire an esprit de corps among the other four members of his crew—J. F. M. Moyle, C. P. Followes, H. Radley, and T. Michie. During downtime at the station, Pengelly even challenged his crewmates to motorcycle races on the aerodrome tarmac to sharpen the crew's competitive edge. The skipper of the Whitley bomber, nicknamed "M for Mother," wanted everyone on his crew at the top of his game. No doubt, some of the British prime minister's oratory rang in Pengelly's ears.

"Only one thing . . . will bring Hitler down," Winston Churchill wrote, "and that is an absolutely devastating exterminating attack by very heavy bombers from this country upon the Nazi homeland . . . without which I do not see a way through."[1]

Forty-eight hours before he was shot down, Tony Pengelly felt fully prepared and sharply motivated to take on the enemy. At age twenty, he'd already served as an officer in the Royal Air Force for two years, since the fall of 1938. He'd seen action as a bomber pilot as soon as the war broke out. His RAF 102 Squadron had flown operational sorties (ops)—dropping propaganda leaflets on the Ruhr River in Germany—on September 4, 1939, the second day of the war. Then, for the first year of fighting, his bomber squadron had played mostly a supporting role. His station's Whitley aircraft had flown operations to Norway in a losing cause. They had bombed German supply lines inland from Dunkirk as the British Expeditionary Force retreated from France in late May 1940. Through the rest of that year, including the crucial Battle of Britain period, which tested principally the Fighter Command aerodromes around London, 102 Squadron was on loan to Coastal Command, escorting naval convoys to sea from Prestwick on the west coast of Scotland. Like most of his air force comrades, F/L Pengelly—a Canadian in the RAF—felt as if Bomber Command was flying in circles. He was sick of Britain's taking it on the chin. He was itching to go on the offensive.

"For the first six months of the war," Pengelly lamented, "I flew at night mostly over Germany to gain operational and navigational experience dropping leaflets."[2]

If the fate of aircrews seemed up in the air, so too was the leadership and bomber strength of RAF Bomber Command. While it didn't concern Pengelly and his crew directly, in the fall of 1940, Sir Charles Portal moved up to commander-in-chief of the RAF, Air Marshal Sir Richard Peirse took over Bomber Command, and Air Vice-Marshal Arthur Harris became Deputy Chief of the Air Staff, second in command to Portal; Harris would presently assume total charge of Bomber Command's strategic bombing campaign.[3] Ironically, as its role suddenly seemed suspended, so did Bomber Command's aircraft strength suddenly diminish. Late in 1940, the British Air Ministry reported a total inventory of 532 bomber aircraft—217 Blenheims, 100 Wellingtons, 71 Hampdens, 59 Whitleys, and 85 Fairey Battles.[4] RAF leadership deemed the Blenheims and Battles obsolete and began moving them to Training Command or the scrap heap. Wellingtons still proved reliable so the RAF called for another hundred of them. Meanwhile, the Hampdens and Whitleys would soon be ready for replacement by more modern aircraft; but for the moment their numbers remained the same. The bottom line was that Richard Peirse's Bomber Command, in the fall of 1940, was reduced by more than half, to 230 aircraft. Operations would be fewer, but more specific and with less impact.

That autumn, nighttimes brought heavy frosts and penetrating cold. Like many crews waiting for news, Pengelly's men dressed in their flying suits for warmth and huddled inside crew huts at the station. They had hung thick curtains as much to hold in heat as to black out the windows and doors. Spartan wall decor included propaganda posters, diagrams reminding aircrew about emergency procedures, and a few favourite pin-ups. And the men sat at linoleum-topped tables marked with indelible glass and cup stains and cigarette burns from hundreds of nights like these. Their talk—of pubs, of home, of women who couldn't resist the attraction of an RAF uniform—reflected their bravado, their boredom, and their apprehension.[5] They all just wanted the CO to come in, announce offensive ops, and get on with it. Inevitably, he did arrive with those orders.

Mid-November brought what aircrew called the moonlight period, a time most Royal Air Force bomber crews welcomed during that phase of the war. If skies were clear, ops to a target would be smoother without clouds buffeting them en route, targets would be more discernable, and the damage they inflicted on the ground would be more photographable. Aircrew also said a moonlit sky seemed to release them personally from the oppressiveness of flying in total darkness or dense, endless cloud. The British Air Ministry had earmarked German marshalling yards and iron smelters as high priority targets, but at the top of the list were synthetic oil plants in western Germany. A nighttime sortie against the refineries at Wesseling, near Cologne, revealed many of the shortcomings of 102 Squadron's weapon of war—the Whitley bomber. But the emergency response aboard one of Pengelly's sister aircraft illustrated the capability of 102 Squadron bomber crews to offset that deficiency.

On November 13, 1940, over Cologne, German anti-aircraft batteries on the ground hit the Whitley bomber piloted by Pilot

Officer Leonard Cheshire. The enemy flak ignited a fire near the fuel tanks and among the target flares still inside the fuselage. With fire and smoke filling the cockpit and his bomber descending rapidly, Cheshire wrestled with the controls to keep the Whitley aloft while his crew ejected the remaining flares and battled the fires. Eventually, his crew extinguished the flames, and after nearly nine hours in the air, Cheshire brought the shredded Whitley back to base safely. For Cheshire, leaving the aircraft—even in a dire emergency—was not an option. The action earned Cheshire a Distinguished Service Order* and inspired the entire 102 Squadron, including F/L Pengelly. Explaining the successful return of his Whitley, Cheshire credited the variable that had overcome any of the Whitley's inefficiencies.

"These eighteen-year-olds," said Cheshire, himself just twenty-three, "are a remarkable breed of men."[6]

If Cheshire's courageous example and the exhilaration of taking the war deep into enemy territory hadn't boosted the sense of purpose around 102 Squadron's crew huts at Topcliffe, the news from northwest of London the next evening certainly would. On November 14 came intelligence reports that the Luftwaffe had delivered its most lethal bombing raid of the war. The same clear, moonlit skies RAF bombers relished had led four hundred German bombers to the heart of Coventry in Britain's West Midlands. The enemy bombers had dropped five hundred tons of high explosives and thirty thousand incendiaries. The attack had destroyed three-quarters of the city's munitions, aircraft, and armament plants, the centuries-old St. Michael's Cathedral, and four thousand houses, more than half the city's residential area. Britons were stunned and appalled. Pengelly had experienced the blitz himself. Earlier in the war, his private apartment had been bombed in a Luftwaffe raid that destroyed most of his

---

* The DSO citation read: "Showing great coolness, Pilot Officer Cheshire regained control of his aircraft, which had lost considerable height and was being subjected to intense anti-aircraft fire, and although the explosion had blown out a large part of the fuselage and caused other damage he managed to regain height. . . . Although the aircraft was only partially answering the controls Pilot Officer Cheshire succeeded in returning to his aerodrome."

photographic equipment. But cameras, lenses, and photo development gear could be replaced; nearly a thousand people had died in Coventry that night—the night immediately preceding Pengelly's last combat flight of the war.

At the briefing for his operation, F/L Pengelly discovered that of the three ops targets slated—Berlin, Hamburg, and the airfields at Schipold and Soesterberg—the largest, Berlin, would be theirs. He'd been to Berlin first on the night of September 23–24 and three times since. This would be his fifth sortie to the German capital. In all, eighty-two Hampdens, Wellingtons, and Whitleys would set out across the North Sea that night and of them fifty bombers would attack sites in and around Berlin. The idea of security in numbers was not something Whitley crews experienced or even preferred. For most of his previous thirty trips—and commonly on Whitley sorties—Pengelly's "M for Mother" Whitley had flown alone. As the Luftwaffe had over Coventry, the RAF operation to Berlin on November 14–15, 1940, enjoyed the assistance of moonlight, but for various reasons only half the attacking force of Whitleys actually reached the city.

At approximately ten o'clock, Pengelly and Moyle, his co-pilot, homed in on their Berlin-area objective and released their bomb load. They then decided to make a second pass over the target so that the Whitley's newly mounted cameras could record the accuracy and damage of their attack. That's when German anti-aircraft batteries around Berlin found their mark. Flak penetrated one of the bomber's two engines and ignited a fire, just as it had two nights earlier aboard Cheshire's Whitley. Pengelly reacted quickly, shutting down the engine in an attempt to prevent the fire from spreading to the fuel tanks inside the wing. Desperately, he turned the aircraft westward for home, but he knew the odds were prohibitive. The loss of one of his Merlin engines effectively cut his power in half. And the results were as predictable as a mathematical equation. Cheshire's heroic dash for home on November 13 had succeeded because he still had two serviceable engines. Pengelly knew the technical specifications of his now one-engine Whitley—even empty of bombs—would prevent him and his crew from making it to friendly soil in England.

To his credit, the experienced bomber pilot did manage to keep the crippled bomber airborne long enough for his crew to prepare for the end. The extra minutes in the air gave each crewman enough time to tighten harnesses, secure parachutes and survival kit, and open escape hatches for evacuation. An hour west of Berlin, the radio operator tapped off an SOS on the wireless to alert RAF Coastal Command of their final descent. Five hundred miles from home, flying on one engine over German-occupied territory in a heavy bomber destined to crash or be shot down, and with just enough altitude to bail out successfully, Pengelly ordered his crew to abandon the aircraft. Then, just as the procedure manual stated, and as they had practised regularly on the ground at Topcliffe, first Moyle the co-pilot crouched and fell backward through the forward escape hatch, next Followes the observer-bombardier, then Radley the wireless radio operator (as well as Michie the tail gunner on his own out the rear hatch), and finally, Pengelly, the skipper, bailed out of the nose of their crashing Whitley. All got out safely.

When Tony Pengelly ran away from his Canadian home in Weston, Ontario, in 1938, two-and-a-half years earlier, to join the Royal Air Force, he'd resigned himself to the RAF life. It meant dedication to a life of service of indeterminate duration. Typically in the Commonwealth air forces, thirty combat operations or about two hundred hours were considered a complete tour of duty. But reaching that plateau merely entitled an airman to a six-month rest from operations (often instructing at a training station during the break) and then a return to combat. Early in the war, when 102 Squadron accumulated the third-worst casualty rate in the RAF, fewer than half all bomber crews were surviving a single tour.

Miraculously, by the night of November 14, 1940, Pengelly had completed thirty-one ops. Had he made it home that night, he might have been entitled to some leave time or at least service behind the lines as a respite. But at that stage of the war, Pengelly's oath of service meant he was in for the duration. The expatriate Canadian had chosen life and loyalty to a centuries-old system of King's Regulations that governed British society, commerce, and military service. And in the Royal Air Force, Pengelly had sworn to uphold its list of directives when serving in a theatre of war. If nothing else, Pengelly was a master of detail, and even as he floated to earth in Germany, he considered his actions methodically and exactly.

"I took my chute off and buried it,"[7] Pengelly said. "Being very optimistic—which you were at twenty—I was going to head west and walk to England, probably try walking on the water."

With equal naïveté, Pengelly started to travel on the wrong side of a public road and nearly collided with a volunteer police officer on his bicycle. Before long he was in the custody of two policemen, in a car, and en route to a local Luftwaffe station. He learned from his captors that they had detained at least two other "M for Mother" crew members, but because Pengelly was an officer, he was destined for a train ride to the district *Durchgangslager der Luftwaffe* (Dulag Luft)—interrogation centre—in Frankfurt-am-Main. Inside a cell with no window on the door, but a view through bars to a nearby wooded area and wire fence, Pengelly again reflected on the appropriate actions as he prepared for his first interrogation. They were lines he'd memorized among the King's Regulations and Air Crew Instructions at initial training school, reminding him "to protect the Security of the Royal Air Force by every means."[8]

His captors brought him coffee and bread, probably to invite his co-operation. He felt unkempt. He hadn't shaved. He was still in his flying suit. Then a German interrogator entered the room. Pengelly thought he looked as if he'd just stepped from a tailor's shop and was terribly polite.

"Good day, Flight Lieutenant Pengelly," the man said in plain English. "How's life in 102 Squadron?"

Pengelly hadn't recalled giving anybody his squadron number. The reference in the regulations to the Geneva Conventions of 1929 came back: "a prisoner of war is only required to give his name, rank, and number."[9]

The interrogation officer offered descriptions of other members of Pengelly's squadron; it proved he knew their names and some of their activities. It also suggested the captor actually knew everything and needed nothing from the prisoner.

Pengelly would have to, as he recalled from the interrogation manual, "stand correctly to attention, maintain rigid silence, avoid attempts to bluff or tell lies, address any officer senior to himself as 'Sir' and . . . don't fraternize; the enemy is not in the habit of wasting his time, whisky and cigars on those who have nothing to give him in return."[10]

The interrogation officer explained to Pengelly that he had been a professor in Austria, had majored in British history, and had even travelled widely in England. And, oh, by the way, he happened to have English cigarettes apparently captured from the British Expeditionary Force during its hasty withdrawal from Dunkirk.

As attentive to the interrogator's methods as Pengelly felt he was, every time his captor edged toward sensitive information, Pengelly reminded himself of the regulations that required him not to try "to fool your interrogators; they will be experts at their job, and in any battle of wits you are bound to lose in the end." Pengelly repeated that he did not have to tell the man anything.

"That's all right," Pengelly's interrogator insisted. "I'll find out some way or other. We're shooting lots of you chaps down."[11]

He couldn't let on, but Pengelly was amazed by the volume of information his interrogator spouted, including turnover figures on the squadron, casualty numbers, and that on one of his combat operations, Pengelly had flown to Italy and back.

Even though the interrogation had ended, and Pengelly felt some relief at having emerged without divulging any secrets of the Service, there were still other parts of that RAF manual at play. Yes, he had offered only his name, rank, and number. Yes, he had seen through the German officer's offer of food and idle chatter and not shown his surprise at how much the German knew about 102 Squadron and its crews. Yes, he had rebuffed the interrogator's attempts to fraternize with him, no matter how good those cigarettes might have smelled. But no, he had not yielded any data about his squadron, where it was stationed, what its strength was, or about the performance of any new designs in aircraft or armament. He hadn't revealed a speck of information about air force training, tactics, or defence systems. F/L Pengelly had indeed lived up to all the King's Regulations stipulated and memorized . . . except one.

All the regulations, while never specifically saying so, implied that included in an airman's duty to King and country, particularly when captured and imprisoned on enemy territory, was an obligation to escape.

"Don't betray those who help you to escape," the RAF document stipulated. It added, "Do keep your eyes and ears open after capture. You may learn much which may be of value both to your country and yourself if you succeed in escaping."[12]

Escaping was a military obligation for which Pengelly admitted there had been no training. None of his instructors at initial training, elementary, or service training in the RAF had explained how to cut barbed wire at night, steal timely documents that would allow him to travel undetected, disguise himself as a German civilian, or dig a tunnel under a fence. All this and more—if he cared to live up to all the obligations of his contract with the King—he would have to learn by trial and error. But Pengelly was a quick study. After just four months in England, in the summer and fall of 1938, he had earned his "certificate of competency for private flying machines"[13] which meant he could fly "all types of land planes." In addition, within his first year in the UK Pengelly had earned his commission as a flying officer in the RAF, making him equally capable in the cockpits of all military aircraft of the day.

Later that first full day in German captivity—November 16, 1940—F/L Pengelly was moved from the interrogation centre to the Dulag Luft prison camp. Curiously, as far as Pengelly was concerned, everybody inside the wire gathered at the gate to see the latest arrival. Among the greeters was a great surprise for Pengelly: the Senior British Officer (SBO) in the camp, Group Captain Harry "Wings" Day. Pengelly hadn't seen his wing commander for over a year; a decorated veteran of the Great War and already age forty when the Second World War began, Day had been shot down on his first op on October 13, 1939. The welcome from Wing Commander Day provided Pengelly's first official lesson as a prisoner of war: each incoming POW had to be scrutinized to verify he was who he said he was. Because his wing commander knew Pengelly and could prove it, any suspicion was immediately lifted about his identity.

But Pengelly's reacquaintance with Day initiated the next phase of his POW education. At Dulag Luft, the German prison camp officials had designated Day as Permanent Staff. They assigned him the responsibility of acclimatizing incoming captured aircrew to their new POW lives. It turned out to be a perfect ploy. Together with captured RAF fighter pilot Roger Bushell and Fleet Air Arm pilot Jimmy Buckley, as well as Middlesex Regiment infantryman Johnny Dodge, Pengelly would help cover Day as he dug a tunnel out of the camp from beneath his prison bed. A precedent had been established.

In June 1941, eighteen POWs broke out of Dulag Luft; all were recaptured, but the effort was the first mass escape of the war.[14] A few months later, when the Germans had transferred all the RAF POWs to *Stammlager Luft* I—or, more commonly, Stalag Luft I— in Barth, the ad hoc escape committee, dubbed "X Organization," masterminded another tunnel breakout of twelve officers. Again the prisoners were recaptured. But by then the escape committee had started pushing back. The Canadian bomber pilot who'd prepared his crewmen carefully should they have to evacuate their crashing Whitley now began preparing to overcome the next adversity.

"Active participation in [escape] work and planning for escape became the most important thing in my prison camp life,"[15] Pengelly said. "The two and a half years I spent behind barbed wire before we began to plan the big escape was all training for that opportunity."

For Pengelly and the others, intent on living up to that final obligation of their Royal Air Force service, the trial-and-error period would seem horribly long, tedious, and frustrating. Pengelly was an officer, a skilled bomber pilot, capable photographer, and born leader. But for him the air war was finished. He would have to focus his talents on the new tasks at hand. Over the next year and a half, the escape committee at Barth successfully dug forty-eight tunnels. Their German captors found every one of them and thwarted every escape.

"That was because at Barth escaping was strictly private enter-prise," Pengelly said. "[But] a man can't forge his own identity papers, dig his own tunnel, make his own wire clippers, escape clothes, maps [and] compasses. . . . From our futility, we knew we would have to organize to be successful."[16]

# BOND OF WIRE

F RANCES MCCORMACK got her first letter from her imprisoned fiancé, a downed Spitfire pilot, just before Christmas 1941. She had met John Weir on a blind date a couple of summers earlier, when friends in Toronto arbitrarily matched them for a night of dancing at the Palais Royale on the Toronto waterfront. Weir cursed his friends for tricking him into the double date, but fell in love with Frances as the pair embraced on the outdoor terrace dance floor overlooking Lake Ontario. The war broke out in the middle of their courtship and because the Royal Canadian Air Force (RCAF) sent John to Winnipeg for elementary flight training, the couple began a long-distance relationship by correspondence. Even when John successfully soloed and graduated to service flight training, the air force posted him to Borden, Ontario, more than an hour's drive north of Toronto, where Frances lived. Still, the two managed to communicate in creative ways.

On a day when John planned to dodge the curfew at the training station and drive to Toronto for an evening date with Frances, he decided to alert her to his plans for a rendezvous. During the day's instructional flight near Toronto, the young pilot trainee simply detoured over the Forest Hill area of the city and "bombed" his girlfriend's residence with a message wrapped in a handkerchief. Neighbours picked up the note attached to a small parachute and rushed it to the addressee: Miss Frances McCormack, 61 Heathdale Road.

"Be down about 8 o'clock or 8:30. If not, I'll phone," Weir said in the note. "No news about a 48 [hour leave of absence]. P.S. Don't say anything about this to anyone."[1]

"You should be a bomber pilot, not a fighter pilot,"[2] Frances later told him.

As much as Weir's after-hours dash to Toronto illustrated his youthful exuberance and ingenuity, it nearly ended his air force career. His Borden flight instructor found out about his student's illegal antics. He lambasted the sprog (novice) pilot about his disregard for the King's Regulations and lack of respect for his fellow pilots. Then he told Weir he'd be reassigned—i.e., washed out of pilot training. When Weir pleaded his case, the instructor decided to redirect his student away from the multi-engine training that would have streamed him toward becoming a bomber pilot. Instead, Weir would train to eventually fly the single-engine, solo cockpit Hurricane fighter aircraft. John Weir couldn't have asked for a more appropriate punishment.

Collisions with authority and protocol seemed routine for Weir, but they never clouded his drive or independence; among many things, he was an avid outdoorsman capable of fending for himself if and when he had to. Later that year, during an instructional flight at Trenton, the young trainee had struggled to bring a Fairey Battle bomber with a burning engine down to earth safely. The episode left his uniform singed, covered in grime, and stinking of glycol from the Battle's burst coolant system. No one bothered to acknowledge that young Weir had chosen to save the King's property and put his own personal safety at risk; nevertheless, when a visiting RAF officer spotted him in a parade lineup with a glycol-stained uniform, he pointed him out as "a rather scruffy looking individual."[3] The nickname stuck.

Frances McCormack felt so moved by Scruffy's passion to join up and serve his country that she decided to resign her paying job as a personal shopper at Simpson's department store to look for war work herself.[4] She found it at Research Enterprises, the company manufacturing ASDIC, the navy device that used sound waves to detect other ships—principally enemy submarines—at sea. Frances knew how to drive so she landed work as the company chauffeur and took great pride in contributing to the war effort this way. Meanwhile, the couple received their parents' blessing to marry and were engaged October 2, 1940, a few weeks ahead of Weir's overseas posting. The two travelled with friends to Ottawa and shared final words at the train station. Frances knew her fiancé felt an allure for the excitement of the war.

"John, I just hate you going away to this war," she recalled saying to him before he embarked.

"Fran, I've had everything my own way all my life," he had told her. "I'm not concerned in the least."[5]

Partly to prove himself and partly because it was serious now, Weir moved deftly into the cockpits of Hurricanes in operational training at Sutton Bridge, northeast of London. Then he moved to active duty with 1 RCAF Squadron, the first Canadian squadron in Fighter Command that daily joined RAF squadrons scrambling to beat back German Dornier bombers during that historic Battle of Britain summer. By the time Weir went operational with 1 Squadron, it had logged an impressive record—1,694 sorties, 29 downed enemy aircraft, another 43 damaged or destroyed—and its Canadian fighter pilots had earned three Distinguished Flying Crosses (DFCs). However, losses had also been severe—three killed in combat, two in accidents, and ten wounded—and it was generally acknowledged that life expectancy of green pilots was six hours of combat or less. Nevertheless, a primed and combat ready Flying Officer (F/O) John Weir reported for active service in October 1940, just as 1 Squadron relocated to Thurso, Scotland, to protect the Royal Navy base at Scapa Flow.

With 1941 came changes. The squadron had replenished its core of experienced fighter pilots. RAF Fighter Command had relocated its aircrew to Digby, in east-central England, and then Biggin Hill south of London. The Canadian squadron had been renumbered 401 and taken into service its first Supermarine Spitfire fighter aircraft. John Weir had also reconnected with one of his oldest pals from Toronto, Hugh Godefroy. Their families had been close. They had grown up, played shinny hockey, and attended school together. They had both enlisted the same day, September 3, 1939, and for the same reason—the German torpedoing and sinking of the passenger liner

SS *Athenia*. They had been posted overseas within months of each other, and they arrived at Digby together. They paired up in combat formations to look out for each other and at Biggin Hill flew their maiden Spitfire sorties together. And they got their baptism of fire over the Channel together. But as uplifting as banding together this squadron of eager young Canadians felt, Fighter Command victories were few and far between that fall. On October 27, 1941, a Biggin Wing sweep over Dunkirk and the resulting dogfight with scores of Messerschmitt Bf 109s produced an all too frequent result.

"The ground crew from 'A' Flight came into the dispersal hut and sat around in dead silence. None of their aircraft had returned," Godefroy wrote. "We had lost Wally Floody, Johnny Small, Blake Wallace, Stan Thompson and Brian Hodgkinson." Three of them had been shot down "on their first ever sweep."[6]

It got worse in November when, during the first week of operations into France, the Biggin Wing lost ten of twelve fighter pilots. Then, on November 8, a flight of Spitfires from 401 conducted a sweep over the River Somme Estuary, where German fighter aircraft swooped down and broke up the Spitfire formation. Godefroy was chased by four Bf 109s. He twisted, turned, and threw his aircraft around the sky to the point of near exhaustion, all the while firing at whatever he saw until his ammunition ran out. He barely made it home in one piece. At the dispersal hut he turned in his escape kit and gave his combat report to the duty intelligence officer (IO).

"Weir and Gardiner are missing,"[7] the IO said.

"Weir missing?" Godefroy shot back, admitting he'd never worried about his friend not returning.

"Blakeslee* reported seeing two Spitfires astern, both on fire," the IO added.

---

* American-born Don Blakeslee joined the RCAF in August 1940, arrived in England in January 1941 to serve with 401 Squadron (earning a DFC), and was transferred to 133 Eagle Squadron in June 1942 as a flight leader. In August 1943 he flew four sorties over Dieppe and was promoted to squadron leader. By the time the three Eagle Squadrons were turned over to the USAAF as the heart of 4th Fighter Group, Blakeslee had flown 120 Spitfire sorties and accumulated 240 combat hours.

It was Wally Gardiner's first ever sweep, but John Weir had accumulated a thousand hours in operational flying. To Godefroy, not seeing the "tough as nails and perpetual clown"[8] John Weir home safe for a celebratory drink and slap on the back "seemed impossible." Nevertheless, the job of informing Weir's parents and Frances McCormack, his fiancée, fell to Godefroy. Of course, the air force would send the obligatory "we regret to inform you" form letter, but Godefroy worried that whatever words of sympathy and explanation he might cobble together would fall short. Nothing seemed appropriate or adequate. And the silence that followed proved equally painful. Later, Frances would learn that when her fiancé's Spitfire was attacked at an altitude of twenty-six thousand feet over Caen, France, Messerschmitt shells had ignited one of his fuel tanks. The resulting fire had burned his hands and face, nearly fusing his eyelids shut. A combination of adrenaline and shock must have masked any pain; he'd managed to bail out and, once on the ground, he'd immediately set about burying his parachute and attempting to disappear into the countryside. To no avail. Soon after, F/O Weir was captured, processed at the Dulag Luft, and became a prisoner of war—*Kriegsgefangenen* or "kriegie"—en route to the airmen's prison at Barth.

Luftwaffe-run prison camps, such as Stalag Luft I, housed captured air force personnel. As opposed to the *Offizier Lager* or *Oflag* prison for non-commissioned officers, the Luft camps generally imprisoned Commonwealth officers shot down in bombers or fighters. As a rule, those officers, even as POWs, were treated with respect. The morning after he was shot down over Boulogne, France, in January 1942, RAF Spitfire pilot Robert Stanford Tuck was wakened by a German lieutenant, who first saluted him smartly. "We are taking you by train to Germany," the young German officer said. "You are regarded as an important prisoner . . ."[9] Throughout his trip to Dulag Luft, Stanford Tuck was fed hot drinks, soup, plenty of bread, and potatoes. He was, after all, a squadron leader.

The architects of Germany's military prison camps could not have conceived of a better containment area than the facility on the outskirts of the medieval town of Barth. Situated on a peninsula jutting out into the Baltic Sea on the north coast of Germany, the grounds and location of Stalag Luft I alone posed a deterrent to escape. Its sandy soils lay flat and virtually without contour; sightlines were perfect for prison guards. A lagoon to the southeast and the open sea to the northeast meant the water table would be relatively high, only six to eight feet underground; so any thoughts of deep tunnel digging appeared to be out of the question. Some pine tree growth beyond the camp perimeter broke the skyline, but not the flow of frigid north winds off the Baltic.

The man-made containment, built in the summer of 1940, consisted of barbed-wire fencing with watch towers manned around the clock by armed German guards. Initially, the camp was a dusty cage, roughly one hundred yards long and seventy yards wide.[10] The perimeter was further accentuated with a ditch excavated just inside the outer wire. Then, just inside that ditch, a second line of wire was strung—at about boot-top level. This wire marked the boundary between the inner camp and a no man's land; prisoners were warned if they ventured beyond the inner wire they would be shot. The compound housing, initially built to hold about two hundred prisoners, was spartan at best. The Germans had hastily constructed low, wooden barracks huts, some with partitioned areas (rooms) containing double-decker bunks for nine to a dozen men (changed to triple-deckers as the number of POWs swelled). The huts lacked insulation, which meant the inside temperature matched the outside in summer and winter, unless the room offered a stove with a modest amount of fuel. And if the chilling winds and primitive accommodation weren't demoralizing enough, the knowledge that just forty miles northwest, out in the Baltic Sea, lay the international border between Germany and Denmark, made Stalag Luft I the epitome of frustration.

"My darling, here I am safe and sound in Germany,"[11] John Weir eventually wrote in the first letter to Frances, in mid-December 1941.

The letter was written on a single, prison-issue, skin-thin piece of paper, which was the allowable limit for POWs. The page measured ten inches by five-and-a-half inches—enough for about three hundred words—and folded in thirds for mailing. Weir wrote that his letters wouldn't be frequent or very explicit, what with the Germans censoring everything. He appeared to be cut off from the rest of the camp, likely in some kind of solitary. He was not the usual upbeat "Scruffy," kidding and romanticizing about things, and he encouraged Frances and the Weir family back in Canada to contact Red Cross authorities to send him parcels because, he wrote, he really needed socks and a shaving brush. Finally, perhaps to ease her mind, he wrote that he had her photograph close by.

By the time he'd composed and mailed his Christmas 1941 letter, ten days later, Weir's demeanour seemed to have improved. Instead of sounding lost, forlorn, and forgotten, he explained that the Germans had been treating them civilly, that his captors had laid out a skating rink area for hockey (all they needed was ice and skates) and that the entire camp was envious of his colour photo of Frances. In addition to wishing her a Merry Christmas, however, Weir added "as education and entertainment" that he was taking language instruction and that he had been put into a barracks with other downed airmen.

"There are quite a few Canadians (twenty-eight or twenty-nine) here," he wrote, sounding more upbeat. "In fact, my darling, it's not bad at all. . . . I hope I'll be on my way back to you soon."[12]

Perhaps the last thing John Weir might have found inviting about imprisonment in an enemy POW compound, Frances would soon learn, was the camp's education and entertainment facilities. She knew that as a younger man her fiancé had actually travelled with his family in pre-war Germany. Even so, discovering that he was enrolling in language study in a POW camp must have seemed a bit odd. Yet there it was, his sudden attraction to studying Spanish, French, and German, and even trigonometry and calculus, if he wanted. Perhaps less odd to his fiancée was Weir's delight that some of his air force mates—Hank Birkland and Wally Floody—were barracked in the same prison hut. Frances would learn later that attending German language instruction inside the camp was preparing her fiancé for life on the run outside the wire, if he could get there. Meanwhile, reacquainting himself with his air force comrades was offering him the means to fulfill that off-handed promise he'd made in his Christmas letter to "be on my way back to you soon."

Unlike John Weir's relatively comfortable upbringing in Toronto, Hank Birkland's background told a tougher, more school-of-hard-knocks tale. Hank was born in 1917, one of a carpenter's seven children, in Spearhill, Manitoba. Like many of his generation—born around the time of the Great War and raised during the Great Depression—Birkland rode the rails, worked for his keep, and chased any and all opportunities as a farm hand, meat packer, door-to-door salesman,[13] and labourer in the ore mines of Ontario and the gold mines of British Columbia. In Sheep Creek, BC, he even returned to one of his favourite childhood pastimes—playing lacrosse. With his size and strength came the nickname "Big Train." When the Second World War broke out, Birkland's enlistment might well have offered him as much a way out of the Dirty Thirties—with three square meals a day, a new suit of clothes, and a paycheque—as it presented a way to defend King and Empire. At any rate, in the fall of 1941, Flying Officer Birkland was in the RAF and piloting Spitfires with 72 Squadron; during a sweep over the coast of France, German anti-aircraft gunners brought his Spitfire down to a crash landing on the beach and ultimately brought him to the same Stalag Luft I barrack hut as John Weir.

Also sharing that hut was Weir's former 401 Squadron wing mate, Wally Floody, shot down just days before him. The six-foot-tall Ontarian was an athlete in every sense. Born in Chatham in 1918, Floody had grown up mostly in Toronto, but during his boyhood summers he enjoyed the family's access to farm holidays, camping out on Toronto Island, and competitive team sports such as basketball, football, and baseball. As a teenager in search of work in the mid-1930s, Floody travelled to north-central Ontario for shift work shovelling mud, rock, and precious ores excavated from mines near Timmins and Kirkland Lake. But so too did Floody find time to play for the mining companies' sports teams[14]—the Preston East Dome Mine baseball team and the Lake Shore Mines Blue Devils basketball team. Floody did not have the matriculation diploma from high school to gain entry to the RCAF, but a letter from his high school principal convinced the enlistment officer, and Floody joined soon after Canada declared war on Germany. In the short span of eighteen months in 1940 and 1941, Floody got married, graduated from the British Commonwealth Air Training Plan, got his commission in the RCAF, and was shipped overseas, only to be shot down on his first op, October 27, 1941.

"I'm having my picture taken . . . in an all-Canadian group," John Weir signed off his Christmas 1941 letter to Frances.

The photo depicted a short but broad-shouldered jack-of-all trades, Hank Birkland, aged twenty-four, imprisoned at Stalag Luft I six weeks; a hard-rock miner and natural team leader, Wally Floody, aged twenty-three, in the Barth camp eight weeks; and the youngest, at twenty-two, John Weir, a natural outdoorsman with a scruffy attitude to match, and just a month inside the first prisoner-of-war camp exclusively built for captured British Commonwealth airmen. Since the Luft was run by Luftwaffe, it's likely the photograph of the three Canadians was snapped by a German airman, who on any other day would have been the Canadians' mortal enemy. But with his prisoners safely contained inside the wire, the Luft guard likely took out a personal camera and snapped the picture as a gesture of ambivalence and respect.

Behind that ambivalence and respect lay one of the strangest contradictions of Germany's prisoner-of-war system. In spite of the racial intolerance and obsessive ideology of Germany's ruling Nazis, who systematically brutalized prisoners from the East, the regime appeared to deal with prisoners from the West with a degree of deference. With some exceptions,* in dealings with POWs from

---

* In the summer of 1944, German authorities delivered as many as 168 Allied airmen shot down over occupied Europe to the Buchenwald concentration camp. Since many of these Allied aircrew, including twenty-six Canadians, had been assisted by members of European underground groups (and were therefore disguised as civilians carrying non-military identity papers), their German captors considered them spies not protected by the Geneva Conventions. At Buchenwald they were subjected to the same torture, deprivation, confinement, work details, and even human medical experimentation that others faced in the death camp. By October, most air force prisoners were transferred to German prison camps under Luftwaffe control.

the Commonwealth countries and the United States, the Germans recognized certain clauses of the Geneva Conventions. Early in the war there was a very practical reason for such regard; some of those same Commonwealth nations, Britain and Canada for example, held German POWs on their side of the battle lines. As well, though the overall responsibility for wartime prisoners lay in the hands of the German supreme commander of the Wehrmacht, control of the camps themselves fell to army, navy, and air force chiefs where the prisons were located. In the case of captured Allied aviators, all camp administration, food and clothing allotment, accommodation, and day-to-day concerns were governed by the command of the air district, or *Luftgau*.[15] Nor did it hurt downed Allied aviators that *Reichsmarschall* Hermann Göring held great sway with Hitler; it was no secret that Göring had high regard for fellow fliers no matter which side they fought for. And up until 1944 that attitude at the top filtered down and was reflected in all treatment of captured Allied air officers. It meant, for example, that captured enemy airmen from the Commonwealth or the United States generally did not have to work inside prisons. Allied senior officers would be saluted by equals and lower ranks on the German side. Allied chains of command would be acknowledged even inside the prison wire. Allied officers could receive mail (including regular Red Cross parcels) and send it. They would be entitled to recreation and entertainment of their own making. That Göring chivalry, a holdover from the Great War, at least early in Germany's war with the West, influenced daily life in Luftwaffe-run POW camps.

When that first photograph of John Weir arrived with a letter at Frances McCormack's Toronto home, it shocked her. For the first time she saw how severely Weir's face had been injured when he bailed out of the burning Spitfire near the River Somme in France. She could see that his eyelids were virtually gone. No doubt she also recognized the starkness of conditions at the prison camp—the barren setting, the primitive huts, the wire-bound world that was his home for the foreseeable future. She marvelled at her fiancé's strength, his sense of humour, and his very clear vision of the future.

"I've been playing hockey a little and I'm really in fine fettle," he wrote, and then added a cryptic note about his living arrangements that may have had more to do with escape activity at the camp than building their future dream home. "I'm still working on a design for our cabin, dear. There are a few architects here who'll help once I get a decent idea to work on. . . . I still have trouble with the children's rooms—how many, four?"[16]

Next to the Britons imprisoned at Stalag Luft I, the Canadians were in the minority and—even inside the prison wire—obliged to respect the authority of the Senior British Officer and his adjutant. At Barth, Group Captain Harry "Wings" Day was the SBO. Formerly a member of the Royal Marine Light Infantry in the Great War, Day had been awarded the Albert Medal for saving the lives of crewmen aboard the torpedoed HMS *Britannia* in November 1918. In the RAF, as the Second World War began, Day served with 57 Squadron, where he earned his nickname, but was shot down five weeks into the war on a reconnaissance operation near Essen, Germany. His adjutant on the Permanent Staff at Stalag Luft I, Lieutenant Commander Jimmy Buckley, had trained for naval aviation and served aboard the Royal Navy's aircraft carrier HMS *Glorious* before the war; however, as British aircrew attempted to provide cover for the evacuation of the British Expeditionary Force from France in May 1940, Buckley was shot down over Calais. Another member of the Permanent Staff at Stalag Luft I was RAF Squadron Leader Tom Kirby-Green, who had piloted thirty-seven combat operations when his Wellington bomber was shot down in October 1941. Inside the wire at Barth, he assisted the SBO as a one-man welcoming committee by entertaining newcomers on his bongo drums, offering bits of exotic food from his Red Cross parcels, and delivering lectures in the library room.

Inside Stalag Luft I, Group Captain Day and Lieutenant Commander Buckley appeared quite compliant to German demands—helping inbound prisoners acclimatize to their new surroundings.

Following interrogation by the Germans, a newly arrived POW met with the SBO and his RAF Permanent Staff, received some necessary toiletries from a Red Cross parcel, and was assigned to a barracks hut. The Luftwaffe administration anticipated that the civilized nature of relations between prison camp officials and the kriegies would defuse any hostility inmates might feel and might even invite a POW to allow vital information to slip out. Conversely, the RAF Permanent Staff expected the Germans to think that British Commonwealth prisoners were resigned to their fate to sit out the war without resistance. In fact, Day as SBO and Buckley as "Big X" (chief of X Organization) were hard at work scouring the camp for ideas, arranging the escape expertise, and executing each new plan.*

"I had worked in the gold mines in northern Ontario," Wally Floody said. "But if you had [an air force] commission and had worked in a mine, the Englishmen figured you had to be an engineer, and if you had worked in a mine you knew a lot about tunnelling in sand. But there was absolutely no similarity between the two."[17]

Thousands of feet below ground level in the Lake Shore Gold Mines near Kirkland Lake, Ontario, Floody could pass other miners in tunnels that were seven feet high and chiselled through solid Canadian Shield. Sub-surface at Stalag Luft I, escapers dug through unstable sand to create passageways barely two feet wide by two feet deep; they worked on their backs or their stomachs and faced the threat of being buried alive with every cut into the sand. Nevertheless, the trio of Weir, Birkland, and Floody became the principal architects and work crew for the first tunnelling expeditions at the Barth prison compound. Since the huts included boards that skirted the exterior walls to the ground, the digging crews simply crawled unnoticed into the two-foot space under the huts. First they built a trapdoor. Then they excavated a shaft straight down and cribbed it

---

* The first official escape meeting took place at Dulag Luft near Frankfurt-am-Main, in August 1940, when Royal Navy airman, Lieutenant Peter "Hornblower" Fanshawe, directed the construction of a tunnel through the fall of the year, but the Germans discovered it just as it reached the prison camp fence.

with wood scavenged from the huts. When excavation ended each day, the diggers would simply cover the entrance with boards, pile sandbags around it, and brush earth on top of the entrance.

Once underground, the dig crews determined where the water table lay; at Barth it was situated just a few feet beneath the surface of the compound sand. But since it proved extremely difficult to keep a tunnel perfectly level, the digging crew often returned to its work on a new day to find depressions in the tunnel filled with water. That forced the diggers to work virtually naked so as not to reveal a pair of pants or a shirt or a jacket covered in wet sand. Additionally, the farther the tunnel proceeded from the hut, the staler the air became. At first, Floody dug narrow shafts upward to allow fresher air into the tunnel. Then the tunnel crew designed its first air pump, consisting of a German jam can with a flop valve and a bicycle pump.

"Geez, if you went down below about four feet you were swimming in fucking water," Floody said. "And putting up air holes wasn't a total success either."[18]

The Germans discovered the first tunnel when it caved in from flooding and multiple air holes. That prompted a sea change among the Luftwaffe guards running the camp. German work crews began systematically stripping the Luft huts of their skirting boards to reveal the space between the floors of the huts and the ground. They also began driving heavy wagons around the compound to collapse any shallow tunnels.[19] They organized a counter-intelligence team called *Abwehr*, or "defence," dressed the men in blue-grey-coloured overalls and equipped them with steel probing rods. The kriegies dubbed them "ferrets" and fought back with a primitive form of security. A prisoner was assigned the job of taking his laundry—perhaps a pair of underwear and socks—close to the front gate of the compound. He would erect a clothesline with a string stretched between two nails to apparently dry his laundry. The moment vehicles, guards, or ferrets approached the front gate, the laundry man would simply remove his shorts and socks from the line. That alerted a system of prisoners, bucket brigade style, that there was a potential threat to the tunnel. Digging could be shut down and a tunnel trapdoor concealed in minutes. What emerged from the desolation of the camp and the persistence of the POWs to work together was an esprit de corps that went beyond the protocol of squadron barracks in Fighter and Bomber commands. The kriegies had fashioned a prison camp collaboration that knit them together into a single cause—theirs was a bond of wire.

"I tried digging in the tunnels," Pilot Officer (P/O) Barry Davidson said, "but I got claustrophobic."[20]

Compared to the other Canadians imprisoned at Stalag Luft I, Davidson, at age twenty-eight, was the old man of the group. He had learned to fly in the middle of the Great Depression and earned his private flying licence on a Tiger Moth at the Calgary Municipal Airport in 1937. The moment he got the certificate, he wrote a letter to Chinese General Chiang Kai-shek, who was attempting to repulse attacks from the Imperial Japanese armed forces; Davidson offered his services to the Chinese "Flying Tigers," but the general politely declined. No matter. Next, he travelled to England, joined the RAF, and became a Blenheim bomber pilot with 18 Squadron. In July 1940, as the German blitzkrieg gobbled up the Low Countries and northern France, Davidson's squadron was dispatched to slow the enemy offensive.

"We found one of the forward new aerodromes they were building . . . around fifteen miles from Paris," Davidson said. "So we lined up on the equipment at the end of the aerodrome with two of our two-hundred-and-fifty-pound bombs."[21]

The German anti-aircraft batteries finally responded and shrapnel ripped through the centre of Davidson's Blenheim, destroying its wing and tail controls. Disoriented and with a dead stick (virtually no control over the aircraft's direction or attitude in the air), he managed to crash-land the bomber on a beach. He hoped it might be a friendly Allied coast. But moments later, his plane was surrounded by German troops informing him and his crew they were prisoners of war. His first letter home to family in Calgary was a simple one.

"Looks like I am in cold storage for the duration,"[22] he wrote.

But if his talents had not properly been put to the test in the air over France, they more than adequately served him on the ground inside Stalag Luft I. Davidson quickly blended into the Canadian kriegie contingent and came to understand that the war had deprived the prison guards of much the same amenities it had the POWs. So, as soon as Red Cross parcels became available to the prisoners of war, Davidson used some of their contents to advance the priorities of the escape committee. Davidson managed to put parcel staples, such as chocolate, coffee, and cigarettes, into the hands of the guards in return for items that would come in handy for the kriegies. Back came tools for tunnelling, the loan of a camera, and the raw materials for forged documents. An avid sportsman, Davidson helped secure sports gear—tennis rackets, baseballs and bats, and hockey skates and sticks—from the YMCA in Morgan's department store back in Canada. The equipment may well have provided kriegies some welcome recreation, but the hardwood from tennis rackets burned long and hot in a barracks stove and a used skate blade often enjoyed a second life as a cutting or digging tool.[23] From the moment he got settled in the POW compound, P/O Davidson became known as "the scrounger."

He wasn't the only one skilled in the art of scrounging. MacKinnon "Mac" Jarrell, from Armow, Ontario, joined the RAF in 1940 and trained as a navigator and bomb-aimer serving aboard Blenheim aircraft. In July 1941, on his twenty-second operation, Jarrell was shot down and badly burned in the episode. The hospital where Mac was admitted happened to have a German-born doctor raised in the United States. Seconded to military medical work, the doctor administered to Jarrell's burns with plastic surgery[24] and nursed him back to health. When Jarrell was finally discharged and sent to a POW camp in central Germany, he joined an escape committee that built a tunnel and, months later, nineteen escaped through it. After his recapture, six days later, Mac was considered high-risk to escape, so the Germans kept moving him from prison camp to prison camp—eight different camps over the next forty-five months.

Once he was cleared by the escape committee at each prison compound, Jarrell joined a crew of scroungers getting to know the German guards and taming them—i.e., bartering with them for the equipment and supplies X Organization needed for its long-term escape agenda. Among other bribing tools, Mac used the flow of tobacco sent from home, including cigarette packs from the Ontario Chinese Patriotic Federation. Also sent from Canada, and innocently cleared by the Luftwaffe administration at the compound, were small wind-up phonograph machines and a regular supply of recordings.

"One record called 'Corn Silk,'" Mac noted in his log, "came in almost every package. It was terrible and the prisoners hated it."[25]

But that was the intention. Eventually, one POW in the compound became so agitated over the horrible sound of "Corn Silk" that he smashed the record only to discover a map of Germany and area had been hidden inside. Suddenly, Jarrell's scrounging crew had additional contraband to assist in the long-range escape plans.

Another western Canadian joined the Stalag Luft I escape committee about the same time that Barry Davidson did. Of course, it had never been Dick Bartlett's intention to become a POW. Born in 1919 and raised on a dairy farm near Fort Qu'Appelle, Saskatchewan, as a boy Dick raised silver foxes, the assets of which underwrote his passage to England and provisional entry into the Royal Navy Fleet Air Arm (RNFA) in 1938. By October of 1939, a month into the Second World War, Bartlett had received his RNFA graduation wings and joined the torpedo training unit perfecting airborne sorties against German shipping across the Channel. By the spring of 1940, as the Nazi occupation of northwestern Europe and Scandinavia began, Sub Lieutenant Bartlett was posted to 803 Squadron flying Skua dive-bombers attacking targets in occupied Norway. The Skuas were manned by a pilot facing forward in the cockpit and, right behind, a gunner facing aft. As the sun rose ahead of them on June 13, 1940, during an attempted attack on the German battle cruisers *Scharnhorst* and *Gneisenau* in Trondheim harbour, Bartlett and his gunner Lloyd Richards took return fire from German Bf 109s.

"A heavy blow [felt like] a kick from a mule,"[26] Bartlett explained later.

Machine-gun bullets and cannon-shell shrapnel had penetrated the Skua's fuselage, its fuel tank, and Bartlett's flight suit up his left side. Unable to evade the fighters and rapidly losing consciousness, Bartlett barely made it over the rooftops of Trondheim, and as the Skua disintegrated—ultimately losing its engine—he crashed-landed into a field. Only three of the fifteen Skuas had completed the attack. Bartlett and his gunner survived their crash, but even as he received treatment at a Trondheim hospital, it didn't take Bartlett long to consider his escape options. Two attempts later, he was put under guard and sent to a series of POW camps in northern Germany and Poland, including Stalag XX-A, where he learned an important covert skill.

"Through friendly relations with Polish labourers at the camp," Bartlett related, "[we] bribed one of the Poles to sneak the components for a small radio receiver into the camp."[27]

The resulting wireless set allowed the POWs to hear BBC broadcasts. But to ensure that the radio was never discovered by German guards or ferrets, Bartlett regularly disassembled it and placed its parts inside a medicine ball; the ball, a bit larger than a basketball and usually weighted with sand, was used by prisoners of war for calisthenics and other sporting pursuits. Without the guards or ferrets ever realizing it, the wireless set was always out in the open, being carefully tossed among the "sports enthusiasts," and consequently under close surveillance by members of the escape committee. Only when the kriegies could safely open the medicine ball was the radio pulled from its hiding place and assembled to catch the BBC news from England.

"[That way,] the radio-equipped medicine ball subsequently travelled from camp to camp [becoming] a continuous source of war news and intelligence,"[28] Bartlett pointed out, and always with S/L Bartlett as its custodian. Despite his standing assignment at Stalag Luft I—protecting the radio—Bartlett was never far from the escape planning among his fellow Canadian POWs.

"I haven't missed any German lectures yet," John Weir reported to Frances in his first letter of 1942 from the Barth prison camp. "I keep myself fairly busy, so the time doesn't drag too much . . . what with learning to cook and stuff." Then, in what seemed a Freudian slip apparently missed by both the German and British censors, Weir concluded that Hank Birkland, Wally Floody, and he "will dig in for the winter;" then he signed off with his now routinely optimistic, "it won't be long before this war is over and we will be home again."[29]

Wally Floody noted from his experience inside several German POW camps that there were only three ways of escaping—over the wire, through the wire, or under the wire. He, Birkland, and Weir had chosen tunnelling as the safest and most efficient way out. At Barth, however, the kriegies tried every possible scenario and the RAF Permanent Staff wasn't about to blunt their initiative. In January 1942, a prisoner tried to escape by hiding in a cart that had just emptied the compound's latrines. Several others attempted to disguise themselves in mock-ups of German uniforms. Another jumped into a snow bank, but was spotted when steam rising from the snow where he was hiding gave him away. Later that winter, three airmen used the cover of a blizzard to cut their way through the wire at the NCO's compound, but a guard spotted the trio and shot Sergeant Johnny Shaw, making him the first fatality of the escape campaign.[30]

Arrivals at Barth continued to mount. During the Battle of Britain, RAF fighter pilots who were shot down most often parachuted to safety on British territory; after Dunkirk and the fall of France, however, surviving fighter pilots who bailed out over occupied France and Belgium most often became prisoners of war. In 1941, for example, RAF Fighter Command claimed 711 Luftwaffe fighters shot down, while sustaining the loss of four hundred Hurricanes and Spitfires, mostly over enemy territory. Similarly, between July of 1940 and January of 1941, RAF Bomber Command lost 330 aircraft, resulting in fourteen hundred aircrew killed, missing, or captured. Over the course of the entire war, more than six hundred Fighter Command and nearly ten thousand Bomber Command aircrew became prisoners of war.* Most of them were captured in Europe and most came through the Luft containment system.

The flow of downed and captured Commonwealth aircrew—perhaps a dozen or two a month at the beginning of the war—became a torrent of hundreds a month in 1941 and 1942; the tide of downed airmen had grown too with the entry of the United States into the war after the Japanese air attack on Pearl Harbor in December 1941. The impact of this ever-growing prisoner-of-war population on Luftwaffe resources—the availability of trained interrogators, transit guards, and bureaucrats, not to mention food, accommodation, and living space—became more than one prison facility could handle. But camp administrators recognized they were facing perhaps an even greater problem—the growing number of dedicated escape artists the camp appeared to be fostering. And with the growing number of escape attempts, *Kommandants* at POW camps across Germany feared reprisals from their superiors should any of the large-scale escape plots succeed.

Meanwhile, Wings Day took full advantage of that fear, even if in truth as few as 5 per cent of the POWs might be described as dedicated escapers. Day's intelligence told him that maybe a quarter of the camp's inmates considered escape an option. To further motivate kriegie escape attempts, he made it known that escaping was an "operational function"[31] in the camp, reinforcing the perception that attempting an escape was an RAF airman's duty. The result was nearly a fever pitch of escape activity at Stalag Luft I; or, as Day described it, he'd been incarcerated "in a kennel with a good pack of foxhounds" all sniffing to get out.

John Weir's letters to his fiancée trailed off slightly in the winter and spring of 1942. In a few notes during January and February,

---

* Between 1939 and 1945, from a total of 125,000 aircrew, Bomber Command lost 55,573 airmen killed, 8,403 wounded, and 9,838 became prisoners of war; 8,325 aircraft were lost. Fighter Command lost 3,690 airmen killed, 1,215 wounded, and 601 became prisoners of war; 4,790 aircraft were lost. Total RCAF casualties included 3,150 killed, 9,890 presumed dead, and 49 who died as POWs.

he wondered if Hugh Godefroy (still flying with 401 Squadron) had found the gold pin John had purchased for Frances as a Christmas present just two days before he was shot down on November 8, 1941. Then, in just a couple of letters in late winter, he explained that hockey was over because the rink had become a mud hole and that the reduced number of Red Cross parcels had left him in need of basic "clothing—pajamas, sox [sic], shoes, slippers, gloves and cap."[32] Yes, Frances had received her Christmas present, but she sensed her fiancé's calls for additional clothes were more for a stockpile than his own personal use. He was up to something.

As it turned out, so were the German prison authorities. Scuttlebutt around the Barth compound suggested most of the officers and air force NCOs were about to be packed off to somewhere in Silesia. In mid-March, Stalag Luft I guards instructed the prisoners to pack their belongings, assembled them for parade, and marched them to the trains outside Barth. Along with the instructions came warnings against any attempts to escape. Roommates Birkland, Floody, and Weir became separated when the Germans loaded POWs into the train cars alphabetically, but that didn't dissuade Scruffy. He teamed up with another kriegie named Mike Wood and the two worked out the details of Weir's escape plan.

Based on maps the escape committee had stowed away in the camp, Scruffy expected the eastbound train would pass through Stettin, which had access to the sea; if the two men could loosen the train windows and jump from the moving train as it slowed through Stettin, maybe they could make it to the harbour and stow away on a ship. Everything went according to plan—preparation of the windows, the jump from the train, safe passage to the waterfront, and refuge overnight until they could find a ship leaving the port. It nearly worked until they ran into an SS officer and were arrested, jailed, interrogated, and shipped off to their intended destination—the Silesian town of Sagan and the new home of imprisoned aircrew, Stalag Luft III.

"Hello, Darling," John Weir began his twelfth letter home to Frances McCormack in the spring of 1942. "We are now well installed in the new camp . . . situated in the middle of a reforestation area with lots of fresh air."33

Scruffy complained that it had been almost two months since he'd heard from anybody in Canada. His fiancée and the Weir family had no idea he had just been shipped from a prison camp where he'd participated in forty-eight tunnel escape attempts, daily goon-baiting (terrorizing the German Officers or Non-coms, or "goons"), and then a nearly successful leap to freedom from the prison train.

"We've been clearing stumps for a kitchen garden (I only hope the Germans give us some seed) and for basketball, volleyball, and tennis courts. . . . Besides that I'm slinging the discus. I hope to be fairly healthy by the time I get back to you. Then all you'll have to do is fatten me up."34

Frances McCormack wouldn't necessarily have understood what her husband-to-be was up to, but clearing stumps, gardening, and pursuing sport while inside the wire at this new state-of-the-art prison camp in Silesia were not at all about filling a cold cellar with fresh produce for POWs' diets or even about keeping fit. These were the grassroots pursuits of a transplanted escape committee already cultivating its next plan.

# "SPINE-TINGLING SPORT"

TREES used for reforestation, especially pines planted closely together, are cultivated that way to allow fast growth upward, not much outward. Stuck into the ground as seedlings perhaps a few feet apart, and with little or no human attention—water or fertilizer—reforestation pines shoot skyward. Their purpose is not to grow freely, but to keep loose, sandy soils from eroding and to create, overnight, what foresters refer to as a "green wall." For some years, farmers along the Bobr River near the town of Sagan in Silesia had protected their sandy soils by planting rows and rows of these fast-growing pines. By the 1940s, thousands of tall, palisade-like pines appeared to cut off the town of twenty-five thousand inhabitants from the outside world. Whether by accident or design, when Sagan's new arrivals—several hundred aircrew prisoners of war—began debarking at the train station and marching down the road to their new quarters, the pine forest seemed to gobble them up for good.

"Situated in the middle of Sagan forest," one aircrew POW said, "one could never see more than a few hundred yards in any direction, except upwards. . . . The lack of view rather enhanced the fenced-in feeling."[1]

In fact, the new prison compound—Stalag Luft III—was carved out of those woods, hundreds of miles from any ocean coastline and even farther from existing battlefields; there was little chance that an escaper could get far enough west to contact the French or

Dutch Underground, or the other direction to find refuge with Soviet allies beyond the Eastern Front. For a year before the prison camp opened in March of 1942, Russian forced-labour workers and eventually some of the first non-commissioned Allied aircrew (whom the Germans could force to work) who were brought there chopped down many of the reforested pines to form a clearing—about three hundred acres of grey-coloured sandy topsoil. The fine consistency of the soil would pose an obvious problem for tunnellers, while assisting any camp officials thwarting them. Working in the tunnellers' favour, however, was the virgin ground, without any previous excavation and (unlike Barth) with a water table hundreds of feet under the surface. In addition, Sagan, less than a mile from the camp, was a busy train terminus with six rail lines intersecting in its marshalling yard. And while that meant smoother delivery of prisoners from trains to platforms and then to the compound, for any observant POW the presence of so many railway lines seemed to provide countless ways to exit town, should he get that far.

The Germans had built two separate and parallel wire fences around the roughly half-mile-square compound. The double-jeopardy fences each stood about ten feet tall and six to eight feet apart. Atop the fences, like a thorny crown, they had installed a barbed-wire overhang that pointed inward toward the prisoners. And between the two fences they had piled and strung additional barbed wire to impede any passage. Illustrating the immense size of the prison, about thirty feet inside the outer fence was an inner warning wire, strung about eighteen inches off the ground; beyond the knee-high wire was no man's land, and any POW caught in it, they were told, would be shot without warning. Guard towers were positioned on each corner and every hundred or so yards along the perimeter of the compound; all were armed with searchlights and machine guns. Eight barrack buildings were built a further forty yards inside the warning wire (each hut sat several feet off the ground on concrete pillars so that ferrets could inspect beneath them at a glance), as well as a wash house, a cookhouse, a couple of latrines, and a pool for rainwater in case of fire. Meanwhile, outside the entire enclosure, the pine forest had been clear-cut back as much as a hundred feet beyond the double fences. The message was evident everywhere: this camp was built to prevent escaping.

When the majority of their occupants began arriving on the first day of spring 1942, there were two compounds ready and waiting. The East Compound contained eight barracks huts; these would house approximately nine hundred air force officer prisoners. The Centre Compound had a dozen barracks to house approximately sixteen hundred non-commissioned air force prisoners. Every POW barrack was a wooden, single-storey hut containing twelve good-sized rooms, and each of those held six double-decker bunk beds and a stove for heat in winter (whenever fuel was provided); before they became overcrowded, two of the dozen rooms in each hut offered a library and recreation room. West of the Centre Compound was the *Kommandantur*,[2] the German administrative compound for the whole camp. To the northeast stood the *Vorlager*, the utility section of the camp housing a bathhouse, an infirmary, buildings to store fuel and supplies, housing for Russian prisoners (the camp's forced labour), and the notorious "cooler"—solitary confinement cells.

For several days freight trains pulled into Sagan Junction disgorging their human cargo—Allied air force prisoners that none of the German *Kommandants* at POW camps across Germany ever wanted to see again. Emerging from the "forty-and-eights"—boxcars built for either forty men or eight horses but often fit for neither—were hundreds of the most experienced escape artists the European air war had produced. German authorities figured it was safer to dump all the bad apples into one basket, a basket that could contain them, than to have them causing havoc at thirty different prison camps all over Germany.

Among the prisoners marched into the new facility near Sagan was the old guard of Royal Air Force men, those who had been locked up in German POW camps for two or three years already. Of course, there was Harry "Wings" Day, who had led 57 Squadron's Blenheim bombers right from the beginning of the war, but was brought down in October 1939—on a Friday the thirteenth. Perhaps the Germans had been the unlucky ones for shooting him down that day; as Senior

British Officer, Day entertained most of the hundreds of escape plans while appearing to toe the line with German camp brass. There was Peter Fanshawe, a Royal Navy pilot shot down June 13, 1940, while attacking the German battle cruiser *Scharnhorst*. One of the original kriegies, "Hornblower" Fanshawe had organized the first escape meetings inside Dulag Luft at Frankfurt-am-Main in August 1940.

There were RAF aircrew men such as Blenheim pilot Mike Casey, shot down over Emden, Germany, on October 16, 1939; and Fleet Air Arm flight commander Jimmy Buckley, shot down near Calais, France, six days later on May 29, 1940. Buckley and Casey had organized the first breakout attempts even before RAF airmen were transferred to Stalag Luft I at Barth. From Warburg and Oflag VI-B prisoner-of-war camp came fighter pilot Douglas Bader (shot down in August 1941), whose Lazarus-like recoveries from combat and crashes had earned him the rank of wing commander, but whose lust for escaping had his German captors threatening to take away both his artificial legs.[3] And from Spangenberg prison came Battle of Britain ace and RAF squadron leader Robert Stanford Tuck, shot down January 28, 1942; he had also made numerous individual escape attempts.

Similarly experienced and equally undeterred by the imposing look of the prison camp were the Canadian POWs. In fact, some of the Canuck prisoners being transported from Spangenberg prison to Sagan had become quite notorious, even among the German hierarchy. When Ottawa-born RAF fighter ace Keith "Skeets" Ogilvie was shot down over Lille, France, on July 4, 1941, William Joyce (a.k.a. Lord Haw Haw, the British-born fascist who became the Nazis' chief English-language broadcaster) announced the victory immediately; normally, processing and publishing such information took days or even months to accomplish.[4] Even earlier, there was the flurry of attention around the capture of Alfred "Tommy" Thompson, from Penetanguishene, Ontario. Like Ogilvie and Tony Pengelly, the twenty-one-year-old Thompson had packed up for England in the 1930s to take advantage of the RAF's Commonwealth-wide enlistment option. Posted to 102 Squadron in 1937 and assigned the job of bombing a German target with propaganda leaflets from his Whitley bomber on September 8, 1939, he and his crew were shot down just five days into the war. Tommy Thompson had the dubious distinction of being the first Canadian airman captured in the war and as such was taken to a special meeting with *Reichsmarschall* Hermann Göring in Berlin.

"He said they discussed hockey," Tommy's son Andrew Thompson said. "[Göring] liked Canadian hockey. That was one topic they talked about. And [Göring] mentioned that my father had gotten him out of bed the night before, when his bomber had flown over Berlin."[5]

Not only was Thompson exposed to Göring, but also to German propaganda cinematographers. Shortly after his capture, they shot newsreel footage and sound of Thompson in his RAF uniform standing at a microphone and speaking about living conditions as a POW.

"Since being taken prisoner here in Germany," Thompson said haltingly to the camera, "my brother officers and myself have been treated with every courtesy and consideration."[6]

Also en route from Spangenberg prison to Sagan was RCAF navigator George McGill, just twenty-three and from Toronto Island. During a combat operation over Wilhelmshaven in January of 1942, McGill was ordered by his pilots to bail out of their burning Wellington bomber. Immediately after the premature order, the two pilots managed to put out the fire and keep the bomber aloft all the way back to England[7], leaving McGill to face years as a POW. And from Barth came F/L Henry Sprague, of Hamilton, Ontario, captured in November 1941 when his Spitfire was shot down over Boulogne by a Focke-Wulf 190.[8] Another Barth alumnus was 102 Squadron bomber pilot Tony Pengelly, as well as Spitfire pilots Hank Birkland from 122 Squadron and Wally Floody from 401 Squadron. Floody's wing (and tunnelling) mate, Scruffy Weir, would arrive a few days later.

All these men had one thing in common. They had experienced years inside the German stalag system. Sometimes alone, other times in teams, they all had plotted and dug tunnels to escape it, and while nearly every one of their attempts had failed, none of the perpetrators had ever given up. Their jailers felt equally assured they could keep their prisoners inside the wire and, with a few exceptions, they had been successful.

When he arrived at the end of his march from Sagan Junction train station, on March 21, and surveyed what his German captors had prepared for the officers and NCOs, Pilot Officer Wally Floody didn't see all the sophistication of the new Sagan camp so much as a preventative system. He considered all the German-designed features of the new facility a compliment to the determination and ingenuity of the kriegies' abilities to find new ways of breaking out.

"It wasn't a punishment camp," he said. "It was the one camp they'd built with all the knowledge they'd acquired during two or three years of holding us prisoners of war. It was supposedly escape-proof."9

The Germans called the new camp Stalag Luft III. The prisoners called it Göring's luxury camp,10 but did so sardonically. Even in the earliest days of captivity there, some of the Commonwealth aircrew POWs weren't prepared to sit still; they set about testing the weakest points of the compound right away. On March 21, the very first day inside the wire, Wings Day joined two other officers in transforming their RAF uniforms to look like German Luftwaffe uniforms (the pants and tunics were not dissimilar in colour), and—being fluent German speakers—tried to talk their way to freedom through the main gate; the bluff didn't work and the three got the obligatory fourteen days of detention in the cooler.

Meanwhile, Jimmy Buckley re-established X Organization* inside the East Compound and began receiving a steady flow of escape

---

* In March 1942, when Commonwealth air force officers arrived at Sagan, Harry Day remained the Senior British Officer and Jimmy Buckley as Big X, chief of the escape committee. In June 1942, Group Captain H. M. Massey arrived at Stalag Luft III and assumed SBO duties. In October 1942, Wings Day, Jimmy Buckley, and others were purged to Oflag XXI-B at Schubin, and Massey to Obermassfeld hospital to treat his injured foot, so the SBO became newly arrived Group Captain D. E. L. Wilson of the Royal Australian Air Force, until Massey returned from treatment in November 1943 and was restored as SBO until May 1944. In March 1943, Day and Buckley participated in an escape from the Schubin prison. Day was recaptured and returned to Sagan just as the North Compound opened, while Buckley disappeared in his attempt to navigate a small boat to Sweden. By that time, Roger Bushell had arrived and had become Big X.

proposals. One scheme—worked out by Bill Nichols, an American in the RAF, and Irish airman Ken Toft—claimed that the mass of coiled wire between the double fences and the distance between German sentry positions created blind spots along the outer barrier. They theorized if the two of them could get across the warning wire to a blind spot at the main fence, they could cut their way through the wire before being spotted. All they needed was a diversion. So, Wings Day and the escape committee organized a series of them. There was a staged fight. A prisoner approached a key sentry box and asked that a phone call go through to the *Kommandant* for an interview. A POW at another sentry box asked permission to retrieve a ball in no man's land. And elsewhere, one prisoner dumped a bucket of water over the head of another. All this distracted the guards long enough to allow Nichols and Toft to snip their way through both fences and the obstruction wire in between. Once the two men emerged outside the double-jeopardy fences, other prisoners orchestrated more diversions to help the escapers get into the pine forest beyond. It all worked. But they were soon recaptured on the run and sent to the cooler too.

It didn't take the seasoned tunnellers long to begin sampling the soil inside the compound and testing the Germans' detection systems. Just as the Canadians had organized themselves at Barth to design, construct, and employ specific tunnelling approaches, a New Zealander and his group had pioneered their own unique tunnelling technique. Air officer Henry Lamond's team would first construct a tunnel about four feet underground and twenty feet long, capable of accommodating three men head-to-toe in a line and closed at each end. Inside the tunnel, the lead digger would pull soil from the front and pass it to the rear. So would the second and the third, advancing the face of the tunnel while enclosing the space behind. The men would work in the nude, pulling their clothes in bundles behind them. They would dig in complete darkness and survive by poking sticks to the surface for air. Lamond's "mole" concept got the green light from Buckley and X Organization that first spring inside the new camp.

In order to make the plan work, the group needed a legitimate excuse to be digging near the double-wire fence. They found one when they realized water from the wash huts drained close to the fences. Day convinced a German duty officer to let the POWs use shovels to trench the water deeper and toward the wire. Over several days Lamond and his two mole mates—Jack Best and Bill Goldfinch—dug the drainage ditch deeper and deeper until they estimated they could begin their horizontal shaft toward the fences without being spotted. Following the evening appell (roll call) on June 30, the three buried themselves in their horizontal shaft and began pulling and pushing the soil to advance their tunnel under the wire. After moling 150 feet, the following night they emerged on the other side of the fence and dashed into the woods. They got all the way to the river near Sagan, stole a rowboat, and managed to make it some distance toward the Baltic when the boat's owner caught up with them and had them arrested.

On most days, since the Geneva Conventions prevented German captors from putting the officer captives to work, any gatherings in the East Compound attracted a lot of kriegies either by accident or design. One September afternoon in 1942 proved no different. Seemingly uninvolved, Jimmy Buckley and Wings Day watched as members of the escape committee assembled a primitive boxing ring in the extreme southeastern corner of the compound. Moments later, as the kriegies began cheering and jeering their arrival, Canadian airmen George McGill and Eddie Asselin entered the ring, donned boxing gloves, and began to spar. Of course, not only was the match a spectacle for the kriegies, but it also captivated the attention of the German sentries, most notably in the guard towers. As it did, and with a nod from Buckley and Day, two POWs dressed like compound workers slipped over the warning wire, quickly hit the dirt in one of those blind spots next to the fences, and began cutting their way through the wire. In just a few minutes, with all eyes riveted on the McGill–Asselin boxing exhibition, the two so-called workers were through the wire and into the woods for at least a temporary escape.

To deter any future above-ground escape attempts, the Germans expanded their sentry staff. The *Kommandant* instituted foot patrols outside the double fences. At night the patrols were augmented with *hundführer*, armed guards with dogs (twenty-four dog handlers and thirty-two dogs). While a guard could survey an area of perhaps thirty-five feet beyond the wire, a watchdog could easily pick up movement or scents across a thousand-foot area.[11]

Meanwhile, to counter the subterranean escape attempts, the German guards dug an eight-foot-deep ditch inside the double fencing in an attempt to deter further moling excavations. That just drew more challenges to the trench; it wasn't long before Canadian digger Joe "Red" Noble and a friend attempted a mole dig from the security ditch, but failed. Then another three-man team tried and was caught. That prompted the Germans to undo the ditch. They filled it back in and resorted instead to a subterranean preventative device they had pioneered at Barth. They buried microphones deep in the ground along the perimeter inside the double fences and posted ferrets on headphones around the clock, listening for the sounds of tools cutting through the soil.[12] It was turning into a tit-for-tat summer. With sentries mounting in number and listening devices going underground, X Organization met to discuss the means of circumventing them. Several familiar tunnelling experts inside the East Compound brought new ideas to the table for consideration.

"The basics are these," Floody told Harry Day and Jimmy Buckley. "First you've got to find a place to sink a shaft. Next, you've got to build a tunnel very deep so the Germans can't hear any digging. You've got to dispose of the sand. And most important, you've got to be able to do all this under the very noses of the Germans."[13]

At the escape committee meeting, Floody suggested they dig two distinct tunnels at the same time, each one thirty feet underground to avoid detection by the buried microphones. If the Germans discovered one of the tunnels, Floody said, the ferrets might let their guard down while the diggers continued with the second tunnel. The tunnelling committee worked out schemes for camouflaging trapdoors in the floors of the barracks huts where the tunnels began. It also hatched a scheme for hiding the real escape tunnels with dummy tunnels. Tunnel diggers would excavate shallow camouflage tunnels that went down a few feet and out about thirty feet before they were terminated. In the floors of the camouflage tunnels the kriegies rigged a trap system through which they would dig an additional shaft fifteen feet deeper underground. That shaft would lead to the entrance of the real escape tunnel. If the Germans discovered the camouflage tunnels, they likely wouldn't spot the deeper shafts. The tunnel crews could then reconnect with the hidden shaft from another location and continue work on the real escape tunnel undetected. Wally Floody and Robert "Crump" Ker-Ramsey began a tunnel from Hut 67, some four hundred feet from the fence line; they figured the Germans would least suspect a tunnel that far from the wire.

"I had started tunnelling in 1941," Floody said. "But by the time we got to Sagan, we were getting pretty expert at it."[14]

Digging deeper into the Silesian sand triggered new problems, however. Each new shift underground meant more diggers emerging with more bags and washbasins of dirt. The volume of soil excavated from camouflage tunnels, vertical shafts, and the two actual escape tunnels began to mount. And because the sub-surface sand was damp and bright yellow in colour, which differed from the fine, dusty grey-coloured sand on the surface of the compound, the escape committee recruited kriegies whose sole job became finding new places and ways of dispersing the excavated sand. Initially, they raked the subsoil into the surface sand beneath the barracks huts, but when ferrets discovered one of the camouflage tunnels, the dispersal crews needed to find new, less obvious hiding places.

The farther down Floody and his diggers burrowed, the tougher it was to breathe. They improvised by fitting sticks together end-to-end and pushing them up to break the surface of the soil above, allowing some fresh air to pass twenty feet down into the escape tunnel. Tunnel sentries, called "stooges," watched for the sticks breaking the surface of the compound soil; their job was to hide the holes—first with their bodies and then by placing a stone temporarily over the air hole. But the air holes proved a half measure. Tunnel diggers, such as Wally Floody, John Weir, and Hank Birkland, could work only a few hours without light or fresh air. When they emerged from their shifts underground, they had to cope with headaches or vomiting. Improvising a solution, Jimmy Buckley found an accordion among the prisoners and had it configured to force fresher air into the tunnel system.

To assist in the dispersal of sand, the diggers changed the direction of one of the main escape tunnels toward the cookhouse so they could hide sand under it. Ferrets discovered the camouflage tunnel and destroyed it. In the process, Floody was caught in a cave-in and nearly suffocated. When Ker-Ramsey and Floody dug their way back toward the main escape tunnel and replaced the camouflage tunnel, they inadvertently weakened the hut foundations above them and the entire dummy tunnel collapsed with Floody still inside. The only thing that saved the veteran tunneller was that his face happened to be over the trapdoor to the vertical shaft; while his teammates dug furiously to reach him, Floody was able to breathe the air from the entrance to the shaft.

When the escape tunnel reached three hundred feet in length, just a hundred feet short of the wire, ferrets raided Hut 67. They tore the building apart and dug far enough to unearth both the dummy tunnels and the main escape tunnel. They blew them all up.

Floody told the escape committee that the elaborate excavation scheme was missing an important ingredient: an equally elaborate scheme to protect the tunnels, the trapdoors, the sand dispersal, and the diggers themselves. In his view, the escape committee had to pay closer attention to security. It needed someone who could be as ruthless as the German prison architects and ferrets. It required the know-how of an individual who could instinctively predict the actions of a prison's inmates and its keepers. It had to find somebody with first-hand knowledge of prison life, well before he fell from the sky and into the Germans' stalag system. It found those qualifications in an RCAF air gunner who had arrived with a civilian record as infamous as his peers' military ones were famous.

"Of the thousand prisoners . . . of Stalag Luft III," George Harsh wrote, "I was the only ex-convict, and so, for me, the psychological adjustment [to being imprisoned] was basically a minor one."[15]

Harsh had lived an entire lifetime, it seemed, before he ever considered risking his second chance at life in the air over German-occupied Europe. The son of a well-to-do family in Milwaukee, Wisconsin, eighteen-year-old George Harsh—fulfilling a "thrill" pact with some buddies at Oglethorpe University in Atlanta—held up a grocery store in 1928. During the robbery, Harsh shot and killed a clerk, was himself shot, then later arrested, charged, tried, found guilty, and sentenced to hang. Plea bargaining saved his life, but relegated Harsh to existence on a Georgia chain gang. For the next twelve years he shovelled dirt for fourteen hours a day, slept in an iron cage, fought off sexual attacks, and eventually knifed another prisoner in a fight over a cake of soap.

In prison Harsh learned how to endure punishment, how to bargain, whom to trust, when and why to fight back, and eventually how to campaign to reform the penal system. Transferred to less severe internment at a Fulton County prison, near Atlanta, Harsh became a trusty (an inmate seeking freedom via legal means), serving as an attendant at the prison hospital and eventually conducting an emergency appendectomy to save a prisoner's life. In 1940 Harsh won a pardon, was freed, and considered his options. He felt the need to begin again with a clean slate. He travelled to Montreal and presently found himself at an air force recruiting centre pleading his case to become an air gunner in the RCAF.

"In one flamboyant *beau geste*,"[16] Harsh wrote, "I was trying to counterbalance my entire past. . . . I was a man trying to prove something."

Overseas Flying Officer George Harsh was posted to 4 Group as a gunnery officer aboard Halifax bombers with 102 Squadron. In Bomber Command's history, early 1942 proved a key period when its commander, Arthur Harris, ramped up the strategic bombing offensive with spectacular one-thousand-bomber raids on Cologne, Lübeck, and Rostock, Germany. This period of Harsh's service, however, also witnessed the improvement of German defences. Harsh and his squadron mates knew well the 4.3 per cent loss rate[17] of Bomber Command raids. That summer, Canadian army, armoured corps, and aircrews had also joined Operation Jubilee, the attack on the French port of Dieppe. On August 19, 1942, 4,963 Canadians spearheaded the morning raid on the seaport in the nine bloodiest hours of Canadian military history; the Second Infantry Division suffered 907 dead and 1,946 captured; the RCAF lost thirteen aircraft, its highest single-day total in the war so far. The setback resonated for everyone in a Canadian service uniform.

Some weeks later, on October 4, RCAF F/O Harsh was not scheduled to fly an operation from 102 Squadron's station at Pocklington, England; however, as gunnery officer he joined the operations officers that night directing the stream of Halifax bombers into the air with signals from an Aldis lamp. The third to last bomber in the flight had a problem. Its rear gunner—on his first op—had a broken gun sight and had no idea what to do. Harsh ordered him out of the turret and went in his place to ensure an experienced gunner was aboard to protect this rookie crew. Everything went wrong that night. Instead of the lightly defended Dusseldorf target, Harsh and his crew found themselves over Cologne and all its night fighter and anti-aircraft defences. His bomber was coned by several searchlights and flak converged on the aircraft, igniting fires and forcing its crew to bail out over Germany. Harsh spent two weeks in hospital for treatment of shrapnel wounds. Then they moved him on to Dulag Luft for interrogation and eventually to Stalag Luft III, where he was photographed, given a kriegie dog tag, and handed over to the SBOs inside the wire.

Over a barracks table, Wing Commander Harry Day conducted the question-and-answer session to verify Harsh was who he claimed to be. Once he'd passed the SBO cross-examination, the serious questioning began. A New Zealand squadron leader wanted to know everything Harsh had witnessed on his way into Sagan: What were the trains like currently? What were present procedures at railway stations? What passes did the guard escort show en route? As Harsh offered his recollections of what he'd seen and heard, the squadron leader made notes on a small "chewable size" piece of paper. Finally, at the end of a very long day that effectively returned him to the life he had led for twelve years in the US penal system, Harsh commiserated with himself about a prospect as dim as it had been his first day shackled to a Georgia chain gang in 1928.

"They tell me you're an American,"[18] a friendly voice suddenly interrupted.

"Yup," Harsh had said, using his best Gary Cooper impression.

"I'm Wally Floody. I got my monthly letter [from home] from the Germans today," he said. "I'm writing my wife, Betty, in Toronto. If there's anyone in the States you want to know you're a prisoner, I'll get her to contact them." Floody explained that by passing on the information in this way, Harsh's family would know he was alive faster than if they waited for official word from the Red Cross or Air Ministry. He was right; Betty Floody was able to notify Harsh's sister of his whereabouts and status six weeks before the official air force form letter arrived with its "we are pleased to inform you" language.

A kriegie friendship and collaboration began in that moment. Floody's generosity left an indelible impression on the latest arrival to Stalag Luft III. In the days that followed, Floody and Harsh often walked the perimeter of the camp, up against the warning wire. It was the only safe place to talk. They shared their histories, their hopes for survival, and the current state of escape committee activity under X Organization. Floody brought Harsh up to date on the growing list of problems facing the tunnel designers and diggers—too much sand to disperse in secret, too many ferrets to track, too many tunnel operations to protect, too limited an inside security force. At the end of one of their exchanges, Harsh walked right into Floody's verbal trap.

"Just how the hell do you guys plan to secure [all] this?"[19] Harsh asked.

"That's going to be your problem," Floody said with a grin. "You, my friend, are going to be in charge of security."

Harsh was not impressed by being dragooned into the job, or by what he realized would become a mammoth responsibility. Floody pointed out that Harsh would be assisted by Canadian officer George

McGill, who had earlier delivered such a convincing escape diversion with his impromptu boxing exhibition that the escape committee immediately recruited him for security. Tom Kirby-Green, who spoke myriad languages (including dialects from his homeland of Nyasaland—now Malawi— in Africa), would become a third member of the security team. And Harsh's final security co-chief would be a fellow American. Albert "Junior" Clark had risen quickly in the military; at age twenty-seven, he was already a lieutenant colonel, and by the summer of 1942 was serving in the RAF. In July he'd been flying a sweep over Abbeville, France, where Luftwaffe fighters shot his Spitfire down; he'd arrived at the East Compound of Stalag Luft III in August, a few months before Harsh, and was also befriended by tunnel designer Floody.

"You know something?" Floody said finally to Harsh. "You're probably the only man in the world who got a job because he's an ex-convict."[20]

Another item on the escape committee's wish list was its own version of MI5, an intelligence service designed to recognize any threat to the secret activity of the escape committee, conceive and organize defence against that threat, and carry out counter-intelligence to mislead or derail all efforts to discover the day-to-day operations of X Organization. Some of the expertise the escape committee needed arrived at the Sagan prison in the form of a Canadian airman shot down over Germany that summer. Born in Toronto and educated in England, Kingsley Brown had two passions as a young man—writing and flying. Beginning in 1928, he wrote for the *Toronto Star*, the *New York Herald-Tribune* and the *Halifax Herald*, and while employed at the latter he learned to fly at the Halifax Aero Club. When war broke out he enlisted in the RCAF and was serving as a Hampden bomber pilot when he was shot down over Bremen, Germany, on July 2, 1942.

Brown recalled his first night at Stalag Luft III in the East Compound barracks hut adjusting to his new surroundings. As new boy he'd been assigned a top bunk, so when the German guards locked the hut doors for the night and the prisoners drew the blackout curtains shut, Brown just sat on his bed, legs dangling. He recalled how, with his head near the ceiling, he was nearly overcome by the stench of body odours and the cloud of smoke from cigarettes and burning candles made of margarine and shoe polish. Despite the haze, however, he began to notice activity at the opposite end of his room, where the stove had been moved aside to reveal a hole in the floor.

"In this eerie light, I watched naked and half-naked men, their bodies shiny with sweat, slipping in and out of the black hole,"[21] Brown wrote.

This was his first exposure to a tunnelling crew, assembling, disappearing down the excavation hole, and then emerging with cloth bags, pails, and tin cans full of sand. Brown was allowed to witness this parade of diggers entering and exiting the trapdoor for the night's excavating only because several kriegies had vouched for him; they had known him in Toronto or at his Bomber Command aerodrome in England and knew he could be trusted. After a few days of orientation, Brown was summoned to a meeting with Group Captain H. M. Massey. Then the SBO, Massey was in his sixties and (before being captured in 1942) had been appointed to liaise with US strategic bombing personnel in Washington, DC; but Massey had felt he ought to witness a bombing operation over Germany first-hand and was shot down on his inaugural op. Massey knew Brown had worked for newspapers and concluded his journalism skills might help the escape committee's propaganda activity.

Thrilled at the prospect of potentially working in connection with those underground operations he'd witnessed, or perhaps joining clandestine radio transmitting, or assisting in production at a secret printing press, Brown reported immediately to his superior, Wing Commander Taffy Williams. Brown found Williams alone in his barracks room. He was seated at a table in front of an open window, working with what looked like empty jars, a pair of scissors, and tiny pieces of paper.

"You're just in time to lend me a hand," Williams told Brown. "We've got a propaganda job."[22]

Williams handed Brown one of the German jam jars he'd procured from a guard. Held inside the jar by a piece of cheesecloth were several bumblebees—very much alive, but not very happy about the arrangement. Williams had a crew of kriegies capturing the bumblebees near the cookhouse and passing them along for propaganda duty. Williams handed Brown a pair of gloves and instructed him to open the top of the jar and gently grab each bumblebee by the wings. Williams then slipped a noose of thread over the abdomen of the bee to where the abdomen joined the thorax and gently tightened the noose; attached to the thread was a pennant-shaped piece of tissue paper on which was carefully written, in tiny script, the propaganda Germans later discovering the bees would read. The kriegies hoped the messages would surprise and offend.

"Deutschland kaput," one side of the pennant said, and on the other, "Hitler kaput."²³

Graduating from his initiation into the kriegies' hierarchy to the escape committee enterprise (with relatively few stings to show for it), Brown moved to a new level of intelligence service. Upon his arrival at the compound, he'd been given a German language textbook that apparently was standard issue to the thousands of non-German workers transported inside the country to work as forced labour. Language was among Brown's specialties and he soon learned that his conversational German was an asset inside the wire. Brown could initiate small talk with the guards to discover valuable bits of information or to determine which guard might be a potential bribery prospect, a so-called "tame" guard. And that work led to joining a sub-committee of the X Organization—known as "Dean and Dawson," after the British travel agency—which forged such documents as identity cards, travel passes, and labour permits. Dean and Dawson, led by Briton Tim Walenn and Canadian Tony Pengelly, put Brown's journalist skills to work, assembling a complete card index of police stations, labour recruiting centres, and industrial addresses for every major town and city in Germany.

As a consequence, Kingsley Brown became something of a fixture in the library or reading rooms in the East Compound. When the latest German newspapers—*Völkischer Beobachter* and the *Frankfurter Zeitung*—arrived in the camp, the former Canadian journalist who was apparently hungry for news (if any guard asked) pored over each edition of the newspapers' classified ads, obituaries, and public service announcements. From his daily readings, Brown might learn the names of real people whose identities could be stolen, the names of police officials who might sanction travel papers, and which industries in what locations might be recruiting migrant workers in Germany or any part of the occupied territories of the Third Reich. While building the card index in the service of Dean and Dawson, Brown met Gordon Brettell, a British pilot officer from Fighter Command. They both spoke conversational German. And that helped them hatch an escape plan for the coming winter.

"The prospect of escape had all the exhilarating fascination of a spine-tingling sport," Kingsley Brown wrote. "And it was this aspect more than any other that beckoned to captives from the free side of the wire."[24]

If digging tunnels, hiding excavated sand, dodging guards and dogs, or tying propaganda notes to the abdomens of bees weren't enough of a sporting challenge, some kriegies tried out-and-out theft. In addition to the data that Brown and the rest of the Dean and Dawson volunteers were compiling from newspapers and public service announcements in the library, Keith Ogilvie contributed on his own. Since his official job inside the wire involved handling the Red Cross parcels[25] arriving for the POWs, Ogilvie had regular contact with the Luft guards and vice versa. One day, he spotted a wallet sticking out of the back pocket of an older guard's uniform. Ogilvie silently lifted it, rushed it along to the forgers to copy, and then informed the distraught guard he'd discovered the wallet on the floor.[26] Worried about the consequences of prison authorities discovering he had lost his papers inside the compound, the guard thanked Ogilvie profusely. In one short, deft act of thievery, Ogilvie had gained temporary possession of valuable identity papers and tamed a prison guard; the man was forever in the Canadian officer's debt.

In spite of the spirited nature of the kriegies engaged in escape attempts, there was no escaping some of the harsh conditions of prison camp life. When his Halifax bomber was shot down by a German night-fighter aircraft over Frankfurt-am-Main, Germany, in December 1942, navigator Don "Tiger" McKim (from Lynedoch, Ontario) jumped into the frigid night sky and a 185-mile-per-hour wind. In addition to the cold and fear he felt, he smashed his head going through the escape hatch and was temporarily knocked out. He came to soon enough to activate his chute, but on the ground was quickly arrested and interrogated at Dulag Luft, arriving at Stalag Luft III on Christmas Eve. His present, on arrival, was a Red Cross parcel and the bottom tier of a bunk bed, closest to the floor and consequently closest to the outside December air.

"I was never so cold in my life," McKim said. "The mattress was made of bags of wood chips, so the cold would work its way through. . . . I didn't take off my clothes. I put all the clothes I had on. My greatcoat. My mittens. Everything."[27]

Following appell outside each day, McKim could anticipate the kriegies' breakfast ration—a slice of German black bread, which often had fine wood chips or sawdust inside to make the loaf go further; the bread ration was a loaf per person per week. There might be a tiny piece of butter or cheese with it and their Red Cross tea or coffee. For later meals, meat and fresh vegetables were rare. The Germans doled out either potatoes or kohlrabi (a coarse vegetable that resembled turnips) to make sauerkraut or thin vegetable soup. Generally, the Stalag Luft III officers remained hungry, but had enough to sustain life and health; in fact, with the aid of Red Cross parcel staples, they generally digested more nutrition and calories than the Germans guarding them.[28]

But Flying Officer McKim never escaped the cold. Because he was only five foot two[29], when he volunteered to help on the escape committee he was assigned to stooge work. That winter and the one that followed, McKim would walk outside discretely noting the arrival, location, and direction of a guard or ferret entering the compound. He would alert the next stooge in the network as to the nature of the goon in the block and which direction he was headed. All the while, he would try to look as if he were just strolling for exercise and pass along his signals while (thanks to his diminutive stature) staying out the sightlines of the guard towers.

"It was certain jobs for certain people," McKim said. "My job required me to be out in the cold. I wasn't capable of doing anything else."[30]

Flying Officer Bob McBride wrote his wife back in Montreal about coping with the cold. Shot down during a torpedoing operation off the coast of France in September 1942, McBride's first postcard to his wife, Jean, simply said, "Wait for me a little longer."[31] As a consequence, she joined the Prisoner of War Relatives' Association, packing parcels for the Red Cross. At one point she managed to pack up and send her husband a bowling set she hoped would provide exercise and diversion.

"The bowling set was marvelous," McBride wrote back. "It burned forever."[32]

Another new arrival at the East Compound that fall was a no-nonsense fighter pilot from Port Alberni, British Columbia. Just twenty years old, Arthur "Jack" Moul had learned to fly on the West Coast at age eighteen. Flying sorties with 416 Squadron, he quickly earned a reputation for his quick hands on the Spitfire's control column and its machine guns. However, on October 23, 1942, during a trip over occupied France strafing German freight trains, a locomotive blew up beneath him, damaging his Spitfire. Moul ditched in the Channel, but was picked up by a German patrol before he could be rescued by RAF seaplanes. Moul arrived at Stalag Luft III in time to become a valued scrounger, working with fellow Canadians Barry Davidson, Red Noble, and Keith Ogilvie searching for guards who could be tamed for the good of the escape committee.

The end of 1942 brought top-to-bottom transformation to X Organization at Stalag Luft III. What had been for Wally Floody and Robert Ker-Ramsey trial-and-error excavation would shortly be elevated to a scale of construction Floody remembered from the mines of Northern Ontario. What George Harsh and George McGill had launched as a ragtag group of inmates scrambling to pinpoint goons and ferrets approaching barracks huts would eventually become so timely a network of spying, tracking, and locating that it would even outstrip the Germans' control of their own guarding system. And the intelligence that had created Dean and Dawson and a library of information for future forgery would soon start generating such sophisticated documentation as to pass for the real thing for hundreds of potential escapers. The catalyst for revamping, expanding, and improving every aspect of X Organization was the arrival of Roger Bushell, the South African-born RAF squadron leader who'd been captured twice—once after being shot down in France in May 1940, and again following his escape from Dulag Luft all the way to the Swiss border the following summer. It was his third escape, during transport to the prison at Warburg, however, that nearly got him free.

En route in a cattle truck, Bushell and several others managed to pry up the floorboards of the truck and drop to the roadway below. One of the three escapers fell under the wheels and was killed, while Bushell and a Czech officer in the RAF, Jack Zafouk, made it all the way to Prague. Meantime, Operation Anthropoid had landed two Czech patriots (trained in Britain) back in the Czechoslovak capital. On May 27, 1942, they ambushed Reinhard Heydrich, the Gestapo chief in charge of the Holocaust of the Jews in Europe; he died of his wounds a week later. Zafouk and Bushell went into hiding but were eventually recaptured, the former being sent to Kolditz Castle prison, the latter rushed to Gestapo headquarters in Berlin for torture and interrogation. His interrogators tried to implicate Bushell in the Heydrich assassination. The Czech family that had hidden the two escapees was executed.

Weighing forty pounds less than when he arrived at Dulag Luft and wearing the scars of his Gestapo grilling in Berlin, Squadron Leader Bushell miraculously emerged from the interrogation ordeal. At the time, rumours circulated that the chief censor officer at the Sagan prison camp had a brother in the Gestapo who intervened and returned Bushell to the Luftwaffe prison system. On the day he arrived at Stalag Luft III, toward the end of 1942, Bushell was wearing his now-tattered air force battledress. That same German censor officer warned the squadron leader if tried to escape and was caught again, the Gestapo would probably shoot him. If he escaped again, Bushell shot back, the Gestapo would never catch him. Unnoticed in a bag of belongings the testy air force officer had tucked under his arm was a civilian suit he'd received from the family that had hidden him in Prague.[33] No doubt Bushell, now the new chief of escape operations, or Big X, was already calculating what he would wear during his fourth escape attempt.

# ESCAPE SEASON

B Y MARCH of 1943, Kingsley Brown had become somebody else. He was quite sane, or as sane as any RCAF airman shot down over Germany, interrogated, and sent to a prison in the middle of Silesia could be. It's just that besides his kriegie dog tags and German prison ID file, Brown also now owned a set of false identity papers. His alter ego was Goleb Plasov[1], a steelworker from Liegnitz, in the former Poland. His father's name was Jakov. His mother's name Natasha. And he—according to a rehearsed story—was in Germany en route to new steelworks in Strasbourg, France. Among his false documents Brown also held a piece of stationery on which the police chief of Liegnitz had inscribed his signature and affixed his official stamp. All the details were accurate. Brown knew they were, since he had personally tracked down the police chief's autograph and seal while doing research for Dean and Dawson, the forgery team. At the same time, Brown and fellow kriegie Gordon Brettell had also received tailored civilian clothing that made the two of them appear to be Bulgarian immigrants. A combination of the papers, German currency, and the clothes—all prepared by X Organization—as well as the two airmen's conversational German to help them deal with checkpoint officials, gave them nearly all they would need to pull off an escape from the East Compound of Stalag Luft III.

Construction that had begun over the winter to the west and a little north of what had been the main prison grounds for Commonwealth air officers appeared to give Brown and Brettell an ideal opportunity. Kriegies in the East Compound spotted crews of Russian workers hacking down more of the reforested area beyond the *Kommandantur*. In a casual conversation with one of the guards, Squadron Leader Bushell had learned that Luftwaffe authorities planned to move inmates in the East Compound to the new North Compound[2] sometime in the spring. As work accelerated, some of the non-commissioned ranks of Allied airmen joined the work crews building the new facility. And since the construction zone had no prisoners housed in it, German guards were few and far between. The escape committee arranged to have Brown and Brettell switch places with two NCOs on the construction gang. On March 27, 1943, four days before the North Compound was due to open, German guards watching over the work crew, including Brown and Brettell in disguise, were distracted with some cigarette trading. The two kriegies quickly hid in wood shavings, waited for the commotion of their apparent escape to blow over, and in the dark climbed the North Compound fence and slipped into the Sagan forest.

Brown remembered the first night as a dash through a Grimm's fairy tale, as the two men used the stars and a compass to navigate their way through forested areas. In the town of Sorau they bought tickets, boarded a train, and hunkered down en route to Leipzig. By coincidence, they shared a cubicle with six soldiers of the Wehrmacht. On the cubicle wall, a poster featured two troops in conversation being overheard by a suspicious-looking civilian. The text on the poster read: "Beware the Third Person! The Enemy has Ears!"[3]

"I've never known the pure joy of living, tempered so deliciously by a sense of danger,"[4] Brown wrote.

If an escape bid seated in the same railway coach compartment as their enemies and the propaganda poster weren't ironic enough, their interrogation four days later sure was. A routine documents check at a railway station in Chemnitz, southwest of Berlin, revealed their masquerade and the two fugitive air force officers were escorted to the local Gestapo headquarters. They expected to be shot. In an office decorated with carpets and potted palms, the district police boss smoked a cigar and fired questions at them.

"Why did you escape?" he demanded.

"It is our duty," they said.

"Correct," he acknowledged. Apparently more interested in talking than listening, the police chief regaled them with his own biography. "I was a prisoner in France during the First World War. I also escaped, but unlike you, I got away." He chatted some more about prison life and then signalled guards to take the kriegies away and to have them sent back to their prison camp. He added finally, "Better luck next time."[5]

Having experienced the thrill of getting beyond the wire and a few days of freedom in his first escape attempt, Brown had another crack at it in December of the same year, with Czech prisoner Joe Ricks along for the ride. That escape was thwarted just as quickly. But it left Brown with an indelible memory. As he and Ricks travelled with armed guards back to Sagan, this time they sat in a train compartment with a member of the Hitler Youth, a Wehrmacht officer who'd lost a leg on the Russian front, and three young schoolteachers—all heading home for Christmas. Someone began to sing. Brown offered a version of "Alouette." Ricks chipped in with a Czech folksong. And the three women began "Silent Night." Everyone joined in, and for those moments, Brown said, the war was forgotten.[6]

The same winter that Brown and Brettell were brushing up their German and getting fitted with their escape disguises for the March attempt, the long-range mass escape plans of X Organization took shape, very much in the image of the new escape chief, Roger Bushell. Whether inside barracks huts far from the probing ears of German ferrets, or pounding the exercise circuit along the inside of the warning wire, during the non-tunnelling months of the winter, Big X had assembled and consulted with his section heads—security bosses Harsh, Kirby-Green, and recently arrived US Lieutenant Albert "Junior" Clark, forgery chiefs Walenn and Pengelly, sand dispersal leader Fanshawe, and, most urgently, tunnel kings Floody and Ker-Ramsey.

Knowing the Germans would soon move most of the Commonwealth and American prisoners to the new North Compound, Bushell calculated the committee's next move. It was decided the current SBO, Group Captain Massey, should approach the camp *Kommandant* and, in a spirit of co-operation, suggest some East Compound officers provide work groups to assist in the construction of the new camp. Feigning goodwill and enthusiasm for the construction work, Floody, Ker-Ramsey, Fanshawe, and Bushell himself all joined the work parties. Between shovelfuls and hammer swings, however, the expert earth-movers calculated the length and breadth and depth of their new home. Floody and Ker-Ramsey paced out and recorded the distances and angles of the place to determine where future tunnels might be built and how creative they'd have to be to put men beyond the wire. One of them even managed to smuggle back a stolen diagram of the projected underground sewage lines.

Not unlike the Centre and East compounds, the North Compound was three hundred yards square, completely surrounded with those reforested pines and with two fences about nine feet high and five feet apart. More bundles of barbed wire filled the space between the double-jeopardy fences, and the warning wire was strung thirty feet inside that fencing. Guard towers—or, as the kriegies described them, "goon boxes"—were situated every one hundred or one hundred and fifty yards. The living quarters consisted of fifteen wooden huts, a kitchen hut (with caldrons for boiling water), a fire pool, and a large sports field, which doubled as the appell area. Each hut contained eighteen rooms; each of the rooms had a dining area, living area, table, stools, lockers, a stove on a tile base in the corner, and double-decker bunk beds (with palliasse, a mattress of woven paper or wood shavings) for eight prisoners. Every hut also had a washroom, lavatory, and small kitchen with a coal stove. The fifteen barracks huts could house up to fifteen hundred air force officer prisoners. Again, north of the barracks, the *Vorlager* contained a coal shed, the hospital, and a building with both the cooler and a room where Red Cross parcels were warehoused and inspected by German guards, and then passed along to the Commonwealth officer in charge of distribution.

Moving was scheduled to take place on April Fools' Day 1943, and the kriegies lived up to the date's moniker. Seven hundred officers (by this time including some three hundred Americans) gathered their worldly possessions—plates, mugs, cooking pans, makeshift gadgets, thread-bare clothes, and Red Cross parcel boxes filled with personal effects, such as photographs, pieces of string, and nails—and assembled for appell. The roll call among the officers that day had the look and feel of juvenile boys lining up for their first day back at school. The POWs broke ranks and clustered around the guards who were searching them. Articles were passed in jest from one man to the next as the inspection descended into chaos. That allowed some vital escape tools—pens and ink, paper, tin shovels, and civilian clothing (including Bushell's civilian suit)—to pass through the screening unnoticed. Miraculously, the antics had also kept one of the escape committee's most valuable possessions undetected. Since the earliest escape committee days at Barth in 1940, pilot Dick Bartlett had carried his exercise medicine ball with him everywhere. Seemingly the kriegies' physical fitness director, the Canadian Fleet Air Arm sub lieutenant was still guarding the hidden wireless radio in that ball.*

Many kriegies knew X Organization had the wireless set, nicknamed "the canary," and that it could receive the evening BBC broadcasts offering the latest world news. Once the canary had been successfully smuggled into the North Compound via that medicine

---

* NCOs brought the first radio to the Centre Compound at Stalag Luft III when they arrived from Barth. They had assembled it from parts gathered by bribing guards and hid it in a functioning accordion until it was confiscated during a snap inspection in January 1943. Officers in the East Compound also brought a radio from Warburg or Barth; it was confiscated in July 1942. In April 1943, parts for another radio were smuggled (inside luggage, a medicine ball, and a biscuit tin) into the officers' barracks. Later, in January 1945, following the evacuation of the POW camp and during the forced march westward, the German *Abwehr* officer, Hans Pieber, actually carried the radio in his briefcase for the Commonwealth airmen.

ball, Bartlett and two other officers assumed the responsibilities of its round-the-clock protection. RAF officer Nellie Ellan operated the radio itself. A second officer recorded the BBC broadcast content in shorthand; the contents were later read aloud in each compound barracks. What most kriegies did not know, however, was that relaying the BBC news was a secondary function of the radio. Once the three custodians of the canary had transcribed the BBC news, Bartlett changed the radio coils to receive signals from the British Air Ministry. These encrypted messages contained intelligence for X Organization. When the canary went silent after each broadcast and intelligence message, it was up to Bartlett to hide it in a most unlikely location—under a latrine toilet in Hut 101[7]. Bartlett and his two companions practised the emergency response if the Germans suddenly descended on the wireless hiding place. If the canary's capture were imminent, Bartlett could destroy its coils, eat any written messages, conceal the wireless under the toilet, and be innocently sitting on the toilet in half a minute or less.[8]

Once inside the new North Compound and dismissed, that April 1, kriegies dashed into the comparatively spacious huts to claim their rooms, where, one man said, there was "almost enough room to swing a stunted cat."[9] Big X ensured that the escape committee was represented in every hut; in each barracks he appointed one officer, Little X, to receive and process all officers' schemes for breaking out of the compound, and Little S to deal with security.

The excitement of the move and the confusion on both sides made this time ripe for all manner of escape attempts. Pilot Officer Gordon King, from Winnipeg, had arrived just in time for the move to new quarters. At age nineteen, in 1940, he knew Morse code, so the air force streamed him into the wireless air-gunner trade, but he was upgraded to pilot training. The RCAF rushed him overseas and sent him, as Second Dickie (observing pilot), on several large bombing operations, including the first thousand-bomber raid on Cologne, Germany, on May 31, 1942. A few nights later, without the security in numbers and piloting a slower Wellington bomber, he and his crew were shot down and captured.

King arrived at Sagan barefoot, having lost his boots when he bailed out. At the train station he faced the mile-long walk to the compound with nothing on his feet; somebody loaned him footwear he'd never seen before—wooden Dutch clogs. They served him well as he joined the officers' work crews preparing the North Compound and then on the walk to his new home on April 1, 1943. King spotted plenty of escape hijinx that first day, including an attempt by Joe "Red" Noble, one of his Canadian barracks mates. Noble spotted a truck loaded with pine tree boughs leaving the camp, jumped into the back, and buried himself among the logs and branches. But a guard in a goon box had spotted him and passed the word to a guard closer to the truck.

"Joe, we know you're in there," the guard shouted. "Come on out."

Noble stayed put, figuring the commotion of moving day would distract the guard.

"Come out, or we'll start shooting,"[10] King remembered the guard shouting more emphatically. And out came Noble.

Not long after he arrived in the North Compound, Gordon King joined a group building its own tunnel to the cookhouse. He remembered it as a scheme to establish a secret passage to the food stores of the building so that they could fatten their meagre rations whenever they wished. The digger at the face of the tunnel was a former fighter pilot, while King worked as "the dish," taking the excavated sand to the entry point and handing it off to a dispersal man.

"We got about halfway to the cookhouse," King recalled, "when a team of horses pulling a wagon walked on the sand above the tunnel and it caved in. The Germans thought it was a big joke. They were elated they'd found it. But at that point tunnelling was just something to do."[11]

While such tunnelling efforts seemed short-sighted, they succeeded in creating a diversion for other escape committee enterprises. Bushell used a similar diversion to send four-foot-three-inch Ken "Shag" Rees through the manhole into the North Compound sewage system to see if human passage was possible. The Welshman returned moments later with bad news; the sewage pipe was only six inches around. At this point in his wartime service, Rees was into his fourth military aviation career. He'd completed a tour with 40 Squadron in 1941, added a second tour based in Malta, then contributed as an RAF instructor back in Britain, and was flying Wellingtons with 150 Squadron in October 1942 when he was shot down and eventually sent to Stalag Luft III. Inside the North Compound, he was effectively commencing his fifth tour of duty, as a member of the principal tunnel-digging team for Roger Bushell's escape committee.

"There were escape attempts going on all the time," Wally Floody said. "The escape committee was vetting people who wanted to try anything . . . even one chap who wanted to go out the main gate disguised as a German shepherd dog."[12]

Two creative kriegies—Czech Ivo Tonder and Australian Geoff Cornish—let their beards grow for a few days. Then they traded Red Cross parcel cigarettes and sweets for some Polish greatcoats, smeared their faces with dirt, and joined a Russian work crew leaving the compound through the main gate. The guard there noticed that the numbers entering and exiting didn't add up, but couldn't distinguish the real workers from the imposters. The seasoned *Abwehr* duty officer, *Hauptmann* Hans Pieber, arrived on the scene. Formerly a member of the Austrian Nazi Party, Pieber had worked at Stalag Luft I outside Barth and then was transferred to the complex near Sagan with the Commonwealth officers the previous year. Pieber recognized the kriegies in disguise and despite the Russians' protestations that the two men were truly members of their work crew, carted Cornish and Tonder off to the cooler. Another escape attempt about that time, a kriegie clinging to the chassis of a work truck, was stopped by the chief of the German anti-escape troops. Staff Sergeant Hermann Glemnitz (dubbed "Dimwits" by the kriegies) had also served the German military prison system for several years. He had worked and lived in England before the war. Nevertheless, he took great pleasure in unravelling escape schemes, whether it was a man hiding in the undercarriage of a truck or tunnel crews burrowing toward the double fence.

Meanwhile, Squadron Leader Roger Bushell seemed equally intent on winning the war of wits. Even if all escape activity at Stalag Luft III did not deliver a "home run"—actually getting Allied air force officers back to Britain—Bushell planned to disrupt as much of the Third Reich's momentum as he could from inside its occupied territory. In the first eleven days of April 1943, Big X and the section chiefs of the escape committee met to determine the number of tunnels to be built, their locations, their trapdoor entrances and projected exits, their depths and direction, their designers, their engineers, their diggers, their soil dispersal units, their security overseers, their routines, and the communications support. Settling into their new quarters in the North Compound were more than seven hundred officers, with just as many skills and aptitudes among them. Each one could now be called on to fulfill every job X Organization required. It all began with Roger Bushell's original meeting among his section chiefs.

"My idea is to dig three major tunnels,"[13] he told the committee. He added that teams would dig simultaneously, that it would take five hundred officers in the camp to do the job, and that if the goons and ferrets found one or two of the tunnels, his view was that one would eventually deliver two hundred or more POW officers outside the wire.

"Now you're talking," Floody said. Already a seasoned tunneller with experience at three German prison compounds, he recognized the brilliance of the plan. Later he commented, "We didn't dream that getting one or two or three people back to Britain was going to change the outcome of the war. But we realized that larger escapes would make the Germans tie down a lot more troops."[14]

The committee had decided a crew would dig one tunnel originating in Hut 123 and running westbound from a trapdoor in concrete and brick that formed the foundation for the chimney in that barracks. It was a location the committee recognized the Germans would suspect, because it was closest to the double fence, but farthest from the main gate of the compound. It offered the most seclusion and therefore aroused the most suspicion.

"We're going to call this one 'Tom,'" Bushell said.

"Dick," the second tunnel, would originate in Hut 122 and also run westbound. Its trap would be concealed beyond a concrete wall and below a pool of water that was run off through an eighteen-inch-square grating in the floor of the hut's washroom shower. Less obvious because it was located inside an inner barracks hut, the tunnel was perfectly concealed.

Meanwhile, the third tunnel, "Harry," would head northbound from Hut 104, under the warning wire, the entire *Vorlager*, and, in fact, beneath the cooler itself en route to the pine forest beyond the northern perimeter of the compound. Its trapdoor had to be excavated beneath a stove in Room 23, through a square of tiles, then through the solid brick and concrete foundation that supported the weight of the stove and chimney, ultimately into the topsoil and sand below. Building the traps to each tunnel entrance took days of planning, manpower, tool assembly, security, and precise timing. Canadian Flight Lieutenant Henry Sprague witnessed the birth of tunnel "Harry."

"That night we staged a diversion, which means we had a party in the block," said Sprague, a veteran of Dulag Luft and Stalag Luft I imprisonment. "The stove rested on tiles in a six-foot-square configuration . . . so during the party some Polish chaps [officers Minskewitz, Wlod Kolanowski, and Zbigniew Gotowski], who were expert cement men, they chipped away the tiles carefully, constructed a platform underneath, re-cemented the tiles—that's all they did that night—and put the stove back in place. That gave us an access point to what later became the vertical shaft to 'Harry.'"[15]

The next step, cutting into the concrete beneath the now movable tile flooring, demanded an equally tricky manoeuvre. First, a pick-head borrowed from the Russian work crews was strapped to a baseball bat handle that Ker-Ramsey used to pound through the concrete. Under Floody's supervision, the digging crew laid blankets to catch the debris and muffle the noise. To mask the smacking sound of each blow, Junior Clark and others organized a team of diversionary kriegies outside the window of Hut 104. There they began pounding pieces of tin and wood as if manufacturing cookware, not an out-of-the-ordinary sight for POWs just settling into their new barracks. Meanwhile, George Harsh's kriegie guards, or "stooges," watched every move the Germans made, whether they were armed guards in the towers, goons on foot patrol, or ferrets wandering the compound looking for evidence of tunnelling.

"We had close to two hundred people in our security force," Floody said. "The moment a German guard or ferret came through the gate, we had one of our security people spot him and signal his whereabouts. . . . I could say to Harsh at any given time, 'How many Germans are in the camp?' And he knew exactly how many, where they were, and when they were due to go off shift. . . . It was complete surveillance."[16]

By contrast, as many kriegies as there were in the ranks of the security system, only a handful knew where the trapdoors to the three tunnels were located; in fact, few knew which huts had been chosen as starting points for the digging. Soon after the move to North Compound, most officers in camp spotted notices going up, inviting kriegies to participate in this baseball game or that cricket match, when really the escape committee was recruiting volunteers for duty in the day-to-day escape operations. Patrick Langford joined right away. As far as he was concerned, too much of his time in the air force had been spent preparing, and not enough spent doing. Born in Edmonton in 1919, Langford had taught himself to ski, ride horses, and play the piano. When the war broke out, he left a good chauffeuring job to join the air force and get into the fighting; instead, because of his high grades in the British Commonwealth Air Training Plan in Canada, the RCAF made him an instructor. After sixteen months of teaching others to fly, he finally got an overseas posting to heavy bombers himself, but in July 1942 his Wellington was shot down over Lübeck, Germany. He bailed out safely, but fire in the disintegrating aircraft burned him across his upper body.

After lengthy hospitalization, Langford arrived at Stalag Luft III just as his fellow officers prepared to move to the North Compound. He seemed eager to join the parade of escape attempts—one plan he presented to Big X involved using a trench the Russians had built as an avenue of escape, and another involved hiding in an exiting garbage wagon. However, the escape committee found a job more demanding and valuable for Pat Langford and his workmate Henry Sprague. They shared the responsibility for protecting the trapdoor to "Harry." As Ker-Ramsey picked his way deeper into the concrete foundation beneath the stove, early in April 1943, the floor in that corner of Hut 104 was exposed for almost ten days. Langford and Sprague used spare palliasses to cover the area whenever guards came near. And with the ferrets staging more surprise inspections all the time, the two kriegies trained themselves to open or close the trapdoor system with lightning speed.

"Sprague and Langford were the fastest trap men in the world," Floody said. "They could open or close the trap in twenty to thirty seconds."[17]

Generating some good-natured chaos during the move to the North Compound seemed innocent on the surface. But it too was serving a greater purpose. As the general population of officers moved into new barracks, claimed bunks, and established routines for sharing kitchens, washrooms, and all other facilities under a barracks roof, the inner circle of the escape committee never rested. Bushell and the section heads began looking for any and all weak points in the Germans' day-to-day maintenance of the stalag. Even the smallest of details—such as haphazard document checks at the main gate in the weeks immediately following the move—might offer the best escape opportunity.

So it was when the first insect infestation of the barracks buildings occurred in the spring of 1943. All it took was the senior Commonwealth medical officer to alert the German medical officer to an outbreak of lice, fleas, or bedbugs and, with not unexpected precision, the prison system responded. Prisoners living in the infested hut would be paraded in parties of twenty-five to the shower house in the woods—four hundred yards outside the main gate—for hot showers and bug inspection. Meanwhile, a delousing team would move into the hut and fumigate it. On June 11, just after 2 p.m. (immediately following a routine relief of every guard in the compound), a delousing party of twenty-five kriegies (each carrying a towel covering a second set of clothes) and two German *Unteroffizier* (NCO) guards approached the main gate. Meanwhile, inside the compound in full view of the guards at the gate, two kriegies—Bill Geiger and Henry "Johnny" Marshall—began a fencing demonstration. Tony Pengelly assembled an apparently impromptu audience that began cheering on the fencers.

"The Germans, who love fencing, had only one eye on business," Pengelly said. "The delousing party reached the gate, its guards shouted something to the guards on the gate, and off it marched into the woods toward the showers."[18]

Before the Germans at the main gate realized anything was wrong, part two of the caper had already kicked into gear. A second group under guard approached the main gate. This time the party consisted of seven Commonwealth wing commanders and group captains and an American lieutenant colonel—allegedly on their way to an emergency meeting with the camp *Kommandant*—with a German corporal escorting them through. One guard gave little notice to the pass the corporal handed him. A second gatekeeper paused and examined the corporal and his pass more closely. A phone call to the *Kommandant* confirmed that the emergency officers' meeting had been fabricated, and a closer examination of the corporal escorting the officers revealed that it was really kriegie Bob van der Stok,[19] a Dutch-born fighter pilot in RAF 41 Squadron shot down a year earlier, in July 1942; as well as the fake German uniform, van der Stok had a dummy gun in a cardboard holster.[20] The camp *Kommandant*, Colonel Friedrich Wilhelm von Lindeiner-Wildau, was furious. The sixty-one-year-old ex-cavalry officer from the Great War and former member of Hermann Göring's personal staff was notorious for his quick temper, but also his sense of humour.

"How do you think of these things? You British!" von Lindeiner said. Then, he began to laugh. He did not attempt to suppress his admiration for the kriegies' fabricated meeting, nor his sense of satisfaction that his men had discovered it. "But we are too smart for you. . . . Of course, we'll have to put you in cells for ten days. Rules, you know."

Meanwhile, it slowly dawned on the guards at the gate that the two guards escorting the previous delousing party might also have been imposters. Indeed, they were Belgian airmen fluent in German and each equally well outfitted in a mocked-up guard uniform, gate pass, and sidearm.

"It was all we could do to keep from looking down the road," Pengelly said. "If there was no commotion there we would know the twenty-seven men were clear—twenty-five who had carried various civilian outfits [maps and concentrated food cakes] wrapped in their towels and two guards, our own men, dressed as German soldiers."[21]

Eventually, a guard ran up to the *Kommandant* and explained he had found towels in the woods and that that shower party had vanished. Von Lindeiner went pale. He immediately dispatched search parties into the woods, had the entire camp population paraded to the sports grounds for roll call, and sent machine-gun armed troops through every hut in the North Compound. Even though it began to rain heavily, he kept the POWs standing on the sports field for five hours.

What Pengelly referred to as "Operation Bedbug" still did not deliver Bushell's home runs—escapers who made it all the way back to Britain—but it proved to be the first significant victory in the psychological warfare between X Organization and the Luftwaffe administration of the North Compound at Stalag Luft III. The temporary escape of twenty-seven POWs required the mobilization of additional German troops to track them down; as many of the kriegies put it, the short-term goal of these escape plots was to tie up German manpower. The events of June 11 had also tarnished the otherwise pristine record Colonel von Lindeiner had enjoyed thus far in the war. Worse yet, even if the *Kommandant* refused to admit it, Operation Bedbug had exposed an important chink in the defensive armour at Stalag Luft III. X Organization's seemingly endless array of ruses, diversions, and masquerades continued to fool the compound staff, at least temporarily. This time, credit for the successful break-out, beyond the wire at least, went to a simple but very powerful section in the escape committee hierarchy—its tailoring crew.

RAF airman Tommy Guest and his master seamsters had, in secrecy, manufactured both civilian clothes and convincing German uniforms from little or nothing. Under normal circumstances, the Germans had allowed sewing equipment inside the barracks so that prisoners could repair their own clothing. However, by procuring blankets, sports jackets, and other garments arriving in Red Cross parcels, Guest and his sewing-machine operators had turned a repair room into a veritable men's garment factory providing the escape committee with all manner of look-alike clothes, from plain business suits to the top hat and overalls of a town chimney sweep. All it took was time, Pengelly added, and "time was our cheapest commodity."[22]

If Colonel von Lindeiner thought the bedbug caper represented the oddest diversion his Commonwealth POWs could create, he was mistaken. A combination of available time and the kriegies' now-expert capability to create something from nothing led to another extraordinary diversion inside the wire. In April 1942, Canadian Flight Lieutenant Arthur Crighton had bailed out of his burning Wellington bomber over Hamburg; all but his tail gunner, Dick Howard, had survived, and eventually the Luftwaffe interrogation and transporting system delivered him to Stalag Luft III. When he discovered, the following spring, that a kriegie had received a set of golf clubs from the YMCA in Norway, Crighton and a number of golf-starved officers in the compound decided to transform a portion of their prison real estate into a nine-hole golf course. One vital element remained missing: golf balls.

"[The] thin elastic strips used to provide insulation for jam, fish, and meat tins in Red Cross parcels [were] rolled around a pebble,"[23] Crighton wrote. "It was finished by sewing on a protective leather covering from an old shoe [around the elastics]."

The resulting golf rounds, in which kriegies could smack the makeshift ball up to fifty yards, were played between the huts, amid kriegies walking along the circuit and across the shifting expanses of sand inside the wire. The only hazards the golfers faced were shots that rolled under the barracks huts and those that ended up beyond the warning wire into territory that truly was "out of bounds." For a while, Crighton and his fellow golfers devised a system that allowed a kriegie with a red scarf on his shoulders to step over the warning wire to retrieve errant fairway shots. Crighton admitted he was never courageous enough to don the red scarf and test machine-gun toting tower guards, but he did face a logistics problem as challenging as manufacturing golf balls from pebbles and elastic bands.

"I was left-handed and left-handed clubs were not available," he said. "[We] melted down a leaden *Keintrinkwasser* jug and fashioned it in a sand mould to become a club head. And a shaft? As factotum of everything musical in the compound, I appropriated the upright staff that supported the lid of the grand piano [in the prison camp]. Thus was constructed the most elegant left-hand five iron in the whole of Kriegiedom."[24]

While Art Crighton appeared to fill his time with repeated rounds of golf on the makeshift compound links, during the remainder of his POW time he occupied himself with his second great passion: music. Before the war, he had studied to play the organ and lead choirs; growing up in Calgary he had earned the prestigious Licentiate diploma of the Royal Schools of Music. In peacetime Crighton had become a respected music teacher and proficient on the organ and the trumpet. Inside the wire, he asked to play trumpet in a concert band and later took over as bandleader.

Since German prison officials appeared to encourage constructive prisoner pursuits, the Germans welcomed Crighton's requests to bring additional live music to the prisoners when the North Compound opened in April 1943. Then, when he sought permission to purchase such instruments as violins and cellos, Stalag Luft III authorities agreed. Crighton also requested wind instruments for a forty-piece symphony orchestra. They opened channels for the YMCA and Red Cross to send reed instruments, trumpets, trombones, and a tuba. Eventually, Crighton the kriegie music director not only led symphony concerts of Mozart, Bach, and Beethoven (which were of course acceptable to the German *Kommandant*), but also organized band performances, marching bands for outdoor events, and a pit band for productions at the compound theatre when it opened in September 1943. Crighton went so far as to assemble an orchestra wardrobe; if prisoners received new uniforms from home (which was permitted) but didn't want to wear them, Crighton commandeered them for his musicians. He insisted that orchestra members wear them.

"The Germans encouraged us," he said. "They knew if we had an orchestra, we weren't digging tunnels."[25]

Escape fever heated up that summer, and not just at the North Compound. For as long as Commonwealth and, more recently, American officers had been imprisoned in the East and North compounds at Stalag Luft III, a growing number of NCO aircrew (by the summer of 1943 they numbered nearly nineteen hundred men) had been penned inside the Centre Compound. By comparison to the officers' huts, the condition of the NCOs' barracks reflected German administration's neglect and the POWs frustration with conditions. Huts had broken windows. Wiring had been torn from the walls. Latrines had been stripped of wallboards for firewood and for shoring up tunnel projects.[26] That June, the Germans transferred all but fifty of the NCOs to Stalag Luft VI in Lithuania. The fifty who remained at Luft III appeared to be the most respectful of the premises; the German prison-keepers decided these fifty men would become orderlies to the incoming officers. They turned out to be the nucleus of the tunnelling effort well underway that summer. The Germans discovered and destroyed it that September.

The same summer, a British air force officer, a Royal Artillery officer, and a Canadian air force officer concocted an escape scenario that would take place virtually in plain view of their compound captors. Serving as crew navigator on a Stirling bomber and shot down over Germany in December 1942, RAF Flight Lieutenant Eric Williams had originally been imprisoned in Oflag XXI-B at Schubin. There he met an artillery officer, Lieutenant Michael Codner. They quickly built a tunnel and just as quickly were recaptured and sent to the East Compound at Stalag Luft III. Just weeks inside their new prison camp, Codner had an epiphany.

"A vaulting horse, a box horse like we had at school," he told Williams. "One of us inside digging while the others vaulted over it. It's foolproof."[27]

Eventually, the two of them worked out the details of their Trojan horse scheme and sold the idea to the British escape committee. With the help of a carpenter who was legitimately constructing frames for stage flats at the theatre inside the compound, they built a strong wooden vaulting horse with stolen wood for the frame and light plywood taken from Red Cross parcel boxes to sheath the horse. And for the comfort of the vaulters, they used cigarette packaging to fashion a cushion on top.

The scheme required a dedicated group of accomplices. Flight Lieutenant Edward Nurse, originally from Newfoundland, then an RCAF instructor, and eventually a Halifax bomber pilot shot down in April 1943, joined the plot. Initially, each day early in the summer, Nurse and the others carried the exercising horse to the spot chosen to begin the escape tunnel. Once the Germans got weary of inspecting the horse,[28] the team began to carry it—containing one tunnel digger, his tools, and about a dozen empty sock-like containers—to a corner of the compound next to the warning wire. Coincidentally, it was the same spot where George McGill and Eddie Asselin had staged their boxing match as a diversion for an escape attempt the year before. As Ted Nurse and the rest of the dedicated POWs conducted vaulting exercises over the horse, the tunneller cut into the sand under the horse, built a trapdoor, eventually a vertical shaft, and then a horizontal tunnel. At the end of each vaulting/digging session, Nurse and the others carried the horse containing the tunneller and the day's excavated sand to a nearby hut to let the tunneller out, dispose of the sand, and plan the next vaulting session.

In the early spring, Oliver Philpot, a thirty-year-old Canadian torpedo bomber pilot who had been shot down over Norway in December 1941, joined the Trojan horse scheme. Originally from

Vancouver, British Columbia, and a veteran of escape attempts from Dulag Luft, Oflag IX at Spangenberg, and Oflag XXI-B at Schubin, Flight Lieutenant Philpot was left behind in the East Compound when the big move of Commonwealth officers to the North Compound occurred in April 1943. Considered a loner, he approached the concept of escaping from a different direction—build an outside identity first, then build a means of escape. And so, as Codner and Williams worked on their two-man tunnel beneath the vaulting horse, Philpot began manufacturing his outside-the-wire persona—a Norwegian margarine salesman named Jon Jörgensen. By midsummer, Philpot took on the additional task of helping to disperse the sand that Williams and Codner were packing into bags inside the horse. Before long they invited him to join the tunnelling as well. From then on it became a three-man escape plan. After 114 days, the tunnel (just thirty inches beneath the surface) extended about one hundred feet eastward under the fence and was ready to deliver its diggers outside the wire.

Escape day was October 29. That morning, the vaulters carried Codner and Philpot inside the horse to the top of the concealed trap to the tunnel. At the end of the vaulting exercise, Codner stayed underground to dig the last leg of the tunnel while Philpot retrieved the last of the full sandbags. At that evening's appell, the escape committee ensured that it could cover Codner's absence. Then the vaulters carried three men inside the horse to the top of the tunnel—Philpot, Williams, and a man to close the trap and seal the three men inside. At six o'clock, after dark, Michael Codner broke through the soil outside the wire with his fist.

"[It was our] first glimpse of the stars . . . in the free heavens beyond the wire,"[29] Williams wrote.

Moments later the three men, shrouded in dark clothes and carrying bundles that contained their civilian suits, travel documents, and food, made off into the woods, undetected. Philpot (as Jörgensen, the salesman) caught a train from Sagan, arriving twenty-four hours later at the Baltic Sea port of Danzig. A day later he managed to stow himself aboard the Swedish vessel *Aralizz*. The captain discovered him and almost had him thrown off the ship, but the ship's sympathetic chief engineer hid him until the *Aralizz* was at sea bound for Sweden. Meanwhile, Codner and Williams, disguised as French workmen, travelled to Stettin where they managed to make contact with the Danish Resistance. Through its members they gained passage on a ship to Copenhagen, and on to Gothenburg in neutral Sweden. The three Trojan horsemen completed their home runs via the British Legation in Stockholm, arriving in Britain by Christmas. They were the only prisoners of war to successfully escape the East Compound.

All three received the Military Cross. For Eric Williams, however, it was small compensation. His wife had died in Liverpool during a German air raid, and two of his three brothers serving in the Royal Air Force had been killed in action.[30] A year of his life lost, caged as a POW at Stalag Luft III, somehow seemed a smaller price to pay.

# SERVANT TO A
# HOLE IN THE GROUND

---

F RANK SORENSEN served his adopted country in deed, with oratory, and to carry on a military tradition. Born in Denmark in June of 1922, he moved with his family from the Danish town of Roskilde to Canada just a week before the Second World War broke out. Frank's father, Marinus Bonde Sorensen, had served in the Canadian Expeditionary Force during the Great War, married Frank's mother, a wartime nurse, and in August of 1939 escaped Denmark and settled the family—two adults and six children—on a farm in the Eastern Townships of Quebec.[1] However, the war drew several Sorensen family members back overseas: Marinus representing Canadian and Danish interests in Britain; Eric, Frank's older brother, in the Canadian Army preparing for the invasion of Italy; and Frank as a Spitfire pilot in the Royal Canadian Air Force with 403 Squadron in Suffolk, England. Just days before he was transferred to RAF 232 Squadron en route to combat operations in North Africa, Frank Sorensen became a voice of freedom on the public airwaves. Because of Marinus Sorensen's Danish ancestry, his status as a Canadian Pacific Railway agent, and his connections with the BBC, his son, air force pilot Frank Sorensen, was invited to speak to Danes in occupied Denmark via the BBC's Radio Free Europe broadcasts.

"Hello, all you Roskilde boys,"[2] Sorensen began his October 15, 1942, broadcast. "Let me first of all speak to those who were boys with me, friends from school and Boy Scout camps . . . I know that there's not one who would not consider it his duty and his part of the burden and fight to make Denmark a free country again."

Just twenty, but already worldly enough to assess what a fascist dictator and his armies had inflicted on the country of his birth, Sorensen blamed German "parasites and thugs" for annexing his homeland, eliminating free speech, and imposing martial law on a passively resistant Danish population. He didn't profess to understand why an older generation had chosen to resolve Europe's differences this way. But in his broadcast, he cited his Danish-born brother, now an engineer in the Canadian Army, and himself, a Danish-born fighter pilot in the RCAF, as models for the way young Danes should respond to German occupation.

"I know how fortunate I and my comrades out here are that we are actively engaged in the battle," he concluded. "For us the problem is simple and straightforward, but . . . it doesn't pay to wait. Let us young people fight together now . . . [until] the Germans once again are driven out of Denmark."[3]

A month later, on November 24, 1942, his squadron boarded SS *Antenor* sailing from Liverpool to Algeria to assist Lieutenant General Bernard Montgomery and the British Eighth Army mount a counter-offensive in the North African desert against Erwin Rommel's Afrika Korps. By mid-January of 1943, with the Allies advancing quickly, 232 Squadron had established a landing strip at Tingley in Algeria, from which its Spitfires conducted sweeps and reconnaissance operations. By March the squadron was flying patrols and escorts in and out of Victoria airstrip in Tunisia. In three weeks, Sorensen flew just thirteen operational sorties[4] and was growing weary of harbour patrols, tactical reconnaissance, and escort operations. However, a letter to his brother Eric described a sudden change in the intensity of the squadron's activity.

"With no more excitement than ground strafing enemy transport once in a while, I welcomed the order by my flight commander one

Sunday morning [April 11, 1943] over Tunis to break away and polish off a few Junker 52s flying low over the Bay of Tunis,"5 Frank Sorensen wrote.

During his descent from an original altitude of twenty-three thousand feet, his flight of four Spitfires encountered enemy fire; one Spit was hit, caught fire, and crashed into the sea. The three remaining fighters in his formation opened fire on the German transport aircraft. Sorensen saw his flight commander fire cannon shells into one of them and looked back to see it crash in a ball of fire; he recalled seeing the troops previously inside the Junker's fuselage flailing about in water mixed with burning fuel and wreckage. Sorensen then focused on catching up to another of the transports heading north toward Italy.

"I sent two of them crashing in flames into the drink," Sorensen continued. "Bags of fun, I thought, until I was reminded by half a dozen Me. 109s that crime does not pay. I wouldn't have met these 109s, if my commander upstairs had not told us to [climb] for I had in mind to go home on the deck [just above the surface of the water]."6

As he climbed, the first Messerschmitt attacked him from behind. Sorensen tried out-turning his opponent three times, expending the remainder of his ammunition as he manoeuvred around the sky. Now there were six more Me. 109s. In ones and twos the enemy fighters engaged him and he dodged fire from a dozen of those attacks. The thirteenth attack found the target as a burst of machine-gun fire hit his engine. Oil sprayed across his windscreen. He was too low to bail out, so he quickly decided to take his chances with a controlled crash landing. He'd forgotten, however, that he regularly left his cockpit safety belts loose (only tightening them for landings), so unable to see ahead clearly and not properly secured into the cockpit, Sorensen prepared for a rough landing on hilly desert terrain.

"I closed my eyes," he wrote. "I hit. I felt I hit again. I could still think and feel. Then I turned a somersault and with a final crash my flying carrier had come to an abrupt stop—upside down. I thought I was dead . . . I took off my flying helmet and goggles, oxygen mask . . . and had a look through a hole in the ground. I had ploughed right into the ground so my cockpit and myself were completely under the ground. I started digging [my way out when] I heard footsteps and then, 'Hands up.'"[7]

Sorensen had crashed right next to a German infantry post. At gunpoint he was pulled from beneath the half-buried Spitfire, quickly searched, thrown into a vehicle, and hauled off to Tunis for interrogation. The Americans bombed the city heavily overnight, but the next day he was put aboard a transport, not unlike the four German aircraft his squadron had shot down the previous day. He and a British officer shot down the same day were escorted to Italy by twenty German paratroopers inside the aircraft and a flight of Me. 109s outside the aircraft. They travelled through Rome, then on to Munich, and to Dulag Luft at Frankfurt, all the while refusing to offer any information and paying for their resistance by receiving very little food and plenty of solitary confinement. P/O Sorensen arrived at Sagan on April 20, "on Hitler's birthday, when every house had a flag out," he wrote.

As it was for so many families on the home front, word of Frank Sorensen's survival of the crash outside Tunis, his transport through Italy, his interrogation by German authorities at Dulag Luft, and his eventual deposit at Stalag Luft III took weeks to arrive. In the interim came the Department of National Defence letter to Frank's mother saying he "is reported missing,"[8] then a long gap with little or no information from either the air force or the government about his fate, and finally—a month after he was shot down—word to Frank's father from the RCAF Overseas office in London that "your son . . . is a prisoner of war."[9]

Meanwhile, Frank Sorensen's letters began wending their way to his grandparents in Hjørring, Denmark, to his father in the UK, and to his mother and siblings now living in Kingston, Ontario. His earliest written thoughts from inside German prison camps were predictably melancholy. His first letter from Dulag Luft, just eight days after his capture, said he was happy, enjoying the good company of other "unfortunate chaps," that he'd asked for his $175-a-month allowance to be sent home to his mother, and that he wanted his father "to write to my squadron and tell them how happy and proud I was to have been one of them."[10] By his fifth letter, notably, the dispirited tone appeared to be gone. He seemed no more or less resigned to his POW plight, but there was something more substantial contained in his letter home than just the words of a kriegie waiting for his imprisonment to end.

"I find time goes by very fast," he wrote in May 1943. "I find plenty to do besides reading and studying chemistry and math. . . . There is plenty of exercise we get when we feel like it—basketball, football, discus, shot put, horizontal bar, horseshoes, and walking 'round the perimeter."[11]

Just as Roger Bushell had done with escape committee section heads Floody, Harsh, and Fanshawe—discussing high-priority issues affecting the progress of tunnelling—by walking the perimeter with newly arrived officer Frank "Sorry" Sorensen, Bushell acquired valuable new intelligence about Erwin Rommel's defeats in North Africa during the winter of 1942–43 and plans for the invasion of Sicily that summer. But having access to Sorensen on a regular basis actually gave Bushell something he hadn't expected; Big X was fluent in German, French, and a few Russian phrases, but he was deficient in Danish. And he recognized if he had any hope of talking his way aboard a vessel sailing the Baltic, simple Danish phrases would be essential. So, pounding the exercise circuit inside the warning wire with P/O Sorensen allowed Bushell to pick up everyday Danish.* But Big X wasn't the only fellow officer Sorensen tutored in Danish. Some time later, Sorensen befriended Flight Lieutenant Eric Foster. As a means of expediting his way out of the camp, Foster feigned insanity. But in the meantime, partly because Sorensen knew that Foster had a Danish wife, he tried to help Eric learn some important phrases. It proved to be a frustrating exercise.

"I tried teaching him Danish," Sorensen wrote, "but for all he learnt, I might as well have taught a horse."[12]

---

* In his 2011 article, "From Roskilde Cathedral School to Stalag Luft III—And the Great Escape," Danish writer Mikkel Plannthin points out that Roger Bushell learned Danish from Frank Sorensen and Arne Bøge, who'd both been born and schooled in Denmark.

Ultimately, Foster's performance around the North Compound convinced the Germans he was mentally unstable and he was repatriated in 1944. But Sorensen's impromptu language instruction, if Big X hadn't already recognized it, illustrated the growing need for X Organization to make conversational training a higher priority among monolingual kriegies. This, in turn, explained one of Frank Sorensen's repeated requests of his family in his regular correspondence.

Given that each kriegie was rationed to roughly four cards and three letters per month, and that the space on official stalag-issued writing paper—ten inches by five-and-a-half inches—was limited to between two hundred and three hundred words, Sorensen's priorities must have appeared odd in his letters home. No doubt, the censors would not have found his references the least bit troublesome. But after the weather, his health, and general POW activity, in both his May 18 and July 12 letters Sorensen reserved space to request certain items from home or via a Red Cross parcel. He asked his mother to send summer season underwear, dehydrated meat, fruit, milk, sugar raisins, oatmeal, maple sugar, chocolate, powdered egg, and onion. Finally, in a quick sentence, he asked a favour of his father.

"Dad, would you send me the thesaurus dictionary, please?"[13] he wrote.

Requesting clothing and food items was commonplace, although emphasizing that the foods be high in energy and dehydrated suggested they might be packed more easily for the trip into the compound, or, conceivably, in the pocket of an escaper, out of it. The special request to his father for the thesaurus, however, had little to do with enhancing Sorensen's literacy or even filling his leisure time with stimulating reading. Contained within the back pages of every thesaurus since its creator, English physician Peter Mark Roget, had first published the book in 1852 was a section called "Foreign Phrases," translated with reference to the applicable English categories into French, Latin, and German. A thesaurus or two or more might well make their way to the North Compound library and reading room, but their circulation would be less about offering readers a lexicon of valuable synonyms and antonyms than about offering them a guide to phrases used in everyday conversation outside the wire.

Assembling a library of language textbooks, including thesaurus donations from the Sorensen family library, likely helped escape preparations a great deal. But finding officers who could properly pronounce the phrases and then get English-speaking kriegies to parrot those phrases back with some credibility was something else again. In that regard, the escape committee had received a remarkable gift, appropriately the previous Christmas, when a twenty-eight-year-old RCAF officer arrived at the North Compound. Gordon Kidder, born in St. Catharines, Ontario, grew up a scholar. He learned French and could speak fluent German as a result of his studies at the University of Toronto in the 1930s; in fact, in 1937, Johns Hopkins University in the US invited him to finish his master's degree in German. Instead, he worked in Ontario's education department and also translated language for an insurance company.[14] When war broke out, he trained as a navigator, and was on his ninth combat operation aboard a 156 Squadron Wellington when it was hit by flak and crashed into the North Sea. Kidder and the wireless air gunner survived in a dinghy until a German minesweeper captured them the next day. Kidder arrived at Stalag Luft III in December 1942.

Flying Officer Kidder was no doubt surprised to find his POW compound not only had kriegies fluent in as many languages as he, but also library facilities to match. Those book rooms became a hub for language classes that not only weren't disguised, but were also encouraged. Had he wanted to, Kidder could have continued his linguistic studies inside Stalag Luft III. By the time kriegies had moved into the East Compound (in 1942) and North Compound (in 1943), some of the most ambitious among them had established courses in business, social science, and the humanities. The courses proved so sophisticated that examining boards in the UK and Canada allowed prisoners of war to earn full credits. While he was imprisoned at Stalag Luft III, RCAF officer Ian Tweddell, from Lashburn, Saskatchewan, received engineering textbooks from the

University of Saskatchewan so that he could advance his studies.[15] Textbooks from the same university helped another kriegie, who'd only received his senior matriculation before the war, complete a credit in political science.[16] College certificates were even available for proficiency in German, Russian, and French. To support the kriegies' educational pursuits, the libraries began to assemble sizable inventories. Thanks to Red Cross and personal family parcels, the libraries boasted hundreds of texts and reference books, as well as detective novels, westerns, and biographies.[17] The Centre Compound library had as many as nineteen hundred books, which explains why Frank Sorensen's emphatic pleas for more specific reading materials passed the censors without arousing any suspicion.

"Yes, the thesaurus dictionary," he wrote on August 11, 1943. "I sure long to get my fingers on that book. No better opportunity learning German, except time and German newspapers. Am studying it though."[18]

By the time Sorry Sorensen had started teaching Roger Bushell and other kriegies some elementary Danish expressions, Big X was receiving the first reports of progress underground. Within days of completing the trap entry to the chimney in Hut 123, Wally Floody, Robert Ker-Ramsey, and Johnny Marshall had penetrated the topsoil into the yellow-coloured sand beneath it, and had begun to excavate the vertical shaft of tunnel "Tom" about three feet square and down thirty feet. To reinforce the walls of the shaft, when he had dug down about the height of a man, Floody had "borrowed" the bedposts from unused double-decker bunk beds around the compound, bolted them together, and then inserted "borrowed" bed-boards as walls behind the posts to shore up the shaft against the loose sand around it.

"We didn't have springs [in our beds.] Each bunk . . . had ten or fifteen boards varying in width from three inches to six inches," Floody said. "We had fifteen hundred officers. That meant fifteen hundred beds. So if you took one board out of each bunk . . . that's a lot of wood for shoring."[19]

With each new five- to six-foot section of the vertical shaft, Floody would need more wood to shore up the walls before continuing his descent. To supply the raw materials, the escape committee had assigned Australian officer John E. "Willy" Williams to lead a crew that constantly cruised the barracks on the lookout for available bedposts, bed-boards, and even nails and screws that could be liberated without being noticed by German guards. When Williams' scavengers liberated the lumber and fasteners, they passed along their found supplies to expert metalworkers and carpenters who engineered the shaft and tunnel construction.

One such expert had come from the same theatre of war as Frank Sorensen. Initially an apprenticed mechanical engineer from Leeds, England, Bob Nelson had branched into aeronautical engineering before joining the RAF in 1937. A talented pilot, Nelson had instructed in Rhodesia until 1941, when he was posted to the Middle East, piloting Wellington bombers against Rommel's Afrika Korps. On his twenty-second operational flight inland from Tobruk his aircraft was hit. He ordered his crew to bail out and crash-landed the Wellington 150 miles behind enemy lines. He endured three weeks in the Libyan Desert (surviving by licking dew from rusty gas cans[20]) and was within three hundred yards of the British lines when he was captured and sent to Stalag Luft III in November 1942. A man of his resourcefulness proved invaluable helping to shore up tunnel "Tom" in the spring and summer of 1943.

By late April, "Tom's" shaft was down thirty feet, "Dick" was nearly that deep, and "Harry" was down about twenty feet. Once Floody had completed the vertical dig in each of the tunnel shafts, Nelson and John Travis, formerly a Rhodesian mining engineer, fashioned a kind of crossroads where the vertical shaft ended and the horizontal tunnel began. At the foot of the shaft, they constructed chambers into three of the walls—one chamber for equipment storage, a second for temporary storage of sand from the tunnel before dispersal, and a third (about six feet in length) to accommodate an air pump. Through the fourth wall of the shaft was the entry to the horizontal tunnel out of the North Compound. For "Tom" and "Harry," the engineers had organized a multi-purpose basement workshop, with fresh air drawn by an air pump from the natural flue of the chimney above, down through the shaft, and along to the tunnel face where the diggers were extending the tunnel.

"The air pump consisted of two canvas kit-bags attached to a central wooden valve box," Nelson wrote. "A reciprocating movement of a wooden frame caused one bag to be compressed in a delivery stroke while the other expanded in a suction stroke. A suction pipeline made from Klim cans [the Red Cross tins about four inches in diameter that had contained powdered milk] ran up the shaft to a fresh air supply and the delivery pipeline was then laid along the floor of the tunnel as it was dug."[21]

Nelson explained that a second Klim can pipeline was laid underground from below each trapdoor to the nearest chimney in the barracks hut. That provided a hidden outlet to expel used air, which otherwise on cold days would have revealed a condensation trail. This way, the regular chimney of the barracks hut gave the tunnel operation a natural draught while a bypass valve in the pump allowed the tunnel to ventilate itself naturally even when no one was underground. The ventilation system also made it possible for a team of diggers, dispersal men, and pump operator to work below with the trapdoor completely sealed above. It meant the work could progress continuously between roll calls.

Digging the horizontal tunnels presented its own set of problems, including excavating on a level plane and in a straight line. The engineers fabricated a level and stole prismatic compasses from the Germans.[22] To calculate the distance travelled underground, they came up with primitive tools, including a premeasured ball of cord. They melted margarine and other combustible fat into candles with pajama string as wicks, ensuring that the sooty by-product went safely up the Klim can chimney; the resulting fat lamps lit the way up each tunnel. Once "Tom" began on the horizontal, Nelson and the other engineers worked with Floody to shore the walls of the tunnel with box frames in a trapezium shape for strength. Each of the bottom and two side boards of the frame, he said, was 21.5 inches long, while the top board was 20 inches long. Because most of the bed-boards were conveniently that length, and featured tongue-and-slot joints, they fit together like a prefab floor, ceiling, and walls. The weight of the earth above the ceiling and against the outside of the walls kept the entire frame rigid. That meant no nails were needed, nor was any hammering required.

"It wasn't very difficult to dig," Nelson said. "[Floody] digging the tunnel would lie inside the existing frame. He would scoop out the earth and the whole roof would collapse on him, but he'd be protected by the wood frame. The tunnel sand would collapse into an arch-like shape. All the sand that had fallen out would be packed behind the wooden frame and the shaft would move forward with the wooden support. . . . The big problem was the risk of collapse because you could get trapped thirty feet underground."[23]

It was about the time the digging team had nearly completed the three workshop chambers at the base of "Dick's" vertical shaft that near-disaster struck. On a day in late April, just after the 9:30 a.m. appell, as the digging shift began, Ker-Ramsey joined Floody underground to finish shoring up the storage chamber and the sand dispersal chamber. A third digger, Norman "Conk" Canton, was shoring the pumping chamber with bunk-bed timber. Suddenly, about twenty feet above the men, a bed-board in the shaft wall cracked and broke, then a frame broke and sand began cascading through the gap and down the shaft. Fortunately for the diggers, the ladder up the shaft hadn't broken, so Ker-Ramsey and Canton clambered upward through the spilling sand, with Floody bringing up the rear. In seconds Floody was up to his waist in sand and unable to move. The first two grabbed his arms and heaved him out before the sand smothered him.

"Much sputtering and shrieking on my part," Floody said, and he cursed for minutes afterward, but then realized his good fortune. He'd become "a little greyer, a little wiser, and a bit more cautious."[24]

It took Floody, Ker-Ramsey, and the others four days to regain the ground they'd lost in the cave-in down the shaft of "Dick." The same kind of setback occurred in the shaft of "Harry" within a few days. Moreover, digging and re-digging down the throats of "Tom" and "Harry" not only put tunnellers' lives in peril, it multiplied exponentially the problem facing the sand dispersal teams. German Staff Sergeant Glemnitz, the chief of the anti-escape guards, had warned all his troublemaking kriegies there was no way to hide the damp, bright yellow-coloured sand from beneath the surface of the compound unless they could find a way to "destroy" it.

At the outset, that apparently impossible piece of magic had fallen to Peter Fanshawe, head of the sand dispersal section. Engineers, such as Nelson, had calculated that each stretch of tunnel, roughly three-and-a-half-feet long by two-and-a-half-feet wide (or twenty-two-cubic-feet), yielded about a ton of sand. Initially, Fanshawe's dispersal men used pots and pans, jugs, washbasins, socks, and makeshift sandbags to dispense with sand in manageable quantities. They could hide it under huts, in latrines, behind wallboards, and even inside Red Cross parcel boxes. But with three tunnelling teams excavating in three sites from morning appell to evening appell, in total likely to generate maybe a hundred tons of sand, his dispersers were running out of places to hide it all. And each time Glemnitz and his team of ferrets found traces of the telltale yellow sand, they increased their spot searches, added unexpected roll calls, and ratcheted up the tension everywhere. The answer?

"Trouser bags,"[25] Fanshawe said at a section meeting of X Organization.

From beneath his tunic and pants, he pulled out a set of suspenders from which hung two cut-off legs of a pair of long, woolen underpants, looking like two sausage bags. (Suspenders and underpants had been sent by the score to POWs in Red Cross parcels in anticipation of the coming cold winter.) A pin was stuck into the lower end of each sausage. By placing the suspenders around his neck and sticking the sausage bags (full of sand) inside his trousers, he could pull a string concealed in his pants pocket. It would release the pin and allow the sand contents of the two sausage bags to flow down the inside of his trousers and onto the ground, where it could be scuffed into the ground relatively unnoticed.

The dispersal team members—now numbering in the hundreds—could fan out across the compound. They could march across the parade square and disperse sand as they conducted a drill. They could cultivate their gardens and hoe the evidence in among the plants. They could even stage fights and mix surface and sub-surface dirt in the resulting dust, and make both nearly disappear. Noting the way his dispersers tended to waddle with eight or ten pounds of sand down their legs, X Organization dubbed Fanshawe's men "penguins." The trick was to find equilibrium, to ensure that, each day, the penguins could disperse roughly the same volume of sand the diggers excavated. Wally Floody noted the diggers were clawing out ten feet of sand per day, while Peter Fanshawe said the penguins could get rid of about six feet per day. One POW noted astutely that kriegies had become servants to an ugly hole in the ground.[26]

John Colwell joined that servitude in June of 1943. Not that he had an aptitude for hauling and hiding sand. But Flying Officer Colwell had experience at just about everything else. The son of a medical missionary, John grew up in India through the 1930s, when his father, a veteran of the Great War in the British Army, decided to move the family to Canada's west coast to own and operate a chicken farm. Riding to and from Nanaimo, on Vancouver Island, to take school and sell the farm's eggs didn't appeal, so when the war began Colwell joined the RCAF, where his skills in math and geometry moved him quickly through the air training plan. By 1942 he was posted as a navigator to 405 Squadron and flying operations with Coastal Command, chasing U-boats and guiding rescuers to downed airmen. Grounded due to bad September weather and a broken engine radiator, Colwell was told replacement parts were a week away.

"No matter," a fellow airman wrote. "John and his crew . . . scrounged a radiator and did the repairs themselves."[27]

By the spring of 1943, his squadron had joined the newly formed 6 Group of Canadian squadrons, with his 405 Squadron flying seven-man Halifax bombers against submarine pens on the coast of France and industrial targets along Germany's Ruhr River valley. On April 3, F/O Colwell was navigating one of the lead bombers in the stream to attack Essen, Germany. They delivered their bombs, but anti-aircraft flak had damaged Colwell's astro compass; instead of a path northward away from heavily populated areas and Luftwaffe night-fighter bases, they were headed west and were shot down near the Maas River, southwest of Rotterdam.

Colwell's first entry in his POW diary was a simple one.

"Made my first parachute jump at 11 p.m.,"[28] it read. Nine days later, Colwell noted that he and a couple of the officers in his Halifax crew, pilot Jim Lago and wireless-operator Bill Hoddinott, "arrived in Sagan about 8 a.m. It was about noon before we were finally allowed into the compound . . . got our Red Cross parcels to start house-keeping . . . in Room 14, Block 120."[29] A few days after he and his roommates figured out who cooked, who cleaned, and who took care of retrieving Red Cross parcels, Colwell began to focus on the rhythm of the North Compound, its periodic escapes, its scheduled and unscheduled appells, and contributing to the escape committee's greatest needs.

"Two Americans got out under the south fence. . . . They searched the camp just after 1 a.m., and identified everyone by card and picture," Colwell wrote on June 17. "We were then moved out into the hall while they searched the room carefully. They lost . . ."[30] Three nights later, "another night search. Jamie [Jim Jamieson], Art [Hawtin], Ach [John Acheson], Mull [W. D. Mullins], and I had our hair all cut off."[31] A day later, he simply noted, "Night search. Started work as a penguin."[32]

Colwell learned about the penguin work shortly after arriving at the compound that spring of 1943. Since none of the officers was compelled to work, he enjoyed the notion of joining a friendly horse-shoe match after appell one day.

"Suddenly, these two Dutch POWs came along and sort of scuffed around in the middle of our game," Colwell said. "I remember thinking it wasn't very considerate of them. And then I saw this sand trickling out of their pant legs and I realized what was going on."[33]

Colwell's diary reflected the experiences of an officer newly introduced to Stalag Luft III and feeling his way into the routine of POW life. He sensed his first priority, self-preservation, was a matter of being accepted by his roommates, assuming a role in Block (or Hut) 120 life, and attending to his health and nutritional needs as best he could. The Allied doctors in the compound recommended that a grown, fairly active man needed three thousand calories in his diet each day; the German rations at best delivered fifteen hundred to nineteen hundred calories in the form of bread, some portions of vegetables, and even fewer of meat. Colwell noted early on that he weighed 148 pounds. His lower calorie intake and his penguin activity consumed those limited calories very quickly. For penguins, each circuit began at the tunnelling hut. One penguin loaded another's two inner pant legs with sand; at capacity that could mean columns of sand two feet long and three inches in diameter down each leg. Then, controllers sent the penguin on a casual walk to a specific dumping site. Controllers also directed penguins to various loading points and dumping sites so that the ferrets wouldn't spot a kriegie repeating a circuit. It was hot, continuous work that summer as Colwell and the other penguins tried to keep pace with the diggers.

Moving sand underground had also become more sophisticated. As each of the three tunnels crept farther and farther from the base of its entry shaft, diggers abandoned their washbasins and jugs in favour of higher-volume transport. The engineers had scrounged the makings of an underground railway system. Willy Williams had retrieved battens that lined the ceilings and walls of the barracks huts; split lengthwise, the battens became one-inch-wide rails nailed to the floor of the tunnel. Bob Nelson and the other carpenters built sturdy trolleys—consisting of chassis and detachable boxes built from beechwood bed-boards, axels liberated from barracks stoves, and wheels of wood covered in tin from discarded food containers. When a shift started, the first digger would wheel himself on the trolley chassis to the face of the tunnel. A second man reeled the empty trolley back with its draw rope and wheeled himself forward. The first digger, facing forward, cut into the face, drew the sand down his body to the second digger, who faced backwards and scooped the sand up his body and into the trolley box. When the box was full he tugged the rope and a third man back at the base of the shaft reeled in the trolley to remove the sand. All the while, a fourth man pushed the bellows in the air-pump chamber, delivering a steady flow of fresher air through the Klim can ventilation system under the railway tracks and floor boards to the face of the tunnel. Gordon King, who had worked as the dish man on the impromptu tunnel to the cookhouse a couple of months earlier, gladly took on the role of air-pump operator.

"I was small and in good shape," King said. "I could stay on the bellows . . . for a shift of eight hours if I had to. We stopped from time to time to rest. Using the cart with the long rope attached, we could bring the sand out much faster. They even put carpet on top of the rails to deaden the sound."34

Matching the digging pairs required a bit of psychology and physics. The section bosses matched John Weir with Hank Birkland, for example. First of all, they were both Canadian. More important, they had dug tunnels together since the first escape efforts at the Stalag Luft I camp back in 1941. But they also compensated each other's work in a unique way. Weir had a tendency to dig harder to the left when he was at the face of "Tom," while Birkland often veered to the right; by the end of a shift one would balance the other. On other shifts, Floody worked at the face of the tunnel and Weir was his second, pulling out the bags of excavated sand. The bond these fellow diggers shared, going all the way back to Luft I at Barth, was paying off.

"One time, Wally was digging and I was passing [the sand] back," Weir said. "Suddenly the candle blew out and there was a helluva wind in my face. I knew damn well what it was. I just went forward as fast as I could and got [Wally] out in a matter of minutes."35

Birkland preferred to dig fully naked and that aggravated Floody; he was afraid the ferrets would notice the scrapes on Birkland's elbows and knees and start paying closer attention to his activities. To hide any telltale scars, tunnel boss Wally Floody insisted his diggers wear long underwear and vests. John Weir's fiancée Frances McCormack might well have wondered why the flow of letters from Weir had slowed that spring; his digging shifts underground increased and lengthened. Further, she was probably puzzled as to why he seemed to be going through his underclothes so quickly.

"This is my forty-seventh letter and I've had a hundred and twenty-three from you so far," Weir began his letter of April 30, 1943. "You wondered what clothes I need? I could do with some light pajamas. . . . Five pair underwear and shirts, sox [sic] could be used. . . . I don't think another May will come with us separated."[36]

Fear of cave-ins, vomiting from pockets of foul underground air, and elbows and knees scraped raw by the sand were just some of the occupational hazards the diggers tolerated. Fat lamps proved extremely helpful in guiding the tunnellers up to and back from the tunnel face, but they too were a half measure. To address the problem, some of the escape committee's engineers came up with a partial solution. They calculated that the wiring in the barracks huts probably had some slack, so clandestinely they stripped away sections of the wall and ceiling boards to track down any excess.[37] When they finished their wire roundup they had spliced together enough wire to bring electricity and lighting to the mouths of all three tunnels. The Germans regularly turned power to the huts off during the day, so for some of the evening tunnel shifts, the electric light was a psychological lift.

Meantime, and suddenly, on June 10, 1943, the Russian work crews—with their axes, picks, and debris wagons—were back at work inside the wire, this time beyond the south fences of the North Compound. The then-SBO, H. M. Massey, learned from Colonel von Lindeiner that the upper command of the prison administration had decided the ever-increasing numbers of American officers flowing through the gates of Stalag Luft III would require a separate compound—a new South Compound—to house as many as four or five hundred USAAF POWs. The inner circle of X Organization met in an emergency session. Bushell and Day were feeling guilty that so many USAAF officers had contributed to the design, creation, and protection of the three tunnels, and it now seemed likely von Lindeiner would complete the South Compound before the kriegies finished any of the three North Compound tunnels. Big X recognized that a lot of American officers might feel cheated out of their chance at freedom. He felt obliged to find a solution.

"We close up 'Dick' and 'Harry' for now," Bushell said. "We go full out on 'Tom.' . . . We might make it before South Compound is ready."[38]

At that point "Tom" had advanced some sixty feet from Hut 123. There were still at least a hundred feet to cover to get the face of the tunnel beyond the double fence and into the protection of the reforestation pines. Bushell asked Wally Floody how much they might advance the tunnel by September if all three digging shifts concentrated on "Tom." Floody told him that digging advanced each tunnel about five to ten feet a day with one team, but simple arithmetic meant three digging teams might move "Tom" westward up to thirty feet a day. Fanshawe agreed that the pace would put pressure on the penguins, but it was manageable.

"It was decided that 'Tom' should be finished before the Americans went," Bob Nelson said. "With the necessity for speed, however, greater risks were taken and the Germans' suspicions were aroused."[39]

With the priority shifting to "Tom," digging and dispersing sand from the two other tunnels came to a stop. The Polish officers who had so expertly created the invisible trapdoors for "Dick" in the showers of Hut 122 and the rebuilt tile flooring at the entrance to "Harry" in Hut 104 returned to seal them up as if they'd never been there. Bushell and Floody then chose the fifteen best diggers, included all of the American diggers available, and divided them into three teams of five for the new push at the face of "Tom." Wally Floody's predictions of ten feet per day proved accurate, and so did Fanshawe's promise to "disappear" the sand as quickly as it came to the surface.

Out of urgency, or perhaps by accident, that summer a number of penguins stumbled on an ideal dumping ground for the now relentless flow of yellow sand gushing from "Tom" like Niagara Falls. And it was incredibly obvious. With few exceptions, neither the Russian workers nor the escape committee "volunteer" officers had disturbed much of the sub-surface yellow sand during the felling of the pine forest or the construction of the barracks huts and sports grounds. The one exception was the structure known as the fire pool, which had required a deep cut a dozen feet into the sand and then installation of a solid brick lining to catch and supply rainwater in the event of a fire. While much of the yellow sand excavated from the pool hole had been hauled away, around the edge of the structure some still lay on the surface. But the pool was right in the centre of the compound, under direct and constant observation by goons in the towers and by some with binoculars hiding in the woods spying on every move the kriegies made inside the wire. The pool perimeter suddenly became a focal point for Fanshawe's dispersers.

"Each penguin nonchalantly sauntered to the edge of the pool with his hands in his pockets," Bob Nelson said. "On reaching the edge of the pool, he pulled the cords which opened the bottom of the containers inside his trousers and allowed the sand to trickle slowly out as he walked. . . . During the summer, many tons of sand were disposed of. Although the sand around the pool got gradually deeper, it was very imperceptible."[40]

Beyond the edges of the pool, Fanshawe and his legion of penguins created numerous other scenarios for making the sand disappear. Whenever a pine stump was removed, exposing yellow subsoil on the surface of the compound, penguins congregated. If a new latrine were dug, penguins would wander by and contribute. One of the American air force officers in the North Compound, Jerry Sage, who had served as a paratrooper in North Africa, used the sports grounds to help the penguins keep up with the flow of excavated tunnel sand. One day, he would organize scores of his USAAF officers to kick up a curtain of dust by demonstrating techniques in unarmed combat. Any and all penguins were invited to participate or spectate; in the midst of the melee, none of the German guards would notice tunnel sand being emptied and mixed into the surface sand of the sports grounds. Other times, Sage staged volleyball matches with penguins two and three deep excreting sand as they jumped up and down cheering on their favourite team.

The day after the summit, "Tom" advanced ten feet and Fanshawe's penguins kept pace. The next day, Floody accidentally triggered another cave-in and had to be pulled out by his ankles before leading a repair of the tunnel frame; they only advanced eight feet that day. The following day it was the same thing, only this time hot margarine from a candle burned his leg. Floody seemed cursed. Nevertheless, by mid-June "Tom" was more than a hundred feet in length. At that point the diggers widened the tunnel to create a halfway house about ten feet long and half a foot wider than the tunnel itself. Floody believed the chamber, roughly beneath the compound fencing, would allow a changeover of crews and trolleys so there was less danger of a long tow rope getting tangled or rubbing against the tunnel shoring and loosening a wooden frame. The engineers calculated that another forty feet would put "Tom" beyond the double wire and under the woods. Then, at a section meeting to discuss timelines, digger Johnny Marshall suggested gradually sloping the tunnel to the surface. Floody considered that too risky; a rope could break or a trolley might run away on them and inflict a real setback. He was sure they could complete the tunnel before the Germans completed the South Compound and moved the US POWs into new huts there. Big X sided with Floody. It was July 3.

Shortly after dawn the next morning, when the Germans had unlocked the barracks doors, and just about the time POWs were beginning to assemble for appell, two men appeared on the sports grounds in a costume—the front and hind quarters of a horse. On the horse's back was USAAF officer Jerry Sage portraying Paul Revere with a tricorner hat and knee breeches made of woolen underpants.

"The British are coming!"[41] he shouted as he brought the two-man horse to a halt.

At first startled, *Hauptmann* Hans Pieber went along with the prank and commenced the roll call, whereupon the American inside the hind quarters poured out the contents of a can of water; the horse was urinating during Pieber's appell.

"*Zwei und achtzig . . . und ein pferd,*" he shouted to the recorder, noting eighty-two prisoners and one horse.

But they weren't done, as John Colwell noted. "Yankee Doodle and his horse . . . then paraded through the huts with a band."[42]

Drummers and buglers came marching through the barracks with about forty other US POWs masquerading as native tribesmen on the warpath. While the horse and tribesmen wreaked havoc on the roll call, Paul Revere, a.k.a. Jerry Sage, and George Harsh threw Roger Bushell out of bed, sat on him, and offered him a sample of their latest creation. The Americans had scrimped and accumulated their rations of sugar and dried fruit from Red Cross parcels for weeks and distilled them into a raisin-flavoured wine. The party continued all day, ending with many of the officers, including Wings Day, being tossed into the fire pool during a water fight. It was Independence Day and the American kriegies weren't going to let it pass without notice.

"The Goons are afraid of something," Colwell wrote in his diary a few days later. "We are having four appells per day and they've been around the last four nights between 1 and 4 a.m."[43] Two days later, he recorded, "Last night, [the Germans] were in the hut several hours. Each room was turned out in turn and searched."[44] Every other day for the rest of the month, Colwell reported searches where "there were dozens of guards and barbed wire used."[45]

During one of those staged volleyball matches with penguins gathered around to empty their hidden sand pouches, Glemnitz came prowling. Bushell and the rest of the escape committee realized he was on to something. Security boss Harsh added he'd seen German guards in the towers all equipped with binoculars. Digger Hank Birkland reported seeing a ferret walking in the pine forest beyond the fences; the German didn't come out. So Harsh and Junior Clark took a closer look and realized the Germans had strategically placed blinds in the woods—piles of brush through which they could use field-glasses to spy on the kriegies without the prisoners realizing they were under surveillance. This sparked a series of after-dark visits from Hans Pieber. The ferret barged into Hut 101, throwing everybody out of bed with shouts of, "*Aus! Aus!*"

It prompted digger Ker-Ramsey to tell Pieber he was wasting his time.

"You think I know fuck nothing," Pieber defended himself in a broken English malapropism, "but I actually know fuck all!"[46]

The war of wits continued. Glemnitz resumed the snap searches. He had narrowed his focus to the western perimeter of the compound, with particular interest in Hut 123. Each time the Germans raided, the escape committee resealed the trapdoor at the entrance to "Tom," waited for the searchers to retreat, and then re-opened the trap and resumed the digging and sand dispersal. Next, Glemnitz arrived with *Hauptmann* Broili, a member of the *Abwehr* counter-intelligence, and about forty soldiers. Following another hut search, he ordered the troops to dig a trench between Hut 123 and the outer double fencing. They went down four feet, where the ferrets used five-foot steel rods to probe even deeper. By that time, "Tom," which was twenty feet below the probing ferrets, had come within about fifty feet of what the escape committee figured was the safety of the pine forest. Floody constructed another halfway house and prepared to dig the last horizontal section and finally the vertical shaft to the exit in the woods. With Fanshawe's penguins under close surveillance from the forest and towers, he suggested redirecting the sand dispersal teams to Hut 122, where Mike Casey and Ker-Ramsey began filling "Dick" with the sand from "Tom." The pace picked up; "Tom" was now two hundred feet long and, Floody figured, within striking distance of the woods.

The ferret chief's next move was uncanny. It was almost as if he knew "Tom" was beneath his feet. Suddenly there were workers felling pine trees all along the pine forest directly in front of where "Tom" was heading. The tunnel would have to go another hundred feet to find safety under the trees. But the penguins' secret weapon, tunnel "Dick," was running out of room; sand had now filled "Dick's" horizontal space, and Bushell refused to let Fanshawe's crew fill the vertical shaft. The next sand dispersal area was dangerously obvious— all the empty Red Cross parcel boxes lying about in the huts—but they would try it anyway. Five days later, August 21, penguin Colwell noted the inevitable.

"The Goons found over a hundred and fifty Red Cross boxes of sand in Hut 101,"[47] he wrote. And at the end of August, "Long morning appell. They searched all the huts and took hundreds of Red Cross boxes. Also my soldering outfit."[48]

For safety's sake, the Poles sealed the trap at the entrance to "Tom" once again. The tunnel was 260 feet long, but forty feet short of the recently extended no man's land to the woods. Still, the escape committee decided that was far enough. Floody would build the vertical shaft to the surface; while potentially out in the open, "Tom's" exit might well be far enough away from searchlights to allow men to escape at night. Since April, the hundreds of kriegies had excavated, hauled, hidden, and disguised the dispersal of more than seventy tons of sand from "Tom" alone. They had built an underground railway and ventilation system, not to mention a security and intelligence system. And while they hadn't delivered the mass escape they'd planned, they had at least escaped detection for more than twenty-one weeks.

Right after appell on September 8, as Wally Floody prepared to send his latest digging crew into "Tom" again to finish excavating the vertical shaft to the surface, Glemnitz suddenly threw up a wall of guards around Hut 123 and led a team of ferrets into the barracks. A couple of hours later, the German staff sergeant jabbed a probe into the concrete floor around the hut's chimney and discovered a chip in the concrete that revealed the trapdoor to the tunnel. Glemnitz beamed with pride at his victory. He had thwarted the largest escape attempt the German prison camp system had ever faced. Other German officials saw the discovery of a 260-foot-long escape tunnel at the heart of the inescapable Luft III quite differently.

"They were amazed, appalled, and at the same time very cocky about their discovery," Bob Nelson wrote. "Nothing like it had been seen. And high officials of the Luftwaffe and Wehrmacht came into the camp to inspect it."[49]

During their inspection, the Germans evacuated the hut and placed a guard at its entrance around the clock. Having unearthed "Tom," it appeared that neither the Luftwaffe *Kommandant* nor the Gestapo chief knew what to do next. So on September 16, they turned "Tom's" fate over to a demolition team.

"The German sappers entrusted with the job . . . did [it] very effectively," Nelson continued, "but at the same time blew a hole through the roof of the hut above the late 'Tom's' trap."[50]

"Tom" (if not Big X) had had the last laugh.

That same week in September 1943, the German police and guards completed the move of American POWs to the South Compound. Without missing a beat, X Organization held its next meeting, with Bushell already planning its next move. Anticipating further Gestapo searches, the escape committee ordered the collection of several thousand more bed-boards and hid them in the still-empty vertical shaft of tunnel "Dick." For the time being, work was suspended on "Dick" and "Harry." In Hut 120, John Colwell, despite losing some of his tools and soldering gear in the purges, began work on a cuckoo clock that would amuse his roommates as well as hide his diary.* And while he had worked diligently as Big X's personal Danish language tutor, Sorry Sorensen was stricken with appendicitis that fall and wound up on a dining table used for emergency surgeries; there, without benefit of anesthesia or sterilized surgical tools, a Russian doctor (also a POW at Stalag Luft III) performed the appendectomy.

"A dog circled the table [and] was rewarded with the appendix,"[51] Sorensen related later. Still, this brush with death didn't seem to blunt the twenty-one-year-old Canadian's drive to escape. Writing home to his parents that fall, he said he would refrain from betting on when the war would end, the way his roomies were, but concluded, "I don't intend being here the winter after this."[52]

---

* John Colwell not only hid his diary and his tin-bashing tools from any German ferrets rummaging through barracks huts at Stalag Luft III, he also hid messages in his writing. He regularly wrote letters home to his mother, Fern, in Hindi—a language in which they were both fluent, but which German censors couldn't decipher.

# "SHYSTERS AND CROOKS AND CON MEN"

ACH OF THEM had plenty of reasons why they shouldn't fall in love, much less get married. Joan Saunders already had a boyfriend, although he seemed noncommittal. Her family had suffered loss in this war; her cousin and his wife had died in the Luftwaffe attack on Coventry in 1940. She had a good wartime job as a bookkeeper at Lougheed, Berg, and Beck's, in her hometown of Leamington Spa, about ten miles from Coventry. The British company manufactured parts for the Royal Navy, including the hydraulics for motor torpedo boats. Like so many things in the UK then, however, the job was temporary. The plant could be hit by German bombing attacks and put her out of work. The contracts from the Royal Navy wouldn't necessarily last. She might be called up to enlist in the armed forces. Or, she might only be able to work there until a man needed the job.

"I was an only child,"[1] she said, and that meant whatever income she could provide her family was minimal, but important.

George Sweanor was an RCAF airman at an operational training unit (OTU) in Britain when he met Joan. Born in 1919 in Sudbury, Ontario, George had grown up through the Great Depression—the eldest of three children—in Port Hope. He'd idolized his uncles, both veterans of the Great War, but read anti-war literature and even wrote an essay entitled, "Who Wants War?"[2] In spite of that, George was fascinated by aviation, periodically coaxing his father to take him down the road to Trenton, Ontario, to see training aircraft airborne. After high school, he took a job with the bank and volunteered for the militia. By 1941 he had enlisted in the RCAF. By the winter of 1942, he'd graduated as a sergeant-observer. And by that summer, he had crossed the Atlantic and been posted to train as a bomb-aimer at the Wellesbourne OTU. On the training course, he got to know a fellow Canadian, Pilot Officer Pat Porter from British Columbia. They would later crew up for combat operations, but that summer they flew training ops and spent time on leave together.

Neither Porter nor Sweanor smoked or drank. They generally avoided the pubs, preferring the dances put on by the towns adjacent to their OTU station. They felt guilty sometimes, since so many local young British men were away fighting in North Africa or at sea with the Royal Navy and merchant navy. The dances usually featured a four-piece band playing soft music, which made the atmosphere conducive to having a conversation. Most military men and local women went stag. And the drill was to select a partner (often a wallflower), dance three numbers with her, escort her back to her seat, then select a different partner.

"If there was one partner you'd like to know better," Sweanor said, "you would try to get her in the home waltz, which permitted you to ask if you could walk her home."[3]

This particular night, Sweanor and Porter arrived by bus at Leamington Spa in search of the main dance hall. As it turned out, a sign on the town hall announced a special dance to raise funds for Red Cross food parcels to be sent to prisoners of war. Admission was more expensive than the regular dance, but the two Canadians wanted to help POWs. Coincidentally, local resident Joan Saunders, age twenty-three, and her girlfriend decided to support the dance fundraiser too. Joan was already seated when the two airmen arrived. On his way into the hall, Sweanor nudged Porter. "That's for me," he said, pointing to a potential dance partner who had "looks, poise, and figure."[4] And for the rest of the night, he plotted to make sure he got Joan Saunders for the home waltz.

"Everybody knew it was absolutely stupid to get married during the war," Sweanor said, "because if you survived, you'd probably be minus a leg or an arm or an eye, and be a burden to your wife the rest of your life. On the other hand, life is so temporary."[5]

Eventually, however, they each realized they had little control over their feelings, and that the war would affect both of them whether they courted or not. In fact, shortly after the couple met, Joan's office was strafed by a Luftwaffe fighter pilot shooting up whatever came into his gun sights.

"His bullets came right through the window, right through my office and my boss's office," Joan said. "It would have gone right through my head, if I'd been sitting there. But it was six in the morning and I always got to the office at eight."[6]

Meanwhile, George realized how close he was coming to the death that the war dispensed daily. Early in October of 1942, Bomber Command was directing Wellington bombers from his 419 Squadron against German targets for the first time since the squadron had arrived at its Yorkshire operational stations. On this night Sweanor's crew was not on ops. Dressed in his best blues to go to a dance, he stopped to speak to F/O Arthur Morlidge, who was going on the bombing raid.

"Can I be of any help?" Sweanor asked.

Morlidge pointed to a letter on his dresser and said, "If I decide to stay over there, would you post that letter for me?"[7]

The letter was addressed to his parents in Lloydminster, Saskatchewan. As readily as he'd agreed to Morlidge's request, Sweanor admitted to an uneasy feeling as he watched his squadron mates leave the Nissen hut for the flight line and the bombing attack to Krefeld that night. The next morning Sweanor saw the padre packing Morlidge's belongings. Bomber Command had lost nine aircraft that night, the one from 419 Squadron had twenty-year-old observer Arthur Morlidge aboard. Sweanor took the letter for posting.

Joan Saunders and George Sweanor were married just after New Year's, on January 6, 1943. As with most events in the UK at that time, the actual wedding happened when the war dictated. At the time, 419 Squadron (now flying brand new Halifax bombers) was standing down, waiting for what Sweanor called "delightfully foul weather"[8] to clear before it resumed flying. His squadron leader, D. W. S. Clark, loaned Sweanor a bicycle to get to and from Middleton St. George, where the couple had rented a single room. His wing commander volunteered his own crew to fly in place of Sweanor's to give the couple two free nights away from the war as a wedding present. His aircrew mates bought the couple a chest of silverware. Air force friend and artist Ley Kenyon designed a wedding card. His pilot, Pat Porter, stood up as best man. And as the couple was married, George Sweanor got a promotion to Flying Officer. Three nights later his Halifax "K for Kitty" was back in the battle order, dropping mines in German shipping lanes off the East Frisian Islands. But the inclement weather persisted, limiting his combat flights to three in January. They made up for the operations scrubbed in January with seven ops in February. Then he was away on a four-week bombing leaders' course, then back on bombing operations against submarine pens at St. Nazaire and German industrial targets at Duisburg and, on March 27, Berlin.

Sweanor counted the op to Berlin that Saturday night among numerous "wrong decisions" in his life. In the first place, although the operation didn't need their services, pilot Pat Porter volunteered his crew to replace one with lesser experience. Although they had flown most operations in Halifax "K for Kitty," she was in for repairs, so they settled for an unfamiliar bomber "E for Edward." Sweanor was sick with stomach flu and could have opted out. As bomb-aimer, however, he was the most mobile member of the crew—serving as second pilot on takeoff and landing, manning the front turret, taking astro shots for the navigator, changing fuel tanks for the engineer, and ultimately lining up and bombing the target. Sweanor didn't want to let his mates down. A decision not to go would have changed his life. Instead, he joined the op.

Early in their outbound flight southeast of Bremen, their bomber was hit by flak, knocking out one of the Halifax bomber's four engines. Unperturbed, Porter felt that they should press on to the target, despite the danger of losing altitude on three engines and perhaps becoming a target themselves. Sweanor released the bombs at a target near Berlin, muttering "my usual, useless prayer that my bombs hit only military targets,"9 and Porter banked for home. But they'd been sighted by an airborne night fighter that quickly caught up with them and raked their aircraft from behind. The attack set fire to the wireless radio area, and shrapnel wounded several of the crew. With the Halifax losing altitude, hydraulic oil fires breaking out, and wounded aircrew, Porter ordered his six crew members to abandon the aircraft. Sweanor went to the cockpit.

"I don't know if I've got any engines left," Porter said, working the throttles.

"Look at the altimeter," Sweanor said. It was unwinding at a terrific pace. "We're in a plunge. We've got to get out of here."10 He made his way to the forward escape hatch so the crew could bail out, but the hatch had been fused shut by the enemy cannon fire. The two gunners aboard reported on the intercom that the rear hatch was fused too, and frozen solid. Sweanor made one more stop in the cockpit to give the pilot his parachute and to open the hatch over his head so Porter could bailout. "Good luck, Pat," he shouted, and then, with an axe in his hands, Sweanor made his way to the rear hatch to help the rest of the crew get out.

Rear gunner Scottie Taylor, who happened to have been a lumberjack in Quebec before the war, grabbed the axe from Sweanor's hands and hacked at the hatch until it fell open. One by one the crew evacuated the Halifax—Murray Bishop, the flight engineer; Gerry Lanteigne, the wireless air gunner (he hesitated and Taylor pushed him out); Alan Budinger, the navigator; Danny London, the mid-upper gunner; and finally Sweanor, who paused for a second.

"I knew I was leaving my last ticket home,"11 he said. One further thought haunted him this night: Joan was pregnant with their first child, and Sweanor revisited the reasons why they shouldn't have gone ahead with a wartime marriage. Would he be maimed? Would he a burden to his wife, if he got back? And if he didn't return, how would his widow and fatherless child manage?

As he fell from the hatch into the night, Sweanor felt a sheet of flame pass over his head. He hadn't realized how much of the Halifax was ablaze. He pulled his rip cord and immediately felt the jerk of the chute; it was barely open when there was a second jerk as the chute caught a tree. Had he delayed just a few seconds longer, he quickly realized, he would have ploughed into the ground with the burning bomber; the chute catching the tree as rapidly as it did probably saved his life. Back in Middleton St. George, in the early hours of March 28, Joan was awake.

"He used to come in [after a bombing operation] about four o'clock in the morning," she said. "I used to reach over and there he was. But this morning I woke up and it was daylight and there was nobody there. And I thought, 'Oh God, he's not coming home.'"[12]

The 419 Squadron padre notified Joan later that day that her husband had, in fact, been shot down. A few days later, the wing commander wrote a letter encouraging her to hope he was a POW. The International Red Cross confirmed that to be true on April 19, 1943. By that time, however, Sweanor had gone from downed airman on the run, to police prisoner, to the subject of repeated Luftwaffe interrogations, and, finally, to prisoner of war and inaugurated kriegie in the newly opened North Compound of Stalag Luft III. During that transition he learned that crew mates—Bish, Bud, Gerry, Danny, and Scottie—had all survived the crash with contusions and shrapnel wounds, but that his pilot, Pat Porter, who had apparently kept the Halifax airborne long enough for his crewmates to chop their way through the rear hatch and bail out, had died in the burning wreckage.

Later, Sweanor learned that forty-three bombers had been shot down in two nights of Bomber Command attacks against Berlin, and that of 301 aircrew aboard those bombers, only fifteen men had survived to be interrogated at Dulag Luft—six of them from his Halifax "E for Edward."[13] Sweanor considered himself fortunate to be among the 5 per cent who survived those end-of-March raids.* He felt well treated by the civilians who'd captured him, sufficiently respected by the police and Luftwaffe officials who'd questioned him, relieved upon his arrival in Sagan that German civilians hadn't lynched him, and grateful that his captors promised there would be Red Cross food once he arrived inside the compound.

"Freed from operations, we could cease contemplating how few hours we had yet to live," Sweanor said. "Our taut nerves could relax."[14]

In spite of the relative ease he felt as he was about to enter the prison camp, Sweanor learned that relief was ephemeral. There was commotion at the gate as a prisoner was caught trying to escape disguised as a Soviet worker. A dozen German guards marched the new arrivals into a large shack for a routine naked search. Sweanor remembered he still had some escape aids—a cloth map of Europe, currency, hunting knife, compass, German-English dictionary[15]— in his pockets; he handed away his jacket to distract the guard and palmed the escape aids as he removed the rest of his clothes. When the guard returned his jacket, Sweanor dumped it on the floor with the escape aids underneath. The final indignities during his introduction to Stalag Luft III were a search of body orifices, a head-and-shoulder mug shot, and fingerprinting. Passing through the main gate into the compound for the first time, he realized the might of the place—its double-fence outer barrier, guard towers, guard dogs, searchlights, and rifle-toting guards. The often-repeated words of Welsh kriegie Shag Rees felt more haunting than humorous.

"So this is where we are going to lose the best years of our wives!"[16] Rees reminded his fellow POWs.

In his first permitted letter home to his wife, George Sweanor wrote a tribute to his Halifax pilot, Pat Porter, who "had not left [the aircraft] via the top hatch as I had thought, but had deliberately

---

* George Sweanor cited statistics from his own research indicating that the life expectancy for a Bomber Command aircrew was five operations, and that of those shot down only 17 per cent survived.

sacrificed his life to save ours. I felt deep guilt being alive. . . . Would I ever be worthy of his sacrifice?"[17] Sweanor and others thought Porter's heroism warranted his receiving the Victoria Cross posthumously, but since so many pilots had died similarly in an air offensive experiencing such high casualty rates, Porter received recognition only by Mentioned in Dispatches. Tangible evidence that his first letter got to Joan arrived at the prison camp about a month later. One day, Sweanor spotted a familiar face coming through the main gate of the North Compound. He waited patiently while the outside guards processed the new arrival and the inside kriegie interrogators passed him. Then he pounced on his fellow 419 Squadron crewmate, Jack Fry. The two men exchanged the latest 419 news. Fry explained that he had been shot down over Stettin on April 20; despite being fluent with his high school German, he'd been unable to get through German checkpoints. Fry assured Sweanor that Joan had received his first letter home as proof he was alive.

Several weeks passed before Sweanor learned about the escape activities that abounded in the compound. His initial contributions were the few bits of escape kit he'd managed to smuggle past the search guards and into the compound. He joined the outdoor gardening units, mixing regular surface soil with the yellow tunnel sand that passing penguins deposited in their vegetable patches. But Sweanor saved some of his best work for the camp-wide security network, serving X Organization as a stooge. He worked in shifts spying on the whereabouts of ferrets, the *Abwehr* men in their blue overalls. Stationed outside at the northeast corner of Hut 101, with a full view of the main gate into the compound, Sweanor would look, for all the world, as if he were just reading a book or playing a game of chess with another kriegie. In fact, he was the "duty pilot," logging every German who entered or exited the compound via the main gate, especially the chief ferret Hermann Glemnitz and his *Unteroffizier* (Corporal) Karl Griese. Because of the nature of his appearance—he had a conspicuously long neck—the kriegies nicknamed Griese "Rubberneck."

One day, the Germans appeared to have vacated the compound, but Sweanor's log showed Rubberneck still somewhere inside the prison camp. The Commonwealth officers working as security stooges narrowed their search to the cookhouse, which they discovered was locked from the inside. They responded by closing the shutters, so anyone inside the cookhouse could no longer see out. Within an hour, Rubberneck emerged embarrassed and fuming. It wasn't long before the duty pilot position at the main gate was openly accepted by both sides. Even by Glemnitz. One afternoon, the *Oberfeldwebel* himself came through the gate, walked up to Sweanor, saluted, and shouted, "I am in. Mark me down."[18]

Sweanor marked Glemnitz in.

"Who else is in?" Glemnitz asked and took Sweanor's logbook. It showed no other ferrets in the compound. Further, it showed Rubberneck and another guard had just left the compound. Glemnitz was not happy. "Book me out!" he bellowed.

Sweanor learned later that the two ferrets had left their posts too early. Glemnitz punished them—one got four days in the cooler, the other no leave for two weeks. The stooges were beating the ferrets at their own game—surveillance. In fact, in early September 1943, when tunnel "Tom" was discovered, X Organization bounced back even when the Gestapo briefly took over the compound. The secret police, who descended on Hut 123 and its occupants, were accustomed to pushing around civilians, not experienced air force officers. At the North Compound, when the Gestapo men set about searching an area, they armed themselves to the teeth, surrounded the offending area, and then ransacked it, placing anything they fancied—pens, pencils, rope, and anything resembling a tool—in a "swag bag" off to one side. As soon as they put the swag bag down, the kriegies created diversions and began pilfering the contents of the bag back. The net gain invariably favoured the prisoners, not the Gestapo.

"To any but the Gestapo," Bob Nelson wrote, "it was a well-known fact that if a workman was sent into a prisoners' compound, two guards also had to be sent to watch the workman's tools."[19]

A perfect illustration of Nelson's assessment occurred about the same time as the Italian army in Sicily capitulated to the Allies in the summer of 1943. Colonel von Lindeiner, sensing a need to compensate for the Mediterranean setback and ramp up German morale, sent in a work crew to begin stringing electrical cable for a loudspeaker to broadcast German radio propaganda into the prison camp. The escape committee noted the workers in their midst and organized a diversion to attempt to steal some of the electrical cable. They were too late. Coincidentally, Canadian officer Red Noble had just completed a term in the cooler, so German guards were releasing him back into the North Compound. In strolled the redheaded Noble, carrying his blanket over one arm. He spotted a spool of wire lying unattended on the ground. Going just a few steps out of his way, but not missing a beat, Noble snatched the wire, tucked it under his blanket, and disappeared into a hut, leaving the workmen flummoxed as to where they'd mislaid the wire. Noble had pilfered more than eight hundred feet of wire, which immediately went into the vertical shaft of tunnel "Dick" for storage and later provided power for the lighting system inside tunnel "Harry."[20]

The impromptu Gestapo inspection of the North Compound that autumn may well have appeared to be a bumbling affair, with the kriegies quickly reversing every measure the secret police instituted or recapturing any contraband their jailers seized. As Nelson observed, the Gestapo did not appear to understand the nature of a Luftwaffe prison nor the means of containing its inmates; he ridiculed the Gestapo "searches [as] very ineffective compared to those of the experienced Luftwaffe ferrets."[21] On the other hand, allowing the kriegies to believe they had the upper hand inside the wire may have been part of a greater Gestapo game plan.

In November 1943, Max Wielen, the head of the *Kriminalpolizei* (*Kripo*) at Breslau visited von Lindeiner at the North Compound and toured the site. A system of buried microphones, which the Germans had installed a year earlier, conclusively revealed that throughout the previous six months "large-scale digging was being carried out by the prisoners."[22] However, Wielen's search of huts and other buildings, according to von Lindeiner, "failed to discover where the tunnels were situated, or at least left that impression in the camp."[23] The

*Kripo* chief's visit to Stalag Luft III was followed by renovations to several of the compound facilities, including construction to enlarge the camp area. Not surprisingly, during such disruptive renovation (and perhaps not coincidentally as escape activity began to intensify), Luftwaffe administrators were forced to remove the microphone listening equipment. Still more remarkable was that the microphones remained disconnected through the fall and into the new year.

Then, early in 1944, von Lindeiner convened a meeting of district security personnel to discuss ways to prevent camp breakouts. He brought in local security chief, SS Major Erich Brünner, who listened to von Lindeiner's concerns that a large-scale escape was imminent. However, Brünner stayed at the meeting barely an hour. He merely chatted with von Lindeiner about the problem, carried out no inspections of anti-escape measures, and refused to order the redeployment of the underground microphone listening system. Dissatisfied with the security chief's response, von Lindeiner went so far as to arrange a meeting among Group Captain Massey, the senior Commonwealth officers, chaplains, and doctors and delivered a special warning to be passed to the prisoners not to undertake a major escape plan.

"Escapers [will] in future suffer very severe penalties,"[24] *Kommandant* von Lindeiner told one of the RAF officers.

This pre-emptive approach was reinforced when the camp adjutant, *Hauptmann* Hans Pieber, spoke to F/L Henry "Johnny" Marshall early in February. Pieber liked Marshall and hinted that the RAF reconnaissance pilot and his fellow POWs might face horrible consequences from higher up the chain of command if they attempted a mass breakout. If they did, he suggested, the Gestapo might respond with lethal force. Pieber's warning to Marshall, as well as Brünner's failure to re-activate the anti-escape defences, and von Lindeiner's veiled warning against mass escapes all suggest that German High Command had already decided it would turn a blind eye to or even encourage a larger escape. And if such a breakout occurred, that would prompt the Gestapo to take matters into its own hands. The

Gestapo, it appeared, was setting a trap for both the Commonwealth prisoners and the camp's Luftwaffe administrators. What made the secret police involvement a greater threat to those involved in an attempted escape was that the German High Command was drafting a restraining order called "*Stufe Römisch* III," or Grade III, which decreed that any recaptured escaped POW—whether he escaped in transit, via a mass escape, or on his own—would not be returned to his military jailers, but instead be handed over to the secret police.*

Inside the wire, with the Gestapo seemingly out of the picture and von Lindeiner and the Luftwaffe guards apparently back in control of Stalag Luft III during the autumn of 1943, X Organization's tunnel activity went on hiatus. While the diggers and penguins enjoyed a well-deserved rest, the pause did not signal a decline in escape committee activity. To be sure, Big X entertained one-shot "wire jobs." Roger Bushell welcomed kriegies presenting reasonably sound escape plans and travel arrangements that might deliver them out of Germany. To assist, the escape committee would supply potential escapers with some currency, compasses, civilian outfits, and wire cutters. Among the attempts, a New Zealander and a Canadian thought they had found another blind spot at the far south end of the sports grounds. On the designated night, they crawled for seven hours, undetected by searchlights or tower guards, and had all but two wires of the outer fence snipped when a patrolling guard spotted and recaptured them. Meanwhile, the escape committee ramped up production in the map-making, tailoring, and forgery sections.

If Bushell's grand plan to have hundreds of Allied POWs escape and fan out across German-occupied Europe was going to succeed, he needed assurance that his escapers would have the appropriate documentation.[25] Through his own experiences and listening to tales from

---

* In interviews and analysis compiled in 1946 by an RAF War Crimes Interrogation Unit, and under the auspices of the Judge Advocate General at the War Office in London, England, authors of the report ask: "Was it a matter of high policy that, in the view of the reprisal measures already planned and in operation in the form of the 'Stufe III' order and the '[Aktion] Kugel' order, at least one major camp break-out was not to be discouraged?"

fellow officers who'd also tried to get back to Britain, Big X knew his escapers would need at least a light grey identity card (*Kennkarte*) or, better, a visa (*Sichtvermerk*), plus a pass (*Ausweise*), and likely a brown card (*Dienstausweise*) legally allowing the holder to be on Wehrmacht property. In addition, if a man were disguised as a foreign worker, he would require *Polizeitliche Bescheinigung*, a police permit authorizing the worker to be in a specific area; *Urlaubsscheine*, a yellow paper entitling the worker to be on leave to get there; or *Rückkehrscheine*, a pink-coloured form that signified the worker was legally en route to his home country.

For Dean and Dawson, the escape committee's forgery section, obtaining accurate samples of these documents amounted to only half the challenge. Equally daunting, the forgers had to procure tools and materials—pens, inks, brushes, and paper stock—to generate the fakes. Initially, Tim Walenn's forgers worked in an empty room in Hut 120, in the row of huts farthest from the main gate. His team of artists, mapmakers, printers, and even carvers spent the better part of a year assembling master documents, finding the ink and paper with which to duplicate them, and then painstakingly replicating. They even built a mimeograph and used razor blades to carve designs into a boot heel for recreating official Nazi stamps with the swastika and eagle emblems. In Hut 120 there were relatively secluded windows, guarded by stooges, where forgers could practise replicating the documents in bright daylight.

In one respect, one member of the Dean and Dawson document factory owed the quality of his forgery to Canada's Group of Seven artists. Born and raised in Toronto, Robert Buckham had been attracted to sketching and painting as a young man. In the 1930s, he signed up for art classes at the Art Gallery of Toronto and attended Saturday lectures from established artists such as Arthur Lismer of the Group of Seven.[26] Before the war he worked in advertising as an art director. When the war interrupted his career, the six-foot-four Buckham was twice refused by the RCAF for his height; but with the war not going well for Britain in 1941, he was finally accepted. He'd flown ten combat operations with 428 Squadron when his Wellington bomber was shot down by a night fighter in April 1943. At Stalag Luft III, X Organization forgery section leaders Tony Pengelly and Tim Walenn were delighted to learn Buckham was an artist.

"I said I was going to major in art there," Buckham said, "and I did."[27]

His steady hand with pen and ink as well as his penchant for colour painting made Buckham an ideal candidate for the reproduction of the *Kennkarte* and *Ausweise* passes. Using the best quality paper they could find in the compound—often the fly-leaves of the library Bibles[28]—Buckham and the others cut the paper to the exact dimensions of the pass. They replicated the background swirl of the master document's watermark (much like currency notes) with pen and ink, and brush and watercolour, then penned in the category headings (first name, surname, date, and place of birth, et cetera). If the document needed a hard back, the forgers glued tracing linen over cardboard and coloured it to match the original. Meanwhile, Jens Muller, a Norwegian air force officer, replicated any official stamps—including date or swastika insignia—by carving a mould in a bar of soap. Once he'd begun sketching and painting for the escape committee, Buckham never stopped. He employed his artistic skills "from morning to night"[29] to paint posters advertising theatre and lecture events. And in his bound, Red Cross–issue diary he drew images of kriegies, their tools, and their surroundings to distract himself from "an empty belly."[30]

When the forgery room drew guards' suspicions, Walenn moved the crew to a kitchen next to where the compound orchestra rehearsed. When the orchestra finished practising, the forgers wrapped up their work too and stowed it in a violin case. The musicians left the hut with their instruments in hand; one carried his violin case,[31] with the forgeries-in-progress enclosed, to Hut 104, where Tony Pengelly hid them in a secret compartment behind a removable wall board.

As well as serving the escape committee as custodian of the forged documents, Canadian bomber pilot Pengelly took on the responsibility of coaxing original documents and other things of value from the German guards who regularly patrolled the compound. Some of the guards weren't necessarily highly educated men, but Pengelly had learned that he could occasionally befriend one by offering him a cigarette and even a short visit to his barracks room for a cup of freshly steeped tea. Pengelly did regular shifts dispensing Red Cross parcels to the kriegies and had been given the authority to "borrow" such luxury items from the parcels to hasten the process. During such visits, Pengelly might share snapshots of his family. A month or two later, Pengelly would invite in the same man and repeat the pleasantries. When the Canadian pilot knew his prey might soon be going on leave, he would offer the bait-covered hook.

"How would you like to take some coffee home?"[32] he would ask the guard.

The German usually jumped at the chance.

Pengelly knew the average German hadn't tasted real coffee since 1936; nor had he enjoyed other delicacies. "And some chocolate for your little boy?"

Often the gift might draw the offer of a favour from the guard, such as, "Can I bring you anything from outside?"

"Yes, if you wouldn't mind," Pengelly would say. "I'd like a hundred toothpicks." Something that inconsequential would be sufficient the first time, but it was oil for the machine. With each trip the guard made, Pengelly repeated the exchange until it got to be habitual—taking a little booty home each leave. And having broken the rules once or twice, the "tame" guard wouldn't likely refuse any of Pengelly's requests, fearing the POWs might expose him. Coffee and chocolate yielded a camera, developing, and printing equipment, and even the short-term loan of passes and visas.

"It was the psychology of binding a man with a thread," Pengelly said, "and gradually strengthening the thread until it was far easier to submit to our bondage than to rebel. They never foresaw where it led . . . and we paid them in wartime Europe's best currency—food that Big X had commandeered from our Red Cross parcels in any quantity he believed necessary."[33]

As well as his police permit, his leave papers, or his permission to be going home, any potential escaper disguised as an immigrant worker, needed paperwork that validated his transit for the purpose of seeking work. Working from published advertisements in German newspapers, Pengelly directed the forgers to draft letters addressed to a real German, in a real company, from a real German in another real company, all on forged letterhead and with forged signatures and corporate stamps. If a guard on the outside needed proof that the immigrant worker was indeed travelling to legitimate employment in Germany, occupied France, or occupied Holland, the fake letter and a kriegie-manufactured map proved it.

"A bigger bunch of shysters and crooks and con men you'd never find anywhere in the world than in a prison camp,"[34] said Don Mac-Donald, a pilot officer kriegie from Winnipeg.

For some of the POWs at Stalag Luft III, the lengths to which X Organization went to dig tunnels, forge documents, and hide the evidence was all part of a cat-and-mouse game conducted inside the wire. For others, the activities comprised what Wings Day had once called an "operational function" of an officer's duty to try to escape while in enemy hands. For those such as Roger Bushell, it was a combination of one-upmanship, spite, never allowing oneself to be idle, and an ideology of never accepting defeat. George Sweanor hadn't experienced the number of years of imprisonment that Bushell had, but he resented Big X's control over the cultivation of German guards and ferrets. If a kriegie were not directly involved in using the Germans for the objectives of the Organization, Bushell made it clear the POW was to back off, remain polite, and stay aloof.

"Underhanded tactics were all part of this war," Sweanor wrote, "but I argued there was room for those of us who wanted to lessen the enemy's will to war by showing him that we were just plain folks, willing to make friends, and to share a few luxuries that the Germans had not seen for years. I never was very good at obeying orders I did not like."[35]

Among the luxuries Sweanor and others seemed eager to share were those found in the new building going up just beyond Hut 119 and in front of the sporting fields. In fact, from his window, Sweanor watched the construction of a theatre in the North Compound.* Under a parole system, the Germans had provided the materials and lent kriegies tools, provided at the end of each day's work every tool was returned intact. Some of the bricks that formed the foundation of the theatre may have come from buildings knocked down during bombing attacks on nearby Sorau, but some of the theatre's other components had obvious origins. Kriegie carpenters took the plywood from all the crates containing Red Cross parcels from Canada and fashioned it into 350 theatre seats, complete with armrests, sloping backs, and tip-up seats. Just like a professional facility, the house floor was raked from a projection room at the rear of the theatre down to an orchestra pit in front of the stage. And beyond the proscenium, the stage itself featured trapdoors, wings, two dressing rooms, and space for lighting, flats, costumes, and props. An extension of the building backstage included a reference library, a lecture room, the chapel, and an ops room.

The magic ingredient at the theatre, however, was the ingenuity of the POWs themselves. Two RAF non-commissioned officers with electrician skills installed indirect lighting in the auditorium and a switchboard panel for stage lighting.[36] Air force officers who had fine arts degrees or who had joined university theatre productions before the war were suddenly in demand as producers, directors, playwrights, set designers and builders, props and wardrobe creators, and actors.

"There was even an electric sign in the foyer of the theatre," remembered Canadian pilot Don Edy, who arrived at Stalag Luft III just after the theatre opened. "They took a wheel and put a strip of tin on the wheel. As the wheel turned [powered by the water], the electric current would pass along the tin. When it came to the end

---

* According to George Sweanor, the Canadian government took thirty-five dollars a month (deducted from his Canadian pay accumulating in Canada) and transferred the funds to the Germans so that Canadian POWs could rent theatrical costumes and musical instruments; similarly, in Canada, German POWs used their allotment to order by mail from the Eaton's catalogue.

of the tin, the current would break and the light would go dark. The light illuminated cut-out letters. . . . So the light would flash on and off announcing the play."[37]

The only memorable entertainment Edy had experienced since his overseas posting in 1941 came while on operations with the RAF in North Africa. As a Hurricane pilot with 33 Squadron, on leave in Cairo, for instance, he'd enjoyed high tea once at the Mena House resort hotel[38] across from the pyramids. In Alexandria, at the Grand Trianon Bar, he'd marvelled at the "Gilli Gilli" boys who passed the hat while one of them placed a baby chick inside Edy's shirt one moment, and used sleight of hand to pull out a garter snake in its place.[39] In February 1942, while strafing a truck convoy with his wing mate Lance Wade near Msus, Libya, Edy's Hurricane took return fire in the engine and radiator; the engine stopped dead and he was forced to crash-land on the desert, where he was quickly captured by German ground troops. Treated for head wounds in Tripoli, he was put aboard a tramp steamer bound for a prison camp in Italy. But the steamer was torpedoed and sunk at sea; Edy clung to debris, was picked up by an Italian cruiser, and eventually delivered to a POW camp in Sicily, then another at Certosa di Padula in southern Italy. He was imprisoned in the monastery (Camp 35) there long enough that he joined some of the British POWs staging musicals, comedies, and revues. One revue, written by POW Neville Lloyd, included a song about life in the camp:

*We're the Padula boys of Camp 35*
*going rapidly 'round the bend.*
*One of our habits is digging like rabbits*
*on tunnels that never end.*
*We lie in bed quite quietly, while the guards*
*are on their rounds.*
*But the moment they're gone, we're at it again*
*with a joy that knows no bounds.*
*We're the Padula boys, Hey, Hey.*[40]

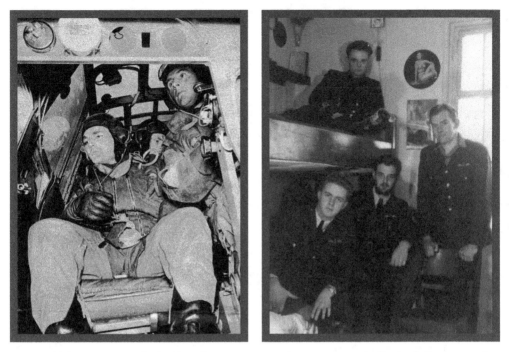

Space inside an RAF Whitley bomber (ABOVE LEFT) was extremely limited. In 1940, after he bailed out of his crashing Whitley, RAF pilot Tony Pengelly found himself in an equally confined space (ABOVE RIGHT, seated on bed, left) in a POW hut at Stalag Luft I (Barth, Germany) with George Guest (beard), Gaynel McCaw and Maurice Driver (top bunk).

(ABOVE LEFT) Long before The Great Escape, a tunnel designing/digging team—(clockwise from lower left) Wally Floody, Sam Sangster, John "Scruffy" Weir, and Hank "Big Train" Birkland—experimented in ad hoc escape attempts at Stalag Luft I. Eventually, under Big X, Roger Bushell (ABOVE RIGHT), at Luft III, X Organization developed plans for a sophisticated mass breakout.

(ABOVE) POW barracks huts in the East Compound of Stalag Luft III (Sagan c. 1942)—looking north to the pine forest and grain elevator—were constructed of wood and set on concrete blocks so German anti-escape guards could spot any illegal activity under them, while armed sentries (RIGHT) surveyed the compound from towers strategically placed along the outside fencing.

This photo, taken from the American South Compound (Sagan c. 1943) and looking northeast toward the German administration area (*Kommandantur*), shows the barren landscape of the appell area of the North Compound broken physically and psycologically by the theatre (left).

RCAF pilots Barry Davidson (LEFT) and Dick Bartlett, once shot down, became chief scrounger and custodian of the secret wireless radio for the escape committee respectively. They developed such skills early in 1940 at Stalag Luft I and were seasoned pros by the time they were sent to Luft III.

Meanwhile, fellow RCAF pilots Keith Ogilvie (LEFT) and Kingsley Brown at Stalag Luft III worked in intelligence—the former fleeced German guards for their wallets, the latter searched the prison library for German officials' identities to steal and for police protocol at train stations and borders—all to assist camp forgers manufacture fake documents for the escapers.

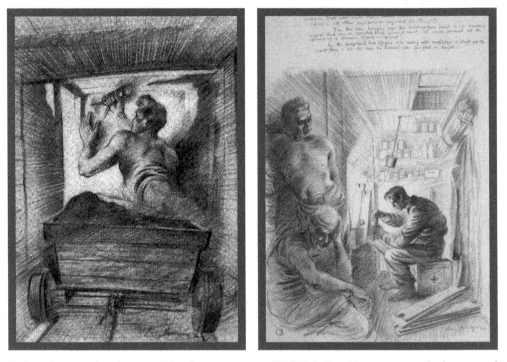

Before the mass breakout on March 24–25, 1944, RAF F/L Ley Kenyon was asked to record images of escape tunnel "Harry." Underground, sometimes on his back, by the light of fat-fuelled lamps, he sketched (ABOVE LEFT) a digger cutting into sand at the face of the tunnel; (ABOVE RIGHT) an underground workshop (tin over worker's head, activated from tunnel trap above, contained pebbles as signal for quiet). In Hut 104 (BELOW) he drew the entrance to tunnel "Harry" through the trap in the concrete foundation under the stove (the entire operation required lookouts—"stooges"—to warn tunnel crews of any approaching German guards).

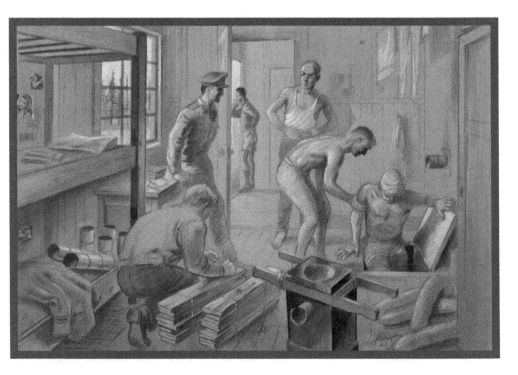

(TOP) Until the Gestapo took over Stalag Luft III (following the escape), the prison camp for Allied air force officers was run by German air force (Luftwaffe) guards. (MIDDLE) Col. Friedrich von Lindeiner (right) was *Kommandant* at Stalag Luft III, pictured here with visiting German Gen. Biewer. (BOTTOM) In preparation for The Great Escape, Commonwealth POWs managed to duplicate the uniforms of counter-intelligence, or *Abwehr*, guards, such as that of Cpl. Karl Griese (far left), a.k.a. "Rubberneck."

(ABOVE) RCAF navigator John Colwell's POW card recorded all of his vital stats but one—as camp tinkerer he could build escape tools out of anything. (RIGHT) In his letters home, RCAF fighter pilot Frank Sorensen asked his family to send thesauruses, which became secret weapons in the camp. (BELOW) Canadians photographed at North Compound c. 1944. Back (l to r): Tony Pengelly, "Mule," Henry Sprague, Ken Anthony, Joe "Red" Noble, Ed Brodrick, Jim Jamieson, John "Scruffy" Weir, Jim McCague, George Wiley, Harold Avery, George McGill, Don Armstrong. Front (l to r): Bruce Baker, Ted White, George Smith, Don "Tiger" McKim, Bill Keetch, Harold Sullivan, G.H. Soper, Colin Monkhouse. (Officers Wiley and McGill were later executed by the Gestapo.)

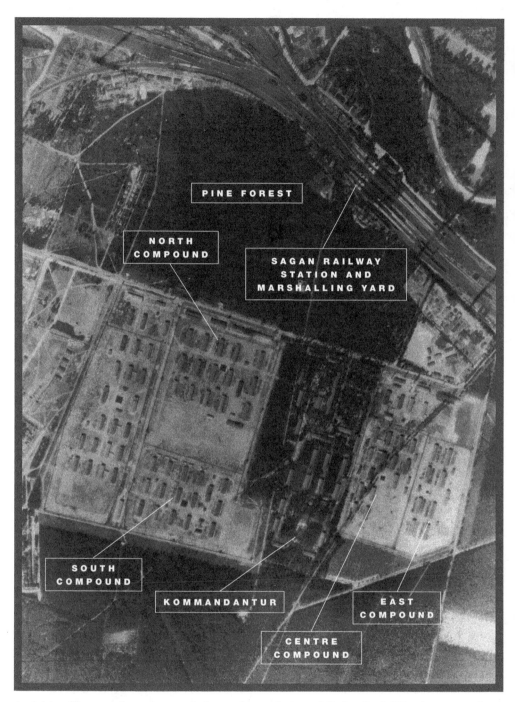

Aerial intelligence photo (c. 1944) shows the evolution of Stalag Luft III prison camp from original East and Centre compounds, opened in 1942, to additional North, South, and West compounds; the prison camp eventually held 10,000 air force POWs. Despite hundreds of attempts, only six POWs completed the "home run"—getting from Luft III back to the UK.

RCAF airman George Sweanor (LEFT) vowed not to get romantically involved while training as a bomb-aimer in the UK, while Joan Saunders felt her work in the British war industry was a top priority. Nevertheless, they fell in love, married, and were separated a month later when George was shot down and sent to Stalag Luft III for the duration.

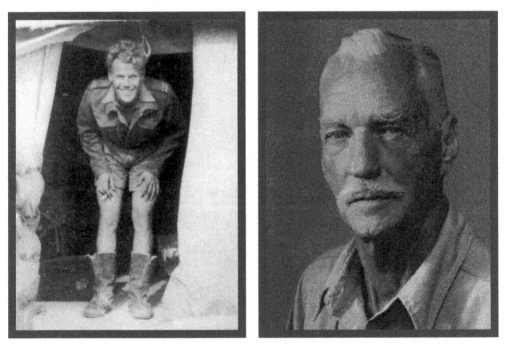

For RCAF Spitfire pilot Don Edy (LEFT), barracks in the North African desert were rustic at best; it got worse in February 1942, when he was shot down, imprisoned first in Italy, and then sent to Stalag Luft III. On the other hand, severe conditions for RCAF gunner George Harsh were nothing out of the ordinary; before being shot down in October 1942 he'd been an inmate in US prisons for a dozen years.

When the Italians capitulated to invading British, Polish, Canadian, and American forces in September 1943, Don Edy's group was on the move again. The Germans assumed control of the POWs and during the next two months transported thousands of them aboard trains from northern Italy to camps in Germany or German-occupied territory; Edy's imprisonments included Stalag VII-A at Mossburg, Fort Bismarck, Oflag V-A at Weinsberg, and, finally, on November 1, 1943, Stalag Luft III.

"I doubt if there is a lonelier feeling in the world than when . . . first taken prisoner of war," Edy wrote. "Everything seems completely hopeless and the thought of being behind barbed wire for God knows how long, maybe years, brings on an immediate depression."[41]

By that time, Edy found himself in a Silesian POW compound that housed about two thousand Allied prisoners of war. He recognized the monotony he would have to fight off, the fear he might never see home or loved ones again, and the anxiety over the civilian hostility that surrounded the camp. He was haunted by the story of a recently arrived Irish officer who'd bailed out over Berlin; he'd survived only because German soldiers, cutting down Allied airmen whom Berlin civilians had strung up on a telephone pole following an air raid, got to him first.[42]

Edy fought off his demons by taking on the role of permanent cook in Room 11 of Hut 123 with roommates Bill Stephenson, Johnny Taylor, Cliff Thorpe, and John Crozier. Edy spent hours preparing the meals, in anticipation of the short time he would have cooking on the top of the one hut stove or in the oven below. He worked with the rations officer to have jam tins cut and bashed into additional cooking and heating surfaces for the hut. With the Klim cans that arrived in the Canadian Red Cross parcels, Edy tried his hand at tin-bashing and soldering; he joined a couple of tins end to end, wound some tin around a pencil for a perking tube, perforated a tobacco tin with nail holes, put a specimen bottle upside down in the lid, and manufactured a coffee percolator.[43] It lasted more than a year. All these important distractions helped Edy forget the state of the war and his state of mind. He enjoyed some immediate relief from his travels and travails as a POW on his very first night at Stalag Luft III. *Macbeth* was playing at the theatre and special arrangements were made for the new arrivals to see the show before it closed.

"Tickets were made available, neatly typed with the date, seat number, and row," he wrote. "I thought this was a little far-fetched in a prisoner-of-war camp, [but] the theatre only held three hundred people; there were nearly two thousand in the camp and everyone wanted to see the shows."[44]

Even German officers who wished to enjoy the inside-the-wire productions had a difficult time securing tickets. George McKiel, a navigator on Lancasters shot down in November 1943, joined the theatre production crew as soon as he arrived at Stalag Luft III; he said the Commonwealth officers quickly decided to reserve the front two rows for the German officers. Further, the kriegies suggested that the plays be recorded for posterity,[45] so in return the Germans gave the actors film to snap photos of the casts. Of course, most of the film made its way to Dean and Dawson for the manufacture of forged passports. The shows ran one or perhaps two weeks at most before the next production went into rehearsal and opened at the theatre. The same night Don Edy attended *Macbeth*, George Sweanor managed to scrounge an extra ticket for another recent arrival to the North Compound—Ley Kenyon, the same RAF gunnery officer who had graciously donated his artistic talent to create a card for the George and Joan Sweanor wedding back in Middleton St. George at New Year's.

"I was amazed at how well [the theatre] transported us out of kriegieland,"[46] Sweanor wrote.

Don Edy nearly had to pinch himself to his senses at the sophistication of the kriegie productions. Most shows had thirty to forty musicians (in air force uniforms) in the orchestra, conducted by Canadian Flight Lieutenant Arthur Crighton, and officers ushering audiences to their seats. There was a full curtain across the proscenium which rose on cue, full lighting on the performances, staging, props, and actors who seemed as if they'd stepped out of Toronto's Royal Alexandra Theatre or Drury Lane in London's West End onto a stage in far-off Silesia in the middle of a world war. Under appropriate lighting, cardboard that the kriegies cut out and painted black became a wrought-iron fence for *The Importance of Being Ernest*. For *Messalina*, the theatre carpentry shop took scrap wood, cardboard, and tin, plus paper swans, and created a fountain with flowing water lit by coloured lights. And the artistic crew took a Red Cross crate, put homemade wheels on it and turned it into the wheelchair for character Sheridan Whiteside in *The Man Who Came to Dinner*. Backstage, actors used oleomargarine as grease-paint makeup.[47] If anyone received colourful wrapping paper in his Red Cross parcel, it immediately found its way onto flats for set decoration. Meanwhile, the same tailors who secretly worked on civilian escape clothes moonlighted by transforming uniforms into suits and coloured sports shirts or pajamas into women's dresses for the dramas. They created wigs from re-braided and re-stitched rope. Perhaps the most astonishing transformations Edy found were in the portrayal of women on stage.

"Our girls were excellent," he said. "At first the boys took quite a kidding, but after the first few productions the kriegies all realized there was nothing funny about it. The plays and dances needed girls and these fellows worked really hard to create feminine characters."[48]

"I was slight . . . and I was young, twenty-one," said Gordon King, one of the air-pump operators inside tunnel "Tom"; King jumped at the chance to be on stage. "[They made me up] into a girl very easily, so I was in *The Man Who Came to Dinner* as the daughter. I had falsies, a wig . . . real professional people doing everything."[49]

George McKiel did his fair share of penguin and stooge service for the escape committee, but among the toughest roles he faced was learning the Katherine Hepburn part in the kriegie production of *The Philadelphia Story*, because "it took me three months to learn to walk and talk like a woman."[50]

When the house lights dimmed and the curtain went up, Don Edy said Belgian airman Bobby Laumans made a beautiful Elaine D'Argent in *Arsenic and Old Lace*, and New Zealand officer Michael Ormond won storms of praise for his "Connie Boswell" act in a revue. Meanwhile, John Dowler made a fitting Frankie in *George and Margaret*, and Kenneth Mackintosh was stellar as Lady Macbeth. Edy remembered playing a lowly executioner in *Saint Joan*, but Malcolm Freegard was memorable in the starring role; and, he remembered, Tony Pengelly was a perfect Clara Popkiss in *Rookery Nook*.

Flight Lieutenant Tony Pengelly claimed that time was a kriegie's cheapest commodity. He expended a lot of it at the theatre as stage manager, producer, and cast member. He most enjoyed memorizing his lines, walking through his roles in rehearsal, and, when it came show time, using makeup, prostheses, wigs, costumes, and a higher register voice to transform himself into countless female characters on the theatre stage. He played ingénues, young wives and old, dancers, singers, goddesses, and witches. Like so many of the men taking on those alter egos on the theatre stage, Pengelly was creating a gift for his fellow POWs and a fanciful distraction from the realities of life in a wartime prison.

"I spent most of the Second World War in drag,"[51] Tony Pengelly later joked.

Still, Pengelly performed his most vital roles elsewhere at Stalag Luft III. From the moment he arrived in the compound outside Sagan—and under the escape committee's direction—he began to pool kriegie artists, calligraphers, cartographers, photographers, and printers to generate a whole array of forged papers. Beginning with documents, letters, and fake identification cards, he worked with four officers. He led ten others drafting the maps that escapers would need once they got beyond the Sagan area. They started their forgery—an hour or two every day at first—making sure that every detail was noted and replicated with utmost accuracy. If a forger happened to use the wrong colour for a forged rubber stamp, he could ruin a year's worth of work. By the time the Dean and Dawson forgery group was operating at capacity, Pengelly had 137 on his staff. Naturally, Pengelly controlled any and all incoming items that might offer information or technology required for the forgery shop. At one point he oversaw the smuggling of an entire typewriter—one piece at a time—into the North Compound.

This led to another of Pengelly's high-priority responsibilities: acting as a chief parcel officer. Almost from the very beginning of the war—when Wings Day was first SBO at Dulag Luft in late 1939—British and Canadian kriegies had decided to pool and redistribute the contents of the Red Cross parcels.[52] In this way the older prisoners of war gave up their seniority for food and toiletries in favour of new arrivals, who had just been shot down, interrogated, and shipped to the prison compound with nothing but what they had on their backs. When parcels arrived at Stalag Luft III, they were not immediately distributed for consumption; they were stored in the building that housed the sick quarters in the *Vorlager* adjacent to the compound.* On average, each week a POW received the equivalent of a full parcel—from the US, the UK, or Canada. Generally, the parcel contents consisted of basic ingredients (what the British called "housewife treats") such as soup, cheese, corned beef, salmon, sardines, raisins, pudding, coffee, tea, butter, jams, biscuits, powdered milk, and occasionally sweets such as chocolate or candy. Since Pengelly was also on the front lines of kriegies taming bribery prospects among the guards, his work, of necessity, required bait to entrap the prospects, or, as he put it, to "oil the machine." Pengelly had the authority from Roger Bushell himself to confiscate any and all parcel items.

"Big X had full control over everything that came into the camp," Pengelly said. "Each [Red Cross] parcel received bore with it a list of contents, and from those lists, Big X commandeered anything he thought the organization could use."[53]

Consequently, civilian shirts, sports jackets, plain blankets, and sheets became fair game for X Organization's tailoring group. Picture books, pen and ink, toilet paper, coloured wrapping paper, and even newspaper clippings helped supply the forgery group. Meanwhile, chocolates and any item considered rare in wartime Germany

---

* While kriegies generally endorsed Wings Day's edict of pooling the Red Cross parcel foods, Canadian F/L Ted Kipp and RAF F/L Ken Toft (fellow-POWs at Warburg) founded Foodacco, an inside-the-wire emporium, which used cigarettes as the primary currency to purchase additional food or delicacies they accumulated. Controversy emerged over whether Foodacco should be free enterprise or non-profit; there was a referendum, but it was overruled by SBO Day, who nationalized the Kipp-Toft free enterprise operation to run as a co-op.

went right into the hands of those blackmailing the guards. In one instance, Pengelly said, they had one guard so well tamed they asked for his passport for an afternoon; the kriegies promised in turn that the guard would not be caught without it and that it would be back in his hands by nighttime. It was, and the guard got a gift for his trouble.

"The camp *Kommandant's* secretary had a boyfriend, a German guard we had tied up pretty well," Pengelly remembered. "The secretary would get correspondence files from the *Kommandant's* desk, give them to her boyfriend, who would give them to us. Big X would read them and then send them back along the same route."[54]

That autumn, fighter pilot Don Edy signed up for a couple of productions at the North Compound theatre—a small part in the operetta *Messalina* and some parallel bar gymnastics in a show called *Six to the Bar*. He had been a POW for just under two years. That November, bomb-aimer George Sweanor acknowledged his twenty-fourth birthday. Back in June, he'd been buoyed by a letter from Joan telling him she'd given birth to a healthy baby girl she named Barbara. More than once Sweanor found himself seated on a stump in the compound, glaring at the barbed wire and vowing he would survive and one day return home to his wife and daughter. He had been a prisoner of war for eight months. Meanwhile, Roger Bushell also got involved in the kriegie theatre productions. Partly to draw the Germans' attention away from his escape committee activities, and no doubt to seek psychological escape from the summer setbacks of 1943, that fall Big X appeared in a production of *George and Margaret*. At age thirty-three and more than three years a captive of the German stalag system, Bushell agreed to prepare the part of Professor Higgins for an upcoming production of *Pygmalion*. He would rehearse periodically through the coming winter in anticipation of an opening night scheduled for March 24, 1944, a night during which he would ultimately be otherwise engaged.

Like so much else at Stalag Luft III, the theatre, while appearing to offer harmless and distracting entertainment to young POWs awaiting the war's outcome, became a disguise for greater pursuits.

# THE PLAY'S
# THE THING

I T SEEMED a world away and it was, but that fall of 1943 the Harlem Globetrotters maintained their winning ways—2,163 victories versus 162 defeats in fifteen seasons. The war was, however, having an impact on the calibre of all professional sports back in North America. At the end of the 1942–43 NHL season, Boston's entire Kraut line of Milt Schmidt, Bobby Bauer, and Woody Dumart enlisted in the forces, which prompted Bruins coach Art Ross to say, "the best forward line today couldn't make the Bruins' third line a couple of years ago."[1] And that fall the New York Yankees won the fortieth World Series, four-games-to-one over St. Louis. The Cardinals committed ten errors in the series. Ironically, pro baseball's commissioner promised the game would go on as long as there were at least eighteen men left to play.[2]

For perhaps that one season, members of the Canadian All-Star Baseball Team, playing games inside the wire at Stalag Luft III, could have thumped the '43 champion Yankees. They had that much talent in their lineup. With the Canadians and Americans housed in separate compounds (since September 1943), contact between the two nationalities of air force officers was limited. That changed, however, when the Americans asked the camp *Kommandant* if they could meet their Canadian rivals in a challenge for softball supremacy.

"The Americans always figured they were better ballplayers than the Canadians," Flying Officer Art Hawtin said. "They were just next to us in the [South] Compound and they got permission to bring their team over."[3]

While baseball was a sport Art Hawtin had enjoyed in the 1930s (he had a Babe Ruth baseball card in his collection), it would not have been his first choice. The fifth of six children born on a farm near Kinmount, Ontario, Art did his fair share of chores, but his favourite physical activity was pole-vaulting; in fact, he stayed in Beaverton High School an extra year as a junior athlete to accumulate more victories and won ten track events in 1938. Along with his blue ribbons, Art gained a valuable skill landing repeatedly in all those high school pole-vaulting pits. On the night of May 13, 1943, as a navigator on a 405 Squadron bombing mission to Germany, Hawtin's Halifax was shot down; he bailed out of the crippled aircraft and landed in the Dutch countryside.

"Landing with a parachute or pole-vaulting over a bar ten or twelve feet high is just about the same," Hawtin said. "I came down in a farmer's field near Dedemsvaart, Holland. . . . I was completely relaxed and I landed safely."[4]

With the likelihood that any Dutch family hiding an evader would be shot, Hawtin agreed to turn himself in. A week later he came walking through the main gate at Stalag Luft III and was assigned to the same room as John Colwell, the dedicated diarist and tin-basher originally from Vancouver Island. Hawtin and Colwell had both served as navigators with 405 Squadron stationed in Yorkshire, so Colwell was able to vouch for his friend in front of the compound SBO. Hawtin's kriegie card identified him as a student. And when he was asked about participating in escape committee activities, he readily volunteered to work as a penguin. But on the day the Americans decided to show the Canadians the finer points of their softball prowess, Art Hawtin turned out to be a pretty agile, hard-hitting left fielder on the Canadian All-Star Baseball Team roster.

Before F/O Hawtin arrived on the scene, baseball had already become an all-consuming pastime at most of the prison camps where

North American POWs were incarcerated. Originally, the prisoners of war played sandlot baseball. The game didn't require a lot of equipment, so the kriegies improvised by using bedposts as bats and baseballs fabricated from old shoes or scraps of leather wrapped together with the rubber seals from empty coffee cans. Eventually, the YMCA back home shipped bats, balls, and some gloves into the camps so that the games at least looked like legitimate softball competitions. Initially, barracks hut played against barracks hut, senior officers versus junior officers, married men against bachelors.[5] The games took on greater significance when the editors of the *Gefangenen Gazette* camp newspaper began publishing box scores and commentary. Eventually, across the six compounds of Stalag Luft III, there were as many as two hundred teams playing on the improvised baseball diamonds of the various sports grounds.

"The Americans made arrangements to play us twice," Hawtin said. "But we had Bill Paton pitching for us. He'd pitched senior ball for the Beaches League in Toronto. They had a pretty good pitcher too . . . but Paton [struck] out sixteen batters."[6]

About the fifth or sixth inning of that first game, umpire Larry Wray went out to the mound to have a confab with Paton. Wray was Senior British Officer and also a Canadian, but he wanted the game to be more competitive. The Americans hadn't hit the ball out of the infield to that point.

"Please let them hit, Bill,"[7] Wray pleaded.

"One ball was hit into the outfield in that game," Hawtin said, adding that the most strenuous part of the game for him was walking to and from the outfield. "The first game we didn't get many runs, but we got enough to win. The second game wasn't even close. I think we won fourteen to one."[8]

Not ones to miss out on such sporting spectacles, the German guards gathered along the baselines to witness the games too. Art Hawtin wasn't sure for whom the Germans cheered—the Americans or the Canadians—but Colonel von Lindeiner was frequently seen beating his cane on his leather boots enthusiastically.[9] While he was quite content to leave the rules on the diamond up to Allied air force officers, the colonel nevertheless kept tight control on other aspects of kriegie baseball, no matter who was winning or losing. Art Hawtin noted in his diary some of the rules the *Kommandant* wanted obeyed rigidly in and around the barracks, but especially near the warning wire.

"Care must be taken that no window panes are broken,"[10] Hawtin quoted from one rule. "Panes broken through carelessness will not be replaced."

"Opportunity will be given twice weekly under the supervision of an interpreter to collect small balls from between the warning wire and the fence," stated another rule. "POWs must furnish a man to collect balls. . . . He must wear some mark which will be easily seen and readily distinguishable at a distance by the guards."

As awkward and silly as the wording of the ball-reclamation rule seemed, its application occasionally proved deadly. Phil Marchildon, from Penetanguishene, Ontario, pitched seventeen winning games for the Philadelphia Athletics in the 1942 major league baseball season before enlisting in the RCAF; a pilot officer and tail gunner aboard a Halifax bomber, he was shot down in 1944. During a kriegie baseball game he witnessed, a ball bounced over the warning wire. A Canadian asked permission from a guard to retrieve the ball; Marchildon wrote that the guard waved the POW to get the ball, but "when the Canadian [was] no more than a foot over the fence [the guard] shot him dead."[11]

And there were flying objects other than fly balls that could get kriegies into trouble near the warning wire. Canadian Frank Sorensen had been a regular "circuit basher" when he first got to Stalag Luft III, walking along the safe side of the warning wire with Roger Bushell, teaching him Danish. But later, when his Danish relatives sent him a glider kit, he test flew the model with its seven-foot wingspan and worried more about its landing than its flight.

"I'm afraid to tow it too high, as it might hit a window or fly over the wire,"[12] he reported in one of his letters home. In fact, on its maiden flight from the appell grounds, the glider caught a gust of wind and flew over the fence. Fortunately, the guard outside the wire wasn't as volatile as some, and tossed it back into the compound.

Meanwhile, letters posted the other way—from his Danish family connections—helped keep Frank Sorensen and fellow kriegies up-to-date on wartime events closer to the front lines. He learned, for example, about the so-called "clearing murders," in which civilians such as Danish author Kaj Munk[13] were executed in retaliation for Danish resistance murders of German soldiers. BBC broadcasts received on the kriegies' hidden wireless were also a lifeline to the Allies' progress in 1943. The balance of the war was tipping in their favour. They learned about Montgomery's pursuit of Rommel at El Alamein in January, the eventual victory of Soviet forces over the German Sixth Army in Stalingrad in February, the successful Bomber Command attacks on Ruhr River dams in May, and the capitulation of the Italian army to joint Canadian-British-American forces in Sicily that summer.

Not surprisingly, there was more at stake on the kriegie baseball diamonds than just the Canadian All-Stars beating the Americans at their favourite pastime. The escape committee took full advantage of the movement of people and sports gear around the compound to camouflage its activities. Some camera and radio receiver parts were small enough to be smuggled inside baseballs, and if a bat were hollowed out, it too could help X Organization deliver contraband between compounds. In addition, prior to the discovery of tunnel "Tom" in Hut 123, in September 1943, American paratrooper Jerry Sage's scheme of mingling penguins and fans helped disperse tons of sand along the sidelines of kriegie football scrimmages, soccer matches, track meets, and baseball games. But with the first snows and nighttime temperatures below freezing in November and December, only the Canadians' maintained outdoor activities, either circuit bashing or playing shinny hockey on the sports grounds. However, neither sand dispersal in the snow, nor above-ground escape seemed practical or inviting during that time of year.

Across from baseball player Art Hawtin in Room 14 of Hut 120 lived the man Hawtin called "the Tin Man."[14] In his diary, F/O John

Colwell continued to keep a record of POW activities. More important, he kept fabricating tools and, with those tools, a steady flow of practical utensils—some overt and others covert—made of tin, wood, wire, cloth, glass, and any other raw materials he could scavenge. Colwell had arrived April 12, 1943, but within a few months he had tailored ten pairs of shorts, an airman's tunic, socks, and a sleeping bag. With the woodworking and tinsmith tools he'd fabricated from scratch, he then became a virtual assembly line, manufacturing useful items for any kriegies in need. Using pieces of tin and steel, and mislaid screws and nails, he built appliances such as coffee percolators, kettles, cooking pots, pie plates, baking pans, toast racks, a fireless cooker, an ice cream freezer, picture frames, a Klim clock, and a metal brace for Group Captain Massey's injured leg. Then, from any Klim tins left over, he secretly began building a suitcase. It took eighty-one tins, but by November the bag was finished. Somehow, he sensed he'd be going somewhere.

"He could make anything out of anything," Hawtin said. "There were twelve of us who moved into a bigger room. There wasn't a thing in the room when we got there. Seven o'clock the next morning he rounded up all the tin cans he could get and we had every utensil we needed within a week. He was a master tinker."[15]

When he moved into a room that doubled their numbers from six to twelve POWs, Colwell felt he needed to build a new oven. At some point in the manufacturing process, he drew a diagram in his diary showing that his Klim tin stove required "120 Klim tins, 25 pounds of clay, a grate and two fire bricks."[16] Colwell also helped organize the menu for Christmas that year. It wasn't lavish, but following appell on December 25, 1943, Colwell's roomies enjoyed a breakfast of sausages with a cheese soufflé, toast and jam, and coffee. At 12:30, they had a lunch of toast and jam and tea. And for Christmas dinner, the cooks for the day—Bill Hoddinott and Art Hawtin—served up macaroni with cheese, roast beef, baked potatoes, Christmas pudding, and coffee. As well, they enjoyed chocolate sent to them by the Canadian Prisoners of War Relatives Association and a package forwarded from the Canadian government with a greeting from the prime minister.

"All Canada joins in warmest Christmas greetings and good wishes to you," the attached card read. "Arrangements have been made to forward to all Canadian prisoners of war a Christmas gift . . . comprising articles such as gramaphone [sic] records and cooking utensils."[17] It was signed W. L. Mackenzie King.

It's difficult to know whether the prime minister realized it at the time, but the gramophone records in the Christmas packages could not have come at a better time. Two huts away from John Colwell's one-man utensil production line, in Hut 103, Al Hake, an Australian airman with a penchant for three-dimensional designing and construction, was hard at work building a more covert utensil—compasses for the escape committee. Chief among the basic components of the compasses, Mackenzie King might have chuckled to discover, were melted-down Bakelite (plastic) gramophone records. Hake and his co-workers cut the plastic into pieces, heated it until it was dough-like, and pressed it into a mould for the compass base about an inch in diameter. They created the directional device with either a sewing needle or a razor blade strip stroked repeatedly with a magnet; the magnetized needle or razor was carefully mounted on a gramophone needle, which stuck up vertically from centre of the Bakelite base, creating the pivot point for the needle or razor. A compass card inside the casing indicated magnetic north (later models actually had luminous chips stolen from the *Kommandant*'s alarm clock). From broken windows, Hake then fashioned a glass face and gently heated it and the gramophone plastic to create a waterproof case around the compass mechanism. It was further sealed with reused window-frame putty. And if there was any question about the authenticity of the compass, Hake and his team pressed a manufacturer's inscription into the bottom of the compass while the Bakelite base was still warm.

"Made in Stalag Luft III,"[18] it read.

It may well be that Mackenzie King had no hint his government's thoughtful gift of gramophone recordings was playing right into the hands of the escapers. But some of the kriegies' relatives received direct, if a bit perplexing, appeals to help supply them with the tools of escape. Since December 1941, Flying Officer John Weir had been writing regularly to Frances McCormack at the family's residence in the Forest Hill area of Toronto. Naturally, Weir's fiancée had become accustomed to his words of longing to be with her. But she also began to understand he wasn't sitting idly by waiting for the war to end. He had told her of his German language lessons, that he had managed to have pictures taken of his fellow POWs, and that he needed several pairs of long johns. Harmless on the surface, the correspondence clearly indicated Weir was up to something. And while Frances might not have deduced her fiancée was one of X Organization's most reliable and productive tunnellers, she probably sensed from his Halloween letter of 1943 that there was a reason behind all of his requests.

"The pajamas you sent in the July parcel just came in time," wrote Weir, referring to what likely became his tunnelling clothes. And then he added a new, emphatic request. "Darling, what we really need are gramophone needles or are they practically non-existent at home too? There are two hundred or more of us here in the compound now. We are all hale 'n hearty, but itching to be home."[19]

Ironically, just weeks later, Scruffy Weir's lingering war wounds would remove him from both the task of finishing "Harry" and the entire escape plan. Dating back to November 8, 1941—the day Weir's Spitfire was hit by Messerschmitt shells and the resulting fuel and cockpit fire nearly blinded him—Weir had coped with no eyelids over his eyes. In the fall of 1943, after "Tom" was discovered and excavating underground was halted, tunnel boss Wally Floody recommended that Weir take an opportunity to have surgery to prevent potential blindness. Weir was transported to a German hospital near Frankfurt-am-Main, where he underwent skin-graft surgery performed by a British surgeon captured by the Germans in the Mediterranean in 1942. Weir would not return to Stalag Luft III until June 1944.

Mid-upper gunner Albert Wallace arrived at the North Compound in late May of 1943. By coincidence, he was shot down the same night as Art Hawtin. Aged twenty-two, Wallace had already worked at two or three civilian jobs, enlisted in the RCAF, graduated as a gunner, become a pilot officer, and completed fifteen and a half bombing operations with 419 Squadron in Bomber Command when he was shot down over Duisburg, Germany. But if he thought spending the night in the mid-upper gun turret of a Halifax bomber was a lonely experience, Wallace discovered, when he first arrived at Stalag Luft III, that life as a POW could be even more isolating. Once he'd been deloused, photographed, and issued a blanket and cutlery by the Germans, he was assigned to Hut 101 and "a friendless room,"[20] where the occupants spoke only South African dialects. Cut out of any conversation, he asked for a transfer and was eventually moved to Hut 104 and Room 23, the very place where tunnel "Harry" had begun.

"I had no idea it was the tunnel room," he said. "I didn't know for weeks that goddamn tunnel was seven feet from my bunk bed. Periodically, the sand would come out, but at first I didn't realize."[21]

Wallace never actually saw the tunnel opened or closed, although he did notice that one of his roommates, Pat Langford, was "extremely security conscious,"[22] almost always sitting on his top bunk, legs dangling over the side and surveying things all the time. Wallace eventually learned that Langford was "Harry's" *trapführer*, responsible for opening and closing the entrance to the tunnel at a moment's notice. In time Wallace would participate in escape activities, but as winter approached he and his fellow kriegies faced a more immediate problem: keeping warm behind the thin, poorly insulated, and underheated barracks walls. Taking a page from the tunnelling efforts, Wallace and several roommates began a nightly ritual—sneaking out of their hut, breaking into the German kitchen facility, filling their kitbags with coal briquettes, and stockpiling them for use during the colder nights.

"We had so much coal in our room, but there was nowhere to hide it," Wallace said. "We put it under our bunks. We put it in our Red Cross boxes to hide it. We'd be in our shirt sleeves, hotter than hell, and guys would come in muffed up to their necks with tuques on and we'd say, 'Oh, it's our new chimney.'"[23]

The supply of extra briquettes dried up when the Germans noticed the sudden depletion at the kitchen and padlocked the coal bin. But Wallace, after a further move to Hut 107, would soon find himself busy with another wintertime activity, in the ranks of the penguin sand-dispersal team. Right after New Year's, Roger Bushell assembled his section heads for the first escape committee meeting of 1944. He sensed that a combination of the ferrets' success in discovering "Tom" in September and the kriegies' relative inactivity through the fall had lulled the Germans into a false sense of security. It was January 7, and he wanted work to resume on "Harry" within days, while the goons' defences were down. The greatest barrier to any progress underground, Wally Floody pointed out, was trying to get rid of the sand with snow all over the compound. The meeting wrapped up without a solution. Then, Fanshawe and Ker-Ramsey hit on an idea. They told Bushell they would explore the space between the raked floor and the earthen foundation of the North Compound theatre. Fanshawe took a fat lamp into the crawl space. He reported that there was enough space under the floor to handle as much sand as "Harry" could ever deliver.

As usual, the toughest part of the transaction—the journey between "Harry" and the theatre—was getting the penguins from one to the other without bumping into ferrets. On January 10, when appell was done, three non-permanent residents of Hut 104 assembled in the large room at the north end of the building. Wally Floody, Robert Ker-Ramsey, and Pat Langford spent a couple of hours removing the square of tiles under the stove that concealed the trapdoor, swinging it open, and descending into "Harry's" vertical shaft. The air was cold; although the trapdoor had been sealed shut for three months, Ker-Ramsey had left a bypass open to allow air to circulate below. Floody discovered that the kitbags on the air pump had rotted through and needed replacing. Still, the greater problem was lack of air circulation farther up the tunnel. A couple of the Klim tin ducts had collapsed a short distance up the tunnel; they were soon repaired to restore the flow of fresh air. Three days after the section bosses reopened "Harry," Floody took his first shift digging and the sand began to move again. About that time, he took a few minutes to dash off a postcard to his sister, Catherine, at home in Toronto.

"My mail has taken its usual winter lapse . . . a four-month gap," Floody wrote late in January, suggesting he might have been slightly distracted. Then he added an ironic sign-off. "Life goes on in its pre-destined rut . . . Your brother, Wally."[24]

Meanwhile, Group Captain Massey got the *Kommandant* to ease the outdoor winter nighttime curfew; kriegies were allowed to walk between the barracks huts until 10 p.m. Massey was reminded, how-ever, that one of the ball-retrieval rules, enacted during the previous season's baseball games, was now in effect. "Snowballing must cease one-half-hour before roll call,"[25] the order said. The kriegies would abide by the snowball rule, but under cover of darkness, a steady line of penguins moved between "Harry" and the theatre carrying some-thing else. Unlike the previous summer's covert activity, the winter penguins didn't have to hide their sand pouches. When a penguin arrived at the mouth of the trapdoor in Hut 104, Langford laid a kit-bag or trouser pouches full of sand over his shoulder. When security boss George Harsh told him the way was clear, the penguin carried his load out the door of Hut 104 straight to Hut 109. And if the route was safe from there, a stooge directed him around Hut 120 through the snow and into the theatre.

Given that Flight Lieutenant Tony Pengelly was stage manager for all the kriegie productions, the goons had little reason to be sus-picious of his late evening presence at the theatre. But when Big X announced the push to renew digging in "Harry," Pengelly worked with the stage carpenters to install false nails in the base of a seat in the back row of the theatre so that it looked secured to the floor but was actually movable. The chair back was also not secured in place. When a trap operator slid the chair back up in the air, then flipped the seat itself forward toward the row in front, a small trapdoor in the floor under the seat was revealed.

"That was a lifesaver, because about a hundred tons of sand came out of ["Harry"]," Albert Wallace said. "I remember going into the theatre one night with my bags full of sand. I was told where to sit because that's where the trapdoor was. I sat in seat number thirteen, pulled my little tickies and out went the sand."[26]

Pengelly explained that when the theatre was dark (had no productions running), dirt was dumped through the trap all evening. Beneath the floor boards of the theatre, meanwhile, the Tin Man (John Colwell) and five other sand-dispersal men worked feverishly to keep the trap under seat thirteen clear and move the sand to the far reaches of the theatre's crawl space.[27] When each penguin unloaded his kitbag or pouch through the trap, the sand fell into a basin that was pulled by rope to a packing point. There, Colwell's crew tamped the sand up tight to the floor between the joists and against the walls. No space was left empty. At the end of an evening's work, as they left the crawl space, each of Colwell's crew would stand over the open trapdoor, slap the dirt from his clothes, and sweep the floor clean of the evidence. Pengelly and his crew would close the trap and reposition the seat and chair back, completing another successful night of making sand disappear.

"One day, we estimated we got rid of a total of twelve tons of sand,"[28] Pengelly said.

If the raked floor and Red Cross crate seats in the theatre weren't all they seemed, neither was the chapel, a room of prayer and reflection built into the backstage area toward the eastern end of the theatre building. Most afternoons between 1 and 4 p.m., when the autumn and wintertime light was at its best, RAF pilot Des Plunkett led a staff of about a dozen draftsmen (with about a dozen stooges guarding in the hallways and outside the windows of the chapel) working on the manufacture of escape maps. The men took the "flimsies" (thin paper linings) from gramophone record sleeves or cigarette packs and drew escape routes on them. Using inks they acquired or manufactured in the camp, the mapmakers then created negatives in jelly, which in turn generated map prints. The final editions of the maps had five legible colours: green for wooded areas, black for railway lines, red for roads, blue for rivers, and yellow for autobahns. Among the map copyists was former architect turned RAF pilot John

Hartnell-Beavis, who knew the value of accurate maps. Shot down in occupied-Holland, he used a silk map from inside his flight jacket to evade German troops for several days before being captured in July 1943. By November he had volunteered his drawing skills to create the jelly stencils that printed up to thirty-five copies of a specific map.

"All our work inks, pens, rulers, dividers, paper, etc., had to be used [so that] it was possible for everything to be concealed in a matter of a few seconds especially when [ferrets were] in camp," Hartnell-Beavis wrote. "If the padre had seen all the secret hiding places and panels in the floor and walls of the chapel, he would have had a severe shock."[29]

The signalling system used by X Organization stooges could be as simple as a red book set in a window as a sign that a ferret was in the area, or a blue towel on a clothesline indicating that all was clear. During the fall and winter of 1943–44, however, the system depended on signals communicated from inside a window in one barracks hut to inside a window in another, and on down the line. Australian air force officer Paul Brickhill* served the escape committee in the security section. He worked out a system of signals passed from one stooge to the next to protect the forgery work going on in the library in Hut 110 and the secret mapmaking going on in the chapel of the theatre. A window or a blind suddenly opened by one stooge would signal danger to a second stooge; that stooge would hold a folded piece of paper in his window, signalling a full shutdown of activity; and those signals would prompt a third stooge near the covert production to tap on the wall. All the forgery in the library or mapmaking in the chapel would disappear in seconds.[30] None of X Organization's stooges considered his work glamorous, but most learned how vital it was, including Flying Officer John R. Harris.

---

* Paul Brickhill was born and raised in Melbourne, Australia; during the war, he was shipped to Canada to train in the British Commonwealth Air Training Plan. Serving as a Spitfire pilot in RAF 92 Squadron, he was shot down over Tunisia in 1943 and sent to Stalag Luft III, where he joined the security section of X Organization. Post-war, his book, *The Great Escape*, provided the first comprehensive telling of the POW and escape experience at Luft III.

"Many a weary hour I spent peering out from behind windows and doors and in all kinds of weather,"[31] Harris wrote.

Born and raised in Toronto and eager to land any job he could after high school, during the Great Depression, John Harris found work as an office clerk with Canadian General Electric. But when the Nazis invaded western Europe and threatened to keep going across the English Channel, he sensed his new job was "to shoot down those Germans blitzing England."[32] As a new recruit with the RCAF in 1941, however, he was streamed to observer training. While still in Canada, he faced greater danger on the ground than in the air. Right after his graduation in August 1942, during a trip home, a freight train crashed into his passenger train on a siding; nevertheless, all passengers survived. Overseas he was posted to 419 Squadron of Bomber Command and his penchant for survival stayed with him. On September 5, 1943, during their eleventh bombing op over Mannheim, Germany, and immediately following the release of their bomb load, Harris and his crew came under attack. The Halifax began to shudder and descend uncontrollably.

"My poor mother isn't going to like hearing about this," was his first thought; then, just as suddenly, all he could see around him were the stars of the night sky. "My God, I'm out of the kite."[33]

Miraculously, either by being sucked through an open machine-gun turret beneath him or blown free by the explosion of the aircraft, Harris found himself floating to earth; he pulled the rip cord for his guide chute, which released the main parachute, and he landed in a forest, the only survivor of his seven-man crew. Following his capture, he was interrogated and eventually packed aboard a Luftwaffe truck for transfer to Stalag Luft III. With him and also shot down that night was F/O John Crozier, flying as a Second Dickie (observing pilot). Crozier was so recently assigned to the station (flying his first op with 620 Squadron) that he was still in his RCAF Blues tunic[34], not his battledress, and considered by the others to be a German spy. The two men—Harris and Crozier—both served X Organization as stooges. The watches could be as long as a couple of hours, and the stooges were moved around so the ferrets wouldn't notice a pattern.

"The system wasn't foolproof," Harris said. "One time I was peering out through a door and up a hallway at what was going on. A German guard came right up beside me. I don't know where he'd come from."[35]

Perhaps a stooge's ability to recover when caught off guard proved as valuable an asset as passing along an alarm. Harris managed to collect his wits quickly and pretended that he had been worrying about the weather before sauntering out of the building. He hoped his performance was sufficiently convincing that the ferret wouldn't bother to trigger a complete search of the building where Harris had been standing guard. It was, and Harris proved he could survive yet again.

"I remember Pat Langford, my immediate superior, he came and chewed me out for not having done my job," Harris said. "Then they discovered that somebody else had slipped up and he apologized."[36]

From the moment "Harry" was reopened, security boss George Harsh spent his days seated within view of the room containing the trapdoor to the tunnel. Stooges on the job—from the duty pilot watching the main gate to those shadowing ferrets—remained in touch with Harsh at all times, so that the second any German entered the compound with Hut 104 in his sights, Harsh could let Pat Langford know. In turn, the *trapführer* warned diggers below to stop any work that might be heard. Then he installed the grill at the top of the tunnel shaft, tucked blankets over it to muffle the sound, closed the trap with the tiles on top, and moved the stove back on top of the trap, simultaneously replacing the extension flue (above the stove) with its usual short flue. All of this happened within twenty or thirty seconds of Harsh's call for a shutdown.

By the third week of January 1944, about ten days after the resumption of digging, "Harry" had advanced fifty feet. Right there—about halfway between Hut 104 and the warning wire—Wally Floody built a halfway house they called "Piccadilly." He planned a second one when "Harry" was two hundred feet in length. They reached that point—roughly beneath the cooler in the *Vorlager* area of the compound—the first week of February, and finished the "Leicester

Square" halfway house by February 10. During that time, they had even been forced to shut down for a week when the moon was full in a cloudless sky. Had they continued to dig and disperse the sand as usual under the theatre, the penguins would have stood out against the moonlit snow. But the escape committee put the excavation downtime to good use.

By this time, Al Hake's assembly line in Hut 103 had manufactured as many as 250 compasses and hidden them down "Dick's" vertical shaft. Des Plunkett's mapmakers had mimeographed approximately four thousand escape maps. Meanwhile, the men in Tommy Guest's tailoring section were making headway on the task of outfitting scores of potential escapees in clothing that would help them blend into the civilian populations of Europe. Using shirts, pants, and jackets from Red Cross parcels, linings from greatcoats, and old uniforms, they shaved the rough surfaces of the cloth and re-coloured them with beetroot, shoe polish, or the dye from book covers. They used the broadsheets of German newspapers to cut out the patterns and sized each piece of clothing to accommodate the escaper.

By the time tunnellers had dug "Harry" as far north as the tunnel would go, Guest's tailors had manufactured as many as fifty civilians suits. They would be worn by POWs made up to look like businessmen, professionals, and travellers going about their daily lives, boarding trains that stopped at the Sagan Junction station. They would be worn by kriegies with sufficient skill in several languages to talk their way through their documents and German checkpoints fluently. For most of the rest—the so-called "hard-arsers"—there would be some documentation, some clothing, and the basic tools of travel: maps, compasses, and kitbags. Without multilingual skills, however, the hard-arsers would have to rely principally on wits and good luck. John Harris, whose forged documents would identify him as Antoine Zabadose, and whose set of stencilled maps would guide him to the Czechoslovak border, was outfitted to look like a Hungarian ironworker.

"I made some effort, though not very successful, to alter the appearance of my greatcoat," he said. "It was almost the same khaki colour as the Canadian army uniform, except that it had flares for sitting on horseback. It was worsted or tan-coloured heavy wool that covered me from the neck to the calf. Underneath, I wore my battle-dress, which I'd had since I was shot down."[37]

Elsewhere in the North Compound, kriegie life—as far as the guards and ferrets could tell—looked normal. The baseball, soccer, volleyball, and other field sports fields beyond the appell area had given way to the Canadians' wintertime pursuit. With the surface of the ground nearly frozen or covered in snow, conditions were ideal for flooding the field into a regulation-sized skating rink for hockey. Players would grade the soil for the rink with homemade shovels and a homemade level—water in a pan—then haul the water from the fire pool several hundred feet away. The first skates were entirely homemade; kriegies took angle irons from benches and screwed the steel to the bottoms of their boots.[38] But true to his kriegieland repu-tation, Alberta-born-and-raised pilot Barry Davidson managed to scrounge the real equipment needed to outfit teams for shinny.

"I wrote Don Mackay, the mayor of Calgary," Davidson wrote. "They got skates and hockey equipment and sent them to the camp. We flooded our rinks with buckets and they were regular sized rinks, so it was a lot of work."[39]

Hockey sticks were hard to come by and maintain. In addition to the city of Calgary's contribution, the YMCA came through with some as well, but depending on the calibre of players and intensity of the play, keeping the sticks in one piece was a challenge. To protect the players from injury, some groups came up with special rules, such as only allowing body checks or shot blocks within a certain distance of the net. However, there were cases of hockey games, indeed an entire season at Stalag Luft III, coming to an end when the supply of sticks simply ran out.[40]

In February, the North Compound theatre staged a homegrown revue. *Between Ourselves*, produced by Peter Butterworth, came com-plete with comedy skits, dance routines, and short dramatic works. Among the highlights, Bobby Laumans was back on the boards in the role of a torch singer and Tony Pengelly joined a Latin dance num-ber with six couples, featuring the female performers made up in

Carmen Miranda-like head gear, capes, and miniskirts. Taking one of the male dancing roles was another Canadian airman, James Wernham. Born in Scotland in 1917, Jimmy had emigrated and settled with his family in Winnipeg, Manitoba. He had worked in a general store and for an accounting firm during the Great Depression years, but enlisted in the RCAF in 1940 and was trained as an observer. Overseas on ops, he became something of a celebrity in May 1942, when newspaper reporters photographed him and his crew[41] (from 405 Squadron) as veterans of "Operation Millennium," the first thousand-bomber raid on Cologne, Germany. Three ops later he was shot down over Holland and captured. At Stalag Luft III, when not tending to other escape committee duties, he devoted his time to the theatre as a means of boosting POW morale.

Another kriegie helping out onstage at the theatre that winter was twenty-two-year-old George Wiley, from Windsor, Ontario. More of a free spirit than most, Wiley wasn't the best student in school and suffered from rheumatic fever as a youth. And he appeared much younger than his years, as if he were underage. Nevertheless, he had the credentials when he enlisted in the RCAF in 1940, about the same time James Wernham did. Wiley flew Kittyhawks for 112 Squadron in North Africa, surviving a crash landing in October 1942 and repeated close calls in dogfights with German fighters through the winter. He was finally shot down in March 1943 in support of the British Eighth Army over Tunisia. At Stalag Luft III, he joined escape committee preparations by assisting John Colwell with sand dispersal under the theatre. That winter, Flying Officer George Wiley took time to write home about his activities on the theatre floor (and below it).

"I've got an important part to play in one of our kriegie plays," he wrote, "and am a bit nervous about doing my part well. May see you sooner than expected."[42]

By the middle of February, *Unteroffizier* Karl Griese, the ferret the kriegies had nicknamed "Rubberneck," was snooping more suspiciously than usual around the North Compound barracks. He periodically ordered impromptu appells in the middle of the morning or the middle of the afternoon. Big X had warned the section chiefs to

be prepared for these unscheduled roll calls. To help attract suspicion
to himself—and away from the others—Bushell made certain he was
spotted in innocuous pursuits, such as attending language classes or
rehearsing his role in that upcoming production of *Pygmalion*. When
the spot searches came, the kriegies made sure they dawdled en route
to the assembly area, a tactic that allowed the tunnel crews enough
time to be pulled from "Harry" and cleaned up before appell. That
month Rubberneck sprang a sudden search in Hut 104, then one in
Hut 110. Then he assembled Wally Floody, George Harsh, Wings
Day, and Roger Bushell and strip-searched them. Next, he brought
in a diviner who passed the divining rod over the ground around several of the huts. There wasn't the slightest twitch. In the last days of
February, when "Harry" was perhaps a hundred feet short of its run
beyond the wire, the escape committee learned that its chief nemesis,
Rubberneck, would be on leave for two weeks.

"I told [Bushell] we could finish 'Harry' before he got back,"[43]
Floody said.

But Rubberneck had a parting shot and delivered a nearly fatal
blow to X Organization before taking his leave. On February 29, during
the morning appell, the pesky ferret appeared with *Hauptmann* Broili
and thirty additional guards. They called out the names of nineteen kriegies, including Wally Floody, George Harsh, Peter Fanshawe, Kingsley Brown, MacKinnon "Mac" Jarrell, Gordon "Nic" Nicoll, Robert
Stanford Tuck, Jim Tyrie, and Gwyn Martin. The entire appell ground
of kriegies held its collective breath as Broili led his select group to Hut
104, on the very doorstep of "Harry." The nineteen were searched for
two hours. Then, without any opportunity to go to their rooms to gather
belongings, the column of kriegies was marched under guard through
the main gate and down the road to a satellite POW camp at Belaria[44],
about five miles away. In one short, sharp dragnet, Rubberneck had
hauled away a half-dozen key members of the escape committee, some
of whom had been in the service of X Organization since 1940, invest-
ing those four years in one real chance to gain their freedom.

"They just wanted to get rid of us," Wally Floody said. "But they
had a pretty good shot at it, because they got the man in charge of

sand dispersal, the man in charge of security, [an intelligence specialist], and myself, a tunnel digger."[45]

Darker more deadly counter-escape measures were occurring in Berlin, even as the dust settled on Rubberneck's surprise purge. Because Heinrich Himmler, *Reichsführer* of the *Schutzstaffel* (SS) and architect of the Holocaust, wished to put greater control of prison camps into the hands of the SS, he gave his blessing to *Aktion Kugel*, or Bullet Operation. Clearly in violation of the Geneva Conventions, it stated that any recaptured escapee officers who were not American or British were to be chained and handed over to the Mauthausen Concentration Camp and either gassed or shot.[46] Himmler's directive also used the code phrase "*Stufe* III" or "Grade III" to cover up all reference to activities surrounding any recaptured POWs. The directive was not handed down as a document, but passed by word of mouth to Colonel Friedrich von Lindeiner-Wildau, the *Kommandant* at Stalag Luft III. The order also gave Lindeiner the authority, should he choose to use it, to execute recaptured POWs in his camp. Von Lindeiner apparently had no intention of resorting to summary executions. In fact, when he received the Bullet Order, he assembled senior officers, medical officers, and padres from all the Stalag Luft III compounds. As explicitly as he could, von Lindeiner relayed the content of the order, almost entreating the officers to halt all escape activity. For the North Compound, however, the die was already cast.

On March 1, 1944, with Rubberneck on leave and several Canadian veteran section heads now removed from the scene, Robert Ker-Ramsey took the lead in the tunnel. Deflated by the loss of key men, but bolstered by the opportunity to complete the final push while their ferret nemesis was away, the tunnellers went back to work. The crew underground doubled, with two diggers at the face of the tunnel, two in each of the halfway houses, a carpenter preparing the shoring, and a man on the air pump continuously. The parade of penguins to the back row of seats in the theatre and John Colwell's packers under the floorboards made the most of the shortened daylight hours and the 10 p.m. curfew. In just nine days, by March 9, the tunnel had extended the one hundred feet that—based on the underground measurements—they figured would put "Harry" beyond the wire, beyond the road, and well into the pine forest. On the tenth day the diggers carved out what would be the base of the vertical shaft to the surface. Over the next five days they gingerly dug upward and—just as Wally Floody had done in the first hours of the tunnelling downward a year before—at the upper end of their vertical dig they built a final solid box frame around four bedposts and a wooden ceiling. It was positioned right below some pine-tree roots, to remain in place until the night chosen for the breakout.

They had tunnelled for eleven months—from April 11, 1943, to March 14, 1944. They had removed and dispersed several hundred tons of sand from three major tunnels. Scrounging from every corner of the compound, kriegies had incorporated 4,000 bed-boards, 90 double bunk beds, 1,212 bed bolsters, 1,370 battens, 1,699 blankets, 161 pillow cases, 635 mattresses, 192 bed covers, 3,424 towels, 76 benches, 52 twenty-man tables, 10 single tables, 34 chairs, 30 shovels, 246 water cans, 1,219 knives, 582 forks, 478 spoons, 1,000 feet of electric wire, 600 feet of rope, and 69 lamps[47] into "Tom," "Dick," and, mostly, "Harry." According to the measured ball of string the diggers unravelled in the tunnel, "Harry" covered 336 feet (nearly 400 feet including the two vertical shafts). They were just six inches away from the sod and roots of the forest floor well outside the wire—six inches to freedom.

The theatre troupe made a couple of offbeat choices to complete its winter playbill. In March, they presented the farcical black comedy *Arsenic and Old Lace.** Next came *Escape*, a 1926 play by celebrated British novelist and playwright John Galsworthy. The storyline followed the life of a law-abiding man who met a prostitute, accidentally killed a police officer defending her, and then escaped from prison. The POW production featured longtime kriegies Peter Butterworth

---

* An air force officer arrived at Stalag Luft III in the winter of 1944 with unused tickets in his pocket to a production of *Arsenic and Old Lace* being staged at the Hudson Theatre in London. His tickets were honoured at the North Compound theatre.

as the shopkeeper, John Casson as the parson, and, of course, taking on the female leads were John Dowler, Malcolm Freegard, and Tony Pengelly.[48] No doubt the irony of the plot occurred to the kriegie performers as well as the German officers seated in the first two rows. But nobody made mention of it. Not even Pengelly had much of the play's subject matter on his mind during the production.

"Up until this last great escape plan was well underway, none of us knew how many were to go out in it, or who,"[49] he said.

During a two-hour meeting in the library room of Hut 110 on March 14, the same day Rubberneck returned from leave, Big X led discussion about the timing of the breakout. The escape committee considered three possible dates—March 23, 24, and 25—the next three nights without potential exposure by bright moonlight, the New Moon period. March 25 was a Saturday, which likely meant additional train traffic and potential congestion along some rail routes through Sagan. They would wait to see what the weather brought on March 23 and 24. The section heads debated whether a mass escape in bad weather, freezing nighttime temperatures, and with snow on the ground might jeopardize any hard-arsers' attempts to get away. Did it make sense to delay a month? The tunnel experts couldn't guarantee the construction integrity of "Harry's" shafts, ceilings, and walls, not to mention the continuing danger of the tunnel's discovery. The decision was to go either March 23 or 24, depending on the weather. The committee hoped between nine o'clock on the night of the escape and 5:30 the next morning it could spring more than two hundred kriegies—one every three or four minutes.

The final agenda item involved Big X and the section heads drawing the names of those who would comprise the list of escapers. The first thirty names selected came from a list of the best German speakers. The next twenty names came from the most prominent escape committee workers. Then, thirty more were drawn from a list of stooges, penguins, tailors, compass and mapmakers, and forgers. Finally, all remaining names of escape workers were pulled from a hat to bring the total number to about two hundred.[50] Escapers would go through "Harry" in the same order the names were drawn.

"When the time came close," Pengelly continued, "we drew lots, intensely, in small groups. Mere slips of paper they were, holding the 'yes' or 'no' of freedom—and for the lucky ones, how long he would be after the first to leave . . . I drew number ninety-three."[51]

The mass escape scenario that the committee chiefs and about six hundred other Commonwealth prisoners of war had built from scratch was just days away from its final act.

# "THROUGH ADVERSITY
# TO THE STARS"

HOLDING the slip of paper with his escape number on it, and sensing all his work falsifying documents for dozens of his comrades at Stalag Luft III was nearly done, F/L Tony Pengelly still agonized over his shot at freedom. He hadn't seen his fiancée in England for more than three years. He hadn't seen Canada since 1938. All the amenities he'd gone without—the food, the people, the shows, the lights, the freedom to open a door and walk down any street whenever he wished—could be waiting at home in Toronto.

"It was the greatest decision of my life as a prisoner of war,"[1] he said.

Weighing on his mind, however, were the details of duty. He had directed the production of many of the escape documents. He knew their design, detail, and delivery better than almost anyone inside the forgery section of X Organization. He wondered whether—on the night of the escape—somebody in his branch of Dean and Dawson should stay behind to check that every identification card was in the right hands of the right escaper as he entered "Harry" on his way out. Nothing could be left to chance. No man could leave with papers that didn't match his disguise. And if Pengelly took his position—ninety-third in the tunnel—and left the job to someone else, might one vital detail be omitted? Could there be a mistake he might have caught? Should someone with his seniority stay behind to help the next escape?

"In the nights when the [barracks] were quiet," Pengelly said, remembering that crucial moment in Hut 104, "I ground it over in my mind. . . . I realized in those nights I lay awake and those days I pounded the circuit inside the wire, that more than a high wire fence had me prisoner now. There was this responsibility, and on my acceptance or rejection of it, depended my chance at freedom."[2]

In the end, Pengelly decided to forfeit his spot. Just twenty-four, engaged to be married to Pauline Robson, and a POW in Germany since the fall of 1940, the wily pilot who'd cajoled countless German guards to loan him their legal papers, and then stepped on the North Compound theatre stage to flawlessly portray female roles, had decided to bow out of the finale. Instead of joining the coming mass escape, he would stay behind. In doing so, he would help give the escape committee a nucleus of old hands to ensure the success of the current breakout and to build up X Organization again for another.

The same kind of decision weighed heavily on navigator George Sweanor's mind. A year older than Pengelly, he had even more to hurry home to, including a new bride and a newborn daughter he'd never seen. But the young RCAF flying officer considered other factors. Despite the sophistication of the security operations in which he'd participated (as the duty pilot inside the main gate), Sweanor still concluded that escaping to Britain was a pipe dream. He realized Stalag Luft III was too deep in occupied Europe and that only those who spoke German had a legitimate chance of getting away. He was also realistic enough to fear the Gestapo's brutality should he be recaptured. He also sensed he had reason to fear German propaganda that had painted Allied aircrew as *Luftgangsters* (air gangsters) and their bombers as *Terrorflugzeuge* (terror aircraft); survival in cities decimated by Bomber Command was not a sure thing either.[3]

"I argued that a mass escape would cause a desired disruption to the German war effort because it would take a lot of people to track us down, but there would be little hope of anybody getting home," Sweanor said. "[So] I felt relieved when my name was not drawn."[4]

A couple of Sweanor's barracks mates did have their names drawn, including George McGill, who had conjured up diversions during earlier escape attempts and then worked as tunnel security assistant to George Harsh; he would be seventy-fifth into the tunnel.[5] Other Canadians' names drawn or chosen by Big X included Gordon Kidder, the Johns Hopkins University master's prospect who spoke German and French fluently; he was thirty-first on the escape list. James Wernham and George Wiley, who had both joined the theatre production crew during the past year, would be thirty-second and thirty-third. Hank Birkland, the Big Train, had dug tunnels in every German compound that had imprisoned him since the fall of 1941; he would go through "Harry" for the last time in the fifty-first position. Pat Langford, the *trapführer* responsible for opening and closing "Harry" almost every day for the previous eleven months was number fifty-eight. Tommy Thompson, the Canadian pilot who'd personally earned the wrath of Hermann Göring for waking the *Reichsmarschall* the September night he was shot down in 1939, would be sixty-eighth; once outside the wire he planned to team up with Flying Officer Bill Cameron, who was in the sixty-second spot. Fighter pilot Keith "Skeets" Ogilvie had won a Distinguished Flying Cross (DFC) for intercepting a Dornier bomber en route to bomb Buckingham Palace during the Battle of Britain; he was seventy-sixth on the escape list. Bob McBride, who'd burned the bowling set his wife sent him the winter before to stay warm, would face the March cold in the eightieth position. A few more Canadians held escape numbers in the eighties and nineties, including Jack Moul, Red Noble and Mac Reilley. Further down the list, Gordon King, who had regularly operated the air pump, held escape number 141. Meanwhile, John Colwell, the Tin Man, who'd hand-built many of the tools of escape while making so much of the sand disappear under the theatre, would be 147. All set to travel outside the wire as Hungarian ironworkers, John Crozier and his roommate John R. Harris had drawn escape numbers 179 and 180.

As Pengelly's forgers put the finishing touches on the fake identity *Kennkarte* and *Ausweise* passes that Crozier, Harris, and many others would need, X Organization moved into fine-tuning mode on other fronts. John Travis's engineers weren't building tools and equipment for the tunnelling anymore; they were transforming sheets of food tins into portable water bottles for the escapers. Des Plunkett's assembly line had completed its last multicoloured, mimeographed maps. For Tommy Guest's tailors there was still civilian wear to stitch and colour, but Al Hake had punched his Stalag Luft III manufacturer's imprint on the last escape compass. Robert Ker-Ramsey and Johnny Marshall began assembling the escapers in small groups to explain how to get through the tunnel. Roger Bushell called for one last levy on the Red Cross parcels, with every ounce of sugar, cocoa, raisins, milk, and biscuits being confiscated and poured into a stewing pot and then a baking oven; the resulting fudge, prepared in Hut 112, could provide a man with enough caloric intake to last him two days.

Otherwise, Bushell remained away from the escape production centres as much as he could—conducting lectures in the library and rehearsing his lines as Professor Higgins in the upcoming theatre production of *Pygmalion*—so that the guards could see him in a normal, innocuous routine. But Big X had one final piece of the puzzle to orchestrate: the logistics for getting more than two hundred men into Hut 104 on the appointed night and through the tunnel in an orderly escape. The first thirty to make their way through "Harry" would attempt to get to the Sagan station in time to catch the earliest trains. Then, using their natural linguistic skills, civilian disguises, and forged papers, they would board passenger coaches and scatter in a half-dozen different directions. The next seventy to make their way through, the so-called "hard-arsers," would be dressed in work clothes, looking like migrant workers in transit. If they couldn't get tickets for third-class passenger seats, they would resort to using compasses, maps, intuition, and darkness to make their getaway individually and in small groups.

Air gunner Albert Wallace had no seniority with the escape committee, but he had served as a penguin hiding sand under the theatre, and could have put his name in the draw. He chose not to. He recognized in himself and others the pent-up frustration of extended imprisonment in the German *Straflager* system. When life boiled down to twice-a-day roll calls, scrounging for food, and shivering inside poorly insulated barracks, he saw comrades become "barbed-wire happy," obsessed with getting out. A Canadian kriegie who had notoriously attempted an escape by cutting through the wire was put in solitary for a month. The resulting claustrophobia turned a trip to the toilet into a run for it; he was shot, though not fatally.[6] Two others had committed suicide, one at Stalag Luft I and the other at Luft III.[7] As depressing and debilitating as compound life became, however, Wallace felt he'd kept his head.

"I had no interest in escaping whatsoever," he said. "We were eight hundred miles from England. Escape through Germany with eighty million people all speaking German and I spoke English? It would take a miracle to get back."[8]

Having spent a little less than a year behind wire at the North Compound, Canadian Spitfire pilot Frank Sorensen was nonetheless feeling the tyranny. Through the winter of 1944, his letters home more often reflected the symptoms that Albert Wallace had seen in some of his roommates. Sorry Sorensen wrote home that the winter had forced the POWs indoors and that "indoor life in a kriegie camp does not make time go any faster."[9] Fortunately, Sorensen had the benefit of fluency in Danish and therefore had received the nod to exit through "Harry" in the first or second wave of escapers on the night of the escape. However, several factors influenced Sorensen's eventual decision to forfeit his higher position on the list. X Organization intelligence suggested the first escapees—fluent in German and dressed like businessmen or travellers—stood the best chance of getting away safely if they caught the fast morning trains leaving Sagan. Sorensen deduced those same express trains would also undergo the greatest scrutiny and surveillance by German police and railway guards. He therefore considered going through the tunnel lower on the list to catch a later, slower train, where his presence would attract less attention.

But Sorensen weighed yet another consideration. Among his closest friends inside the wire was James Catanach, an Australian officer who'd grown up in a tightly knit family, and Arnold Christensen, a New Zealand officer who shared Sorensen's Danish heritage. Both Catanach and Christensen had been imprisoned longer than Sorensen had, and in the grand scheme of the mass breakout, their successful escape seemed to hold greater emotional significance, at least in the way Sorensen looked at it. So, for strategic purpose or matters of the heart or both, he chose to trade his earlier spot on the escape list for a higher number and later exit through the tunnel.[10]

Canadian Fleet Air Arm pilot Dick Bartlett faced a slightly different dilemma before the breakout. For nearly four years he had successfully moved the kriegies' wireless radio, hidden inside a medicine ball, from one prisoner-of-war camp to another, right under the Germans' noses. At the North Compound, he had safely concealed "the canary" in a non-functioning toilet. Based on his service, Bartlett was assigned the sixteenth position on the escape list, and paired with Norwegian pilot officer Halldor Espelid in the fifteenth spot. Then, in the weeks leading up to the breakout, another Norwegian flying officer, Nils Fugelsang, was shot down and imprisoned at the North Compound. Bartlett figured that Espelid and Fugelsang, with their linguistic advantage, together stood a better chance of evading capture and getting home. Bartlett chose to give up his spot to Fugelsang and stay behind.[11]

Circumstances leading up to the breakout also put an end to Barry Davidson's hopes of escaping through "Harry." The former Blenheim pilot shot down in July 1940 had served on the original escape committee and in time had become X Organization's leading scrounger. A born baseball and hockey player, but also a poet, diarist, and artist, Davidson had shone brightest in the art of friendly persuasion, taming Germans guards—offering them Red Cross chocolate, coffee, and cigarettes—to lend him the makings of tools or identity documents. In the pre-breakout lottery, he had won the seventy-eighth position on the escape list. But then, almost on the eve of the breakout, his strength became his weakness.

"I had been seen talking to Fischer, one of the guards, shortly before the escape," Davidson said. "He hated the Nazis and had sympathy for the POWs. We had such a good security system that [X Organization] knew the Germans had seen me talking to him. . . . My relationship with this guard would have risked his life had I gone. . . . So Roger Bushell asked me if I'd step back and not go out."[12] Reluctantly, Davidson agreed.

A couple of days past the official arrival of spring, the Sagan area of Silesia still had six inches of snow on the ground. But the air above the ground was mild. The escape committee met in Hut 104 on March 23 and decided to delay the breakout one more day. There was more snow that night, but when the committee met in Hut 101 on the morning of March 24, the members knew a decision had to be made right away to give Ker-Ramsey the day to prepare "Harry" for the wear and tear of the escape and to allow Pengelly the time to have all required documents signed and date-stamped "March 23." More discussion focused on the plight of the hard-arsers in the snow and cold of the night. Wings Day and Roger Bushell agreed the hard-arsers' chances of escaping were slim anyway, but even if they were only on the loose for a few days, the resulting chaos across Germany rounding them up would have as desirable an effect as if they all got back to Britain. Bushell gave the decision his blessing and then walked to the North Compound theatre where his understudy, Kenneth Mackintosh, got the word Big X would not be onstage as Professor Higgins that night. *Pygmalion* would have to open without him.

All day long the atmosphere was electric at the North Compound. Behind closed barracks doors—all with stooges at the watch—kriegies collected their forged maps, compasses, and food rations and stitched them into clothing pockets. Meanwhile, Ker-Ramsey, staying behind like Pengelly as an escape committee veteran, made last-minute adjustments underground—covering the trolley tracks with fresh blankets to muffle the sound, installing new tow ropes (passed through the main gate by the *Vorlager* on the premise they would be used for a North Compound boxing ring) on the trolleys, and installing light bulbs (taken from the huts) in every socket available along the full length of "Harry."

After sunset, about six o'clock, those on the escape list had last meals prepared by their roommates. John Travis, the tunnelling engineer, cooked up a concoction of bully beef fritters and a gruel of boiled barley, Klim powder, sugar, and raisins for two of his barracks mates—Roger Bushell and Bob van der Stok. Van der Stok, the Dutch flyer, was going out in the first twenty of the escape order. When they'd finished eating as much of Travis's fritters and gruel as they could, Bushell got into the suit he'd smuggled into the compound from Prague a year before and van der Stok emerged in his escape apparel; unlike the fake German corporal's uniform he'd used during Operation Bedbug, van der Stok wore a civilian business suit, handmade by Tommy Guest's tailors.

"How do I look?"[13] he asked his roommates.

"Immaculate," Gordon King told him as they examined the tailoring and the quality of his passes and identity documents forged by Dean and Dawson. King knew van der Stok had been a medical student in Holland prior to the war and spoke several different languages, including German. He planned to connect with the French Underground to get across the Pyrenees to Spain en route to Britain. He was going through "Harry" in the eighteenth spot.

In Hut 112, George Wiley had gathered up his things and joined fellow Canadian James Wernham in 104 to await their call. Wiley appeared anxious about his first escape attempt and approached his roommate Alan Righetti. He handed Righetti his watch and a few other personal things, asking him to pass them along to his mother back in Windsor, Ontario, if things didn't work out. Righetti, a veteran of earlier escape attempts, joked that Wiley would likely be home before Righetti, but he accepted the watch and Wiley's final wish.[14]

Just before 7 p.m., the clockwork movement of men to Hut 104 began. Under the direction of block commanders at each hut in the compound, and with stooges positioned at windows, men trickled into Hut 104 at thirty-second intervals. They were assigned rooms in which to wait for their escape number to be called. Once that happened, they were guided into Room 23 and to the trap under the stove. The committee had appointed marshals among the escapers; each marshal ensured his allotted ten men were all set. Within an hour the priority escapers were in position, ready to go. And even though their spots were way down the list, so too the hard-arsers began to make their way to Hut 104.

"In the room where we were, we tried to play bridge," John Harris said. "I was with three other would-be escapers. I was with Johnny Crozier because he was the one with the set of maps."[15]

At 8:45 p.m., the first man in the escape sequence, Les "Johnny" Bull, hustled down the ladder in the shaft beneath Hut 104, stretched himself face down on the trolley, and dog-paddled his way to Piccadilly, the first halfway house, a hundred feet up the tunnel. Once there, he jerked the rope for Johnny Marshall, who would act as an underground conductor for the first hour and—once his ten men were through—exit the tunnel in the number eleven position. Marshall retrieved the trolley by reeling in the rope, climbed aboard, jerked the rope ahead, and Bull reeled him up to Piccadilly. They repeated the exercise to get to Leicester Square, and finally to the base of the exit shaft at the north end of "Harry." Their job was to remove the ceiling boards at the top of the exit shaft and make the final cut through the sod in the pine forest. Behind them, Czech flyer Arnost "Wally" Valenta (second), Roger Bushell (third), and Bernard Scheidhauer, a Free French officer and fourth on the list, prepared to do the same. At the bottom of the entry shaft two Canadians got into position in the pump room. *Trapführer*, Pat Langford, would help get men up the tunnel and reel in the empty trolley; then, with his group of ten on their way, he would take his turn as the fifty-eighth on the list. Meanwhile, Gordon King, the diminutive Wellington pilot from Winnipeg, volunteered to pump the bellows through the night until his turn came, way down the list.

"I was a hard-arser," King said. "I had a map of the area, a little package of food, and my compass, just waiting my turn."[16]

Also in position along the escape route through "Harry" were experienced tunnellers Red Noble, Shag Rees, and Hank Birkland. They had agreed to position themselves at the halfway houses and haul ten men to their location before joining the escape. The eleventh, twelfth, and thirteenth men in the order—also with underground experience—would haul the next ten through and hand off the responsibility to the next three.[17] The plan called for a controller to remain outside the exit hole in the woods to get twenty men on their way and then hand off the controller job to the twenty-first man. Everybody was in place. The only piece missing was the completion of the exit hole up through the sod in the woods.

About ten o'clock, the German lock-up guard from the *Vorlager* went through the North Compound closing shutters and barring the hut doors from the outside for the night. Shortly afterward, King, Ker-Ramsey, and Langford began to wonder what was wrong. Seventeen escapers had been in position since 9:30, but nobody was moving through "Harry" yet. The first two men up the exit shaft— Les Bull and Johnny Marshall—had been battling for thirty minutes to open the exit to the tunnel, but the wooden ceiling at the top of the shaft was wet, swollen, and wouldn't budge. Bull and Marshall, both dressed as civilians bound for the early morning trains, had to strip down to their underpants so as not to soil their business suits and try to free the wood and break through the soil above. Bull finally succeeded in prying the boards loose, and then, using a small shovel, broke a hole through the soil and snow above. He felt the cool air of the winter night on his face as the hole widened and he could see the night sky above, the stars unobscured by wire. Up the last rungs of the ladder, he poked his head through the hole. The sight was both awesome and terrifying.

Just as the tunnel engineers had planned, the exit to "Harry" was well outside the wire. However, the reason Bull could see so many stars as he peered up the exit hole was that there was no tree canopy blocking his view. There was nothing overhead. "Harry" was short of the pine forest by ten feet. Worse, the goon tower was just forty feet away. Worse still, the path of two sentries posted outside the wire— one pacing between the tower and the gate to the east, the other walking to the west fence and back—passed within thirty feet of the exit hole. Even without moonlight, at ground level a sentry would spot anyone moving in the open against the blanket of snow in an instant. All this Bull reported to Marshall and Bushell, who'd by now reached the base of the exit shaft. Amid the frustration and panic rising among the lead group, Bushell weighed the options. They could put the whole thing off and dig farther, but the digging and dispersal units had virtually shut down and were in escape mode. And with the compound-wide final preparations, there was a good chance ferrets would stumble across something to draw them to Hut 104 and "Harry's" trapdoor. Then it dawned on Bushell: they couldn't postpone the escape. All the documents were dated March 24, 1944.

Just as quickly, the solution dawned on Les Bull. At the edge of the woods, closest to the exit hole, lay a blind, a tangle of timber and brush. Birkland, Clark, and Harsh had spotted the ferrets hiding behind it spying on kriegies during the push to complete tunnel "Tom" the previous summer. Bull concluded if they attached a signal rope from the top of the escape shaft ladder, up through the exit hole, and out to the blind, a controller behind the blind could signal with a tug on the rope when the way was clear of German sentries. It was settled in an instant. They tied a new rope to the top rung of the ladder and—when the sentries were out of view—Bull unravelled the rope to the blind and prepared to signal the next man, Johnny Marshall, through. Bushell quickly scribbled the sequence on the wall at the base of the shaft, so each man would read the note and know what to do.

"Pause at top of shaft. Hold signal rope tied to rung. Receiving two tugs, crawl out. Follow rope to shelter,"[18] it said.

Bull got into position behind the blind in the woods and waited for the sentries to come back into view, stop at the tower, turn, and retrace their steps out of view. He tugged twice on the rope and Wally Valenta popped up, wriggled through the snow across the distance to the blind, and entered the woods. A few minutes later Roger Bushell, number three, did the same. Big X had planned to travel with Robert Stanford Tuck, but with the British ace purged to Belaria a month earlier, his new partner was Bernard Scheidhauer, the fourth man through the exit and into the woods. The improvised "controller in the blind" system meant the interval between men was now longer than the planned two or three minutes, but at least the system was working.

Deeper into the pine forest, the kriegies stood up without fear of being seen. For two years those pine trees—a green wall—had been a physical and psychological barrier keeping them from the outside world. Now it concealed them from the compound they'd just fled. Among the first groups assembling in the woods were Wally Valenta, Johnny Marshall, Des Plunkett, and Freddie Dvorak, all bound for Valenta's and Dvorak's homeland, Czechoslovakia. Next, Roger Bushell and Bernard Scheidhauer, who planned to hook up with the French Underground in Alsace and Paris. Shortly afterward came the two Norwegians, Halldor Espelid and Nils Fugelsang, who'd taken Canadian Dick Bartlett's sixteenth spot, along with New Zealander Arnold Christensen and James Catanach, one of whom had switched with Canadian Frank Sorensen; they were headed through Berlin to the Danish frontier. The eighteenth man out of the tunnel, in his "immaculate" suit, was Bob van der Stok; he too was making his way toward the station with intentions of getting across France and through Spain back to England. They exchanged "see you in London" send-offs, and then dashed into the night. They had all been instructed to vary their routes into the railway station. There were three options: stairs to a walkway west of the station, directly across the tracks to the eastern entrance of the station, or through a subway that ran under the tracks into the station.

Bushell and Scheidhauer as well as Plunkett and Dvorak emerged from the woods and approached the station just as an express train en route from Breslau to Berlin arrived at Sagan. The first two entered the station in plenty of time to purchase their tickets and board. Meanwhile, Plunkett and Dvorak were blocked at the eastern entrance to the station by a passing Russian work party; when they diverted to the subway under the tracks, they were stopped by a railway worker and a guard. However, at exactly that moment, there was confusion all over the station and marshalling yard because an air-raid siren sounded and the station lights went out. The two kriegies took advantage of the moment and dashed aboard the express without tickets. Dutch airman Bob van der Stok got caught in the same confusion; he was just outside the southern entrance to the subway under the station tracks. A soldier questioned him, and van der Stok explained he was a foreign worker trying to board the train. Conveniently for van der Stok, the soldier insisted he follow instructions and enter the air-raid shelter, which in turn led him conveniently to the subway under the tracks to the station and boarding platforms.[19] But by now, the entire Sagan area was in blackout against a looming Allied bomber attack.

It was just before midnight when the sirens sounded at Stalag Luft III. Wings Day, twentieth in the escape sequence, had just begun his climb down the entrance shaft. By the time he reached the bottom of the ladder, the Germans at the *Kommandantur* had cut electrical power to the entire prison facility. Everything above and below ground fell into darkness. The single benefit from the blackout was that it snuffed boundary lights and tower searchlights too, which expedited the escapers' dash from the exit hole into the woods.

Back inside the North Compound, however, "lights out" required hut shutters to be opened and fat lamps in the hut rooms doused; it also sent the *hundführer* and their dogs patrolling through the compound. Inside Hut 104, dozens of hard-arsers lay still in hallways and in bunks throughout the perceived danger of the air raid. With electricity cut off to "Harry" as well, tunnel travellers couldn't judge the distances, the whereabouts of the halfway houses, or even how close they were to the tunnel walls. Ker-Ramsey was quick to realize the additional danger of throwing already jittery escapers into total darkness in such a confined space, and he immediately began lighting fat lamps along the tunnel. The escape schedule was falling further behind. Instead of taking two or three minutes, it was now taking a man at least six minutes to travel the full length of "Harry" and up the exit shaft.

As he moved northbound through the tunnel, Wings Day helped Ker-Ramsey light the lamps, then completed a hauler shift at the base of the escape shaft before exiting the hole himself. But the anxiousness around the blackout amplified the tension in the tunnel. Most of the first thirty-five men, including Canadians Gordon Kidder, James Wernham, and George Wiley, carried suitcases; while they were only made of cardboard or plywood, some were bulky and difficult to pass through "Harry" without making separate trolley trips. Some of the men and bags caused derailments of the trolley. Others bumped into shoring and caused small cave-ins. Tom Kirby-Green, thirtieth in the tunnel, derailed between Piccadilly and Leicester Square and his shoulders bumped a weakened shoring. It broke and sand caved in, burying him from his waist to his shoulders. Canadian digger Hank Birkland, on duty at Leicester Square, realized the problem, crawled back to Kirby-Green, and freed him from the sand. Birkland then worked feverishly in the darkness to clear the sand and replace the shoring boards. Bob Nelson faced a similar problem a short time later near Piccadilly.

"Due to the cold weather, people were wearing warmer, thicker clothes, and being hauled through . . . they pulled down some of the roof support and collapsed the sand," Nelson said. "When I was hauling [James Long] through, the roof fell on top of him. I had to pull him out and then when he got past me, I then had to go up the tunnel on my elbows and toes to repair the roof and clear the sand that fell in."[20]

As Birkland completed his repair and dispersal of the sand that had collapsed on Kirby-Green, above ground the air-raid sirens were sounding the all-clear across the POW complex and the Germans restored the electricity to their tower searchlights and consequently to "Harry's" underground lights. That's when Birkland, the Canadian who'd spent much of his waking life the past year digging inside Stalag Luft III tunnels, travelled through "Harry" for the last time and got his first taste of life beyond the wire. He moved out of the tunnel and into the woods, marshalling the next ten men on their way. Then he joined British air officers Les Brodrick, Denys Street, Edgar Humphreys, and Paul Royle as they made their way westward, away from Stalag Luft III and Sagan.

With the lights back on inside "Harry," at least those in transit could now see where they were going. However, now the escapers weren't lugging suitcases through the tunnel, but blanket rolls, additional layers of clothing, and pockets bulging with extra food and survival supplies. And if, in addition, the hard-arsers happened to be broad-shouldered, passage along the tunnel and through the halfway houses proved just as difficult and sluggish. Word went back up top to Ker-Ramsey, the above-ground controller, who began inspecting men as they were about to climb down the first shaft. As difficult a decision as it became, Ker-Ramsey had to relieve some men of their bulkier bedrolls, extra clothing, and survival supplies. That meant that hard-arsers such as Canadians Pat Langford, Bill Cameron, Tommy Thompson, George McGill, Keith Ogilvie, and Bob McBride had to dump some extra clothing or blankets they were carrying for warmth, but they did so sensing a stronger urge to escape than to carry protection against the March cold.

"They hoped for the sake of fellas like myself, going hard-ass, that . . . our chances of hiding out in the woods or getting something to eat would be a little better," Ogilvie said, "but it was really cold and frosty."[21]

By four o'clock in the morning, the experienced members of the escape team had been clearing documents, hauling trolleys, rescuing escapers, re-shoring walls and ceilings, re-dispersing sand, and coaxing the system for more than seven hours. About sixty men had been relayed through "Harry" in that time. Dawn was less than two hours away, so Pengelly and Ker-Ramsey made the decision to call off anyone holding an escape number greater than one hundred. They were all told to stow their forged documents away, eat their escape rations, and hide whatever escape clothing they could. The escape committee hoped it could squeeze twenty or twenty-five more men through "Harry" by 5 a.m. and then close the tunnel down before the Germans learned anyone had escaped.

Meanwhile, there was another holdup at the exit hole. Roy Langlois had just relieved Canadian George McGill at the ferret blind in the woods when he signalled another halt in the flow of escapers; he'd heard a shout coming from the guard tower. One of the sentries pacing along the fence was summoned by the tower guard—the two had apparently agreed to switch places for some reason. Then the tower guard climbed down, crossed the snow-covered road, and began walking directly toward the tunnel hole. Langlois, still hiding behind the blind in the woods, thought for sure the goon had spotted the steam rising from the tunnel hole. He was coming straight for it. Then, suddenly, the guard stopped, took down his trousers, and squatted to relieve himself. Five minutes later, the guard departed, Langlois tugged on the rope, and escapers began moving again.

It was close to 4:50 a.m. when the controllers in Hut 104 decided it was time to shut things down. They needed to determine who the final escapers would be and give the trolley haulers—Shag Rees, Red Noble, and Tim Newman—enough time to haul them to the exit hole and then get themselves up the escape ladder and out as well. Then, the trap over "Harry" back in Room 23 of Hut 104 could be resealed and rooms around the stove returned to normal. It appeared the last group of escapers would include Lawrence Reavell-Carter, Keith Ogilvie, Michael Shand, Len Trent, Bob McBride, Roger Maw, Michael Ormond, Ian Muir, Clive Saxelby, Jack Moul, and Frank Sorensen. Mac Reilley had taken Tony Pengelly's number, ninety-three, but just missed the cut-off.

"There I sat in Hut 104, waiting the night away," Reilley wrote. "Frank Sorensen . . . was sitting with his legs reaching for the ladder to descend into the tunnel when it all ended."[22]

Langlois was still positioned at the blind just inside the pine forest, marshalling his group of ten men to safety. He directed Spitfire pilot Ogilvie and burly air-gunner Reavell-Carter to his position just hidden by the pines. Next, Michael Shand, another Spitfire pilot, emerged from the tunnel exit and began crawling through the snow toward Langlois at the end of the signal rope. Right behind him was Len Trent, the Victoria Cross winner from New Zealand. Suddenly, Shand and Trent felt the rope guiding them to the blind jerk again; it was Langlois, trying to get them to stop. A guard, formerly pacing close to the fence, had deviated from his sentry's path and was stepping through the snow right toward the escape hole, as if something had attracted his attention. Shand and Trent stopped dead in the path. The guard kept coming, nearly stepping into the hole; he still hadn't seen the two air officers prostrate on the snow. Then, recognizing

Shand's human shape in the slush path to the woods, the guard lifted and aimed his rifle.

"*Nicht schiessen!* [Don't shoot!]" Reavell-Carter shouted as he jumped from behind the brush pile in the woods.

Startled by the kriegie shouting and leaping into the open, the guard pulled the trigger on his rifle, but the bullet didn't hit anybody. Reavell-Carter had no choice but to surrender. Trent did the same. When the guard finally shone his flashlight down at the exit hole, next to where he was standing, there was Bob McBride, perched on the top rung of the ladder and waiting his turn to crawl out; with no other option available, he also surrendered. To add to the alarm, the guard began blowing his warning whistle.

That night, Don Edy had slept fitfully in Hut 123, where tunnel "Tom" had originated. He remembered the eerie stillness of the dawn broken with that single rifle shot at the north end of the compound. He and his roommates didn't dare go to the windows to see the Germans' reaction. They just stayed in bed and listened.[23] George Sweanor had gone to bed fully clothed, wearing socks, boots; he'd even stuck food in his pockets[24] because he figured when the Germans got wind of the escape there would likely be an all-day appell and probably ration cuts. When he and his roommates heard the gunfire and whistle blowing, they pried open the shutters covering a window at Hut 119 and saw some of the escapers in Hut 104 attempting to race back to their home huts. More gunfire and the *hundführer* racing into the compound soon stopped that.[25] Inside Hut 104 the secretive quiet was suddenly broken.

"All hell broke loose," said Gordon King, who'd been at the base of the entry shaft pumping air through the bellows much of the night. "Some of [the kriegies] stupidly ran out of the hut. They could have been shot doing it."[26]

Tunnel controller Ker-Ramsey and forgery chief Pengelly reacted to the rifle shot in an instant. They passed along the order throughout Hut 104 for all forged papers and escape kits to be destroyed. Within minutes there were small fires burning up and down the halls and in every room of the hut. The next order was a full retreat from the tunnel. In moments, Tim Newman was thundering back from Piccadilly halfway house to the entry shaft, Ian Muir right behind him. Michael Ormond wasn't long after. Finally, the trolley haulers—Red Noble, Roger Maw, and Shag Rees—began to withdraw. As he turned to retreat from Piccadilly, Rees was squeezed out of the way by the two escapers who'd been at the base of the exit shaft—Jack Moul and Clive Saxelby. With the tunnel mouth discovered, Rees felt for sure there'd be a ferret on his tail in seconds. And yet each time he looked ahead all he saw was "Sax's bum blocking the way."[27]

With the last man up the shaft and out of "Harry," the trap was sealed as quickly as it ever had been over the previous year. The stove was replaced. And blankets that had been used to muffle the sound and hide any excess sand quickly disappeared into nearby bunks. By the time a *hundführer* entered the block, a few minutes later, much of the obviously incriminating evidence had vanished. The German guard gathered a few greatcoats lying around in the halls and waited. His dog curled up on the coats and went to sleep.

"Our mad haste was really unnecessary," John R. Harris said. "A German guard coming on duty had accidentally sighted [escapee Michael Shand] leaving the tunnel exit and fired a shot, more to attract attention . . . than in hopes of hitting the fleeing prisoner. By the time he succeeded in summoning support and the Germans realized what was going on, we could have burned half the camp down."[28]

For the moment, the real action was happening at the exit end of the tunnel. The sentries were marching Bob McBride, Len Trent, Roy Langlois, and Lawrence Reavell-Carter to the guardhouse. In spite of the rifle shot, most of the compound guards inside were still asleep. As the guards were roused by the sentries, the escapers took advantage of a nearby stove and jettisoned their forged papers into the fire. When he arrived, *Kommandant* von Lindeiner was livid. He demanded to know the number that had escaped, which kriegies had led the escape, and where the tunnel had originated. Finally, he told the four foiled escapers the Gestapo would soon be involved.

"They will shoot you," he predicted, "get rid of the lot of you."[29]

(ABOVE) Under a parole system, German prison officials supplied materials and tools (provided they were all returned each day) so Commonwealth POWs could build a fully functioning theatre in the North Compound in 1943. (TOP RIGHT) Air force officers such as Tony Pengelly (right) took a ribbing for portraying women on stage, but audiences found their looks and performances totally convincing. (BOTTOM RIGHT) Arthur Crighton arranged for donated instruments and uniforms to outfit the theatre pit orchestra. (BELOW) Commonwealth POWs volunteered an array of theatrical talents—as writers, directors, actors, set designers, stage managers, and lighting specialists. Their North Compound theatre had seating for 350 on chairs made from Canadian Red Cross parcel boxes.

Stalag Luft III POWs—particularly those from North America—organized dozens of baseball teams; this one was typical, featuring (back l to r) "Gee" Rainville, Slim Smith, Joe Loree, Stephens, Jimmy Egner, Jimmy Lang, Randy Ransom; (front l to r) Art Hawtin, Earl Clare (team captain), Tommy Jackson, Glen Gardner, Ernie Soalier.

(MIDDLE) Ice hockey games didn't end with regulation time or even sudden death goals, but when the last of the hockey sticks (donated by the Red Cross or stores in Canada) broke beyond repair. (BOTTOM) Boxing matches inside Stalag Luft III, such as one with George McGill and Eddie Asselin in 1942, offered exercise and a diversion while other POWs attempted to escape.

(ABOVE LEFT) RCAF navigator Don McKim, seated at his observer's table during training, and (ABOVE RIGHT) RCAF gunner Albert Wallace, posing atop the Royal Bath Hotel in the UK, did most of their wartime service at Stalag Luft III, in part assisting The Great Escape. (MIDDLE) Without monthly Red Cross parcels containing basic cooking ingredients and so-called "housewife treats," most POWs agreed they wouldn't have survived. (BELOW) Secret photo shows officers operating the hidden wireless radio set inside Stalag Luft III; one tuned in the BBC broadcast, the other took shorthand to share information with fellow officers.

(ABOVE) RAF officer Ley Kenyon captured the climax of The Great Escape in his sketches, including February 29, 1944, when German guards fortuitously transferred key players of the escape committee to a neighbouring prison, and (BELOW) the night of March 24, 1944, when escapers realized their tunnel "Harry" came up short of the pine forest, requiring a rope system to signal when German sentries had passed and another escaper could crawl out and make a run for it.

After German guards discovered the mass breakout and recaptured 77 of the 80 escapers, they displayed the contraptions the POWs had built inside tunnel "Harry." (ABOVE) Prison guard Karl Griese (left) and a second guard show off a tunnel trolley inside shoring box frames (they've got them upside down—frames were narrower at top). (BELOW RIGHT) Griese (a.k.a. "Rubberneck") operates a ventilating pump that kept fresh air flowing underground through nearly 400 feet of Klim tins soldered together. (BELOW LEFT) Guard demonstrates sand-dispersal sacks hidden under POWs' coats and inside trousers. In over a year of tunnel excavation at Stalag Luft III, "penguins" dispersed several hundred tons of sand from tunnel "Harry" alone.

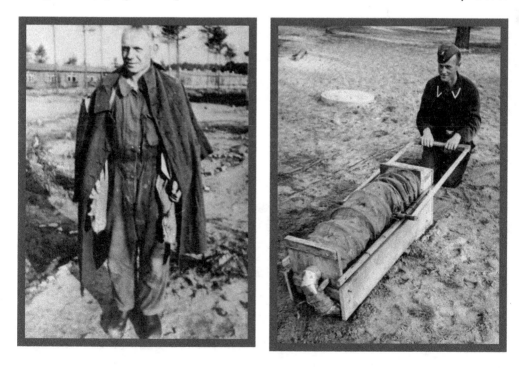

(ABOVE) Senior British Officer G/C Herbert Massey (right) speaks to German officer Hans Pieber, who guarded Commonwealth air officer POWs at both Stalag Luft I and III; also in charge during the forced march in the winter of 1945 (he then knowingly carried the POWs' secret radio to receive BBC broadcasts about the war). (BELOW) Controversial crime investigator and SS officer Arthur Nebe is said to have soured on Nazi philosophy (extermination of European Jewry and executions of Russian civilians) and joined the plot to kill Hitler in July 1944; however, he was guilty of choosing 50 of the recaptured Great Escapers to be executed.

(LEFT) In 1962, at a movie set built to look like Stalag Luft III near Munich, Germany, former escape tunnel designer Wally Floody (middle) chats with James Coburn (left) and Charles Bronson during the filming of *The Great Escape*. (BELOW) Playing the part of an American in the RAF, James Garner (left), becomes the POW camp "scrounger," a role actually performed by a Canadian. Steve McQueen's character, Capt. Virgil Hilts, was totally fabricated. (BOTTOM) Floody became technical advisor for director John Sturges (left) as well as actors McQueen and Angus Lennie (right). The finished feature film cost $4 million and grossed more than $11 million in 1963.

(ABOVE RIGHT) This secretly photographed image of Allied air force officers being force-marched from Sagan, Poland, was taken in January 1945. Indicative of their skill to adapt, in just hours, the POWs transformed prison camp tables, chairs, and bed boards into sleds and backpacks to carry survival gear. (ABOVE LEFT) Just before their liberation in western Germany, the POWs posted signs to prevent being shelled or strafed by friendly forces.

Throughout the winter forced march, RCAF pilot Frank Sorensen carried in his pocket this Ley Kenyon sketch of the memorial (built in 1944) to the 50 murdered officers—the stone monument remains intact northwest of the Stalag Luft III site today.

On the involvement of forces outside the camp he was right. Within an hour of the discovery of the tunnel, seventy German troops equipped with helmets, machine guns, and Schmeisser automatic pistols arrived at the compound and surrounded Hut 104. Even von Lindeiner, Hans Pieber, and Broili had their revolvers drawn. Over a hundred kriegies began to emerge from the barracks building to face an armed force that didn't seem the least bit interested in upholding the Geneva Conventions. Outside Hut 104, snow began to fall. The ferrets forced many of the men to strip to their skin. Every man was searched. All the civilian clothes accumulated or altered by Tommy Guest's tailoring crew were thrown into a pile, leaving most of the kriegies in little more than their underwear against the cold. John R. Harris was wearing clothes that looked more like his uniform, not civilian clothing, so he didn't have to strip. He tossed a blanket that hadn't been confiscated to a fellow kriegie without any clothes. Harris had forgotten, however, that he and his partner still possessed an obvious connection to the escape.

"Did you burn the maps?"[30] Johnny Crozier, his escape buddy, suddenly asked.

"What maps?"

"The ones I gave you inside," Crozier reminded him.

Des Plunkett's mapmakers had given most of the hard-arser kriegies maps that would guide them away from Stalag Luft III. Since Crozier and Harris would be travelling together outside the wire, the pair had been given a set of nine stencilled maps showing them the country from Sagan south to the Czech border. But in the confusion following the rifle shot and the closing of "Harry" an hour earlier, both men had forgotten to destroy the evidence.

"You never gave me any maps, Johnny," Harris insisted.

That's when Crozier realized they were still in his pocket. The Germans could quickly determine the routes the other escapers might be taking if they suddenly came into possession of the stencilled maps in Crozier's pocket. He and Harris had to get rid of them. And fast.

"Fortunately, I had read many thrillers in my boyhood," Harris wrote. "We could eat the maps. And that's just what we did, along with the help of any other prisoners to whom we could surreptitiously pass a map. Some of those fellows never spoke a friendly word to Johnny or me again."[31]

Nine stencilled maps were the least of the *Kommandant* von Lindeiner's worries. Inside Room 23 of Hut 104, a ferret who had entered the tunnel from the exit hole outside the wire had made his way back to the entrance shaft. With "Harry's" entire length now exposed and nothing left to hide, Red Noble opened the trapdoor to let the man out. Noble and Shag Rees were then ordered outside, where Rubberneck relished the moment of humiliating his nemeses, tearing off their civilian clothes. Noble and Rees pushed back, ready to fight. Rubberneck reached for his revolver. Von Lindeiner intervened and had the two kriegies marched, in the nude, to the cooler. But the German colonel had yet to face the toughest truth of the entire episode.

"At last an appell was called," Don Edy remembered, "and everyone was turned out onto the sport field under heavy guard. The Germans were beyond themselves with rage. So we did nothing to provoke them further."[32]

Out came boxes with the name and photograph of every prisoner in the compound neatly catalogued and filed. It took two hours, but every man was identified and accounted for as he stood in the snow. More stressful to von Lindeiner was the process of elimination: Who was missing? As the list of escapers rose eventually to the seventy-six who had managed to get away from the North Compound, George Sweanor watched the *Kommandant*'s face grow pale. Eventually, he left the compound. Von Lindeiner knew that not only had he failed to keep prisoners of war from escaping, but he was also now in danger of violating the *Aktion Kugel* and *Stufe Römisch* III orders by not immediately handing over the four escapers his men had recaptured at the exit hole to the Gestapo.

"Gentlemen," Hans Pieber said to the kriegies as von Lindeiner left the compound, "you should not have done that to him."[33]

After the camp offices had completed the inventory of those present or absent, all remaining kriegies were dismissed back to their huts, except those from Hut 104. They stood virtually naked under guard for another hour before the Schmeisser-wielding guards allowed them to dress and re-enter their block. That afternoon, von Lindeiner learned that sixteen escaped officers had been recaptured and were being held at the Sagan civil police station. In spite of the two German High Command orders to the contrary, he demanded his prisoners be returned to the camp. He placed dozens more phone calls, notifying railways stations, airfields, border crossings, and even port authorities along the Baltic about the breakout.

Meantime, Max Wielen, the head of *Kripo* at Breslau, issued *Kriegsfahndung*, a nationwide manhunt order, and then *Grossfahndung*, the highest alert to police stations across the region, advising them to hold recaptured prisoners under the *Stufe Römisch* III order. Just as Big X had hoped and expected, the manhunt diverted the energies of police, SS, armed forces, Hitler Youth, the Home Guard Air Raid Precaution personnel, and civilian searchers—some seventy thousand Germans[34]—away from the war effort to the recapture of the officers who'd escaped from Stalag Luft III.* Later the same day, Saturday, March 25, the German counter-intelligence chief, SS Major Brünner arrived at the Sagan-area prison compound with orders to arrest von Lindeiner in preparation for his court-martial over the escape. The sixty-four-year-old colonel suffered a non-fatal heart attack over the matter.

The North Compound experienced an eerie calm after the original storm on Saturday. All the stories of the events of the mass escape the previous night circulated from hut to hut around the camp. However, scuttlebutt about the seventy-six escapers remained scarce. Von Lindeiner was replaced with a temporary *Kommandant*. Initially, that didn't change things, but the sequence of events that had sealed von Lindeiner's fate was about to overtake the kriegies and the escapers as well.

A Canadian flying officer from Winnipeg was shot down the same weekend as the breakout. At twenty-six, Gordon Venables was older

---

* Paul Brickhill suggests information gathered from the tamed German guards at Stalag Luft III put the total number of Germans—military and civilian—involved in the search for the escaped POWs closer to five million.

than most RCAF aircrew, and when he tumbled into a farm field that night he broke his leg. F/O Venables came through the prisoner-of-war delivery system in the middle of all the post-escape upheaval. Luftwaffe medical staff set his leg, but he was soon on the move to Stalag Luft III. He was fortunate not to have been swept up and dispensed with in the *Stufe Römisch* order, but still endured a rough passage to the POW camp. German civilians were riled up by increased Allied bombing attacks on their cities and by the highly publicized mass escape.

"I had a broomstick for a cane,"[35] Venables said. "We arrived at the train station. People were everywhere. To my surprise, a compartment was cleared of passengers for [the guard and me. We] had to change trains at Frankfurt. The city had been heavily bombed . . . with severe damage and loss of lives. He told me to stay close to him as the people were very angry and liable to turn on me. He put me in the cab of the engine, away from the civilians [until] we arrived at the POW camp near Sagan."

On April 1, 1944, exactly a week after the breakout, the Gestapo arrived at the North Compound and the mass searches of men, belongings, and barracks huts resumed. As usual, the Gestapo men appeared ham-fisted as prison guards, until they started handing out summary judgments. When they inspected "Harry," the first thing they spotted was the string of lights up the tunnel. They grilled all the German electricians involved in maintaining the camp, forcing two to confess that the theft of the wire had gone unreported. Gestapo men promptly shot the two men. Next they shot the supervisor for not acknowledging the loss and punished two more prison guards for possessing morsels of food that had come from the prisoners' Red Cross parcels. The newly installed *Kommandant*, *Oberst* Braune, announced there would be four appells a day. He closed the theatre, stopped all mail in and out, and dumped wagon-loads of raw human sewage down the entry shaft of tunnel "Harry."[36]

What kriegies had known as a "spine-tingling sport" at best, and an uncomfortable existence at worst, was taking a deadly turn.

# THE HATE CAMPAIGN

T HE FATE of the hard-arsers—as Big X had accurately predicted—was pretty much in their own hands. Or, in the case
of New Zealand officer Michael Shand and Canadian officer
Keith Ogilvie, their feet. When the guard outside the Stalag Luft III
fence fired his rifle, Shand, who was already in the woods, bolted in
one direction while Ogilvie crawled for about a hundred and fifty
feet, stood up, and started to run in another direction.[1] Whether
from fear of being caught by prison guards and interrogated by the
Gestapo or just from the shock of the late winter conditions on his
system, Skeets kept on running for most of the next forty-eight hours.
Perhaps the last kriegie to get away that morning, he had planned to
make his way toward Czechoslovakia, but all that mattered initially
was to get clear of the compound and the search parties that would
inevitably be on his trail. He simply ran west, but since snow covered
much of the countryside, he tried to find less travelled roads to put
as much distance between himself and the compound as quickly as
possible.

"I ran out of food and it was still wet in the trees and the snow.
And you couldn't sleep," Ogilvie said. "Bloody miserable."[2]

By Sunday night, he'd managed to cover almost forty miles and
had reached a major road heading south toward the Czech border.
But the moment he left the relative cover of remote roads and forested areas, Ogilvie—dressed in army battledress and a greatcoat—

was spotted by members of the German Home Guard near Halbau, Germany, and taken to a local inn. Knowing his escape bid was over, en route to interrogation, he tore up the maps and forged identification in his pockets[3] and discreetly dropped the pieces when the guards weren't looking. The inn proved to be a holding cell for several recaptured kriegies. Before long, Ogilvie was joined by RAF officers Charles Hall and Brian Evans as well as Canadian countryman Tommy Thompson. The three had linked up with another Canadian, Bill Cameron, outside the wire in the pine woods shortly after the Germans sounded the alarm at 5 o'clock on the morning of the escape. Within a few hours, Cameron began suffering from exposure to the cold. Hall, Evans, and Thompson wrapped him in all the warm clothing and blankets they could spare, left him some rations, and pressed on.[4] Cameron was soon recaptured near Sagan, the others by the Home Guard in the same region as Ogilvie.

Until early 1944, German police had held very little jurisdiction over recaptured prisoners of war and generally, after brief questioning, returned them to German Armed Forces; in short, the Gestapo could not punish them. In February 1944, however, Heinrich Himmler's *Aktion Kugel*, or Operation Bullet, had wrenched control of recaptured POWs from the military, in this case the Luftwaffe at Stalag Luft III, and given it to the Gestapo. Under Bullet, recaptured prisoners other than British or American were to be taken to Mauthausen concentration camp and exterminated. It didn't matter whether the escape occurred in transit, in a mass breakout, or singly— all recaptured POWs would be turned over to the secret police, not the military authorities, as quietly as possible.

By coincidence, the same weekend of the mass breakout from Stalag Luft III, the leaders of the German Prisoner of War Directorate were en route to Berchtesgaden. They arrived at the Führer's Bavarian headquarters in the midst of a tempest. Hitler, Heinrich Himmler, Hermann Göring, and Wilhelm Keitel had been conferring since word of the mass escape from the North Compound had arrived. Amid the accusations and laying of blame, Hitler decreed that all recaptured escapers would be shot. Göring protested. Ultimately, the weekend conference at Berchtesgaden decided on the number of Commonwealth air officers to be executed. That night, Himmler issued the "Sagan Order" to the POW Directorate and quickly altered the operations at police and military prisons across Hitler's occupied Europe. Those moves had life and death consequences for the prisoners of war detained in them.

The Sagan Order began by describing the increased number of POW escapes as "a menace to internal security." Adolf Hitler had initially demanded all eighty Commonwealth air officers who made it out of the tunnel be shot. Ultimately, however, the Sagan Order decreed that "more than half of the escaped officers . . . after interrogation . . . are to be returned to their original camp and to be shot en route." Had Hitler's order been carried out to the letter, the Sagan Order might have meant forty killings. But the arithmetic appeared to be lost in the Gestapo's eagerness to retaliate. Fifty would be killed. Finally, the order spelled out how the killings would be covered up, by declaring that "the recaptured officers were shot whilst trying to escape."[5]

The man given the job of choosing which fifty men would die was *SS Gruppenführer* Arthur Nebe. At age fifty, the former First World War explosives soldier turned police detective had served the Nazi Party, the state police, *Kripo*, and the SS *Reichssicherheitshauptamt*, or RSHA. Three days after the escape from Stalag Luft III, Nebe began receiving daily telegrams on those kriegies the manhunt had recaptured. He then sat in his Berlin office with each POW's identity card and his record sheet and played god. The factors influencing Nebe's decision were the prisoner's age and life status: middle-aged with a family, he lived; not too young and unmarried, he died. In addition, if the POW had led groups of escapers because of his fluency in various languages—a so-called "linguist"[6]—the Gestapo considered him dangerous and therefore expendable. The air officer's place of birth was a deciding factor too: almost all men of non-British origin and "an unduly high percentage of men from the Dominions"[7] received Nebe's death sentence. His decisions were passed to subordinate Gestapo officials, first Max Wielen, the *Kripo* chief, and then to the

chief of the Breslau Gestapo, *Oberregierungsrat* Wilhelm Scharpwinkel. It was up to Scharpwinkel to organize the execution squads and
fulfill the Sagan Order.

Late in the evening on Sunday, March 26, security guards escorted
Keith Ogilvie and thirty-four other escapers to a Gestapo prison at
Görlitz, ironically near the Czech border where so many of them had
been headed. Three days later, Gestapo interrogators there questioned Ogilvie about the escape and its organization.

"I'm a British officer and it's my duty to escape,"[8] he parroted
back, and then remained silent to further questioning.

During his interrogation, an interpreter translated his statements
as a female typist recorded them. When the questioning ended, the
interpreter turned to Ogilvie and said, "The young lady [typist] said
you are lucky. You have escaped in a soldier's uniform. Therefore you
will be tried before a military court. The others will not be so lucky."[9]

Tommy Thompson's interrogation at Görlitz, also on March
29, proved more confrontational and frightening over the issue of
whether he was who he said he was and the protection of his rights as
a military officer. When the Gestapo interrogator demanded information about the breakout, Thompson refused to answer.

"I must warn you," the interrogator said. "You are not the in hands
of military authorities, but . . . the secret service. Anything might happen to you without protection and you may never go back to your
camp."[10]

"Despite whose hands I am in, I [am] protected by the Geneva
Convention," Thompson protested.

The interrogator half laughed, and even when Thompson presented his identity tags the man waved them aside. Ultimately,
Thompson managed to convince his questioner that his clothes
were indeed military dress. "You are lucky," the Gestapo man said
finally. "You are recognized as military. The rest are wanted for civil
investigation."

The contradiction of the next hours for Ogilvie, Thompson, and
others, proved to be watching Commonwealth officers clearly dressed
in the air force battledress (he saw George Wiley in his Canadian blue

battledress and John E. "Willy" Williams in his Australian airman's tunic with flight-lieutenant stripes visible) being led away from the prison. Following his interrogation, Keith Ogilvie was returned to a cell with fellow escapers Charles Hall, Neville McGarr, and Paul Royle; the cell was so small that all four men had to either stand or lie down at the same time. A few days later, Ogilvie spotted a German corporal he knew from Stalag Luft III outside his Görlitz cell.

"Say, Horst, when are you gonna get me out of this place?" he asked.

"Oh, Mr. Ogilvie, tomorrow morning you'll go,"[11] the guard said. Indeed, the next day Luftwaffe guards arrived and escorted Ogilvie and seven others back to Sagan. Only one of his cellmates—Australian Paul Royle—was with him; Briton Charles Hall was taken from Görlitz prison March 30, and South African Neville McGarr disappeared April 6. Some time later, the eight survivors of the Görlitz imprisonment and interrogation learned the fate of the other twenty-eight kriegies held there.

On Thursday, March 30, *Oberregierungsrat* Scharpwinkel and his staff arrived at Görlitz to carry out the Sagan Order. First the Commonwealth officers—Squadron Leader Ian Cross, Flight Lieutenants Mike Casey, Tom Leigh, and George Wiley, and Flying Officers John Pohe and Al Hake—were collected by the dozen Gestapo men in civilian clothes and pushed into three waiting cars. Other recaptured officers looking through prison windows knew Hake was suffering from frostbite and assumed the men in civilian clothes were escorting the air force officers in the cars to a hospital. They were actually going to the local *Kripo* headquarters for interrogation.

"I went to Görlitz," Scharpwinkel* said, "for the purpose of getting a picture of the prisoners. As I speak English, I put one or two

---

* *Oberregierungsrat* Wilhelm Scharpwinkel, chief of the Gestapo at Breslau, was arrested by the Soviet Army on May 10, 1945. In August 1946, the Soviets allowed Captain M. F. Cornish of the British Intelligence Corps to travel to Moscow to interview Scharpwinkel (under Soviet supervision). His voluntary statement (quoted here) was taken September 19, 1946. He died in a prison in Moscow, October 17, 1947.

questions to the prisoners . . . Were they married? Had they children? I did not ask any questions about how the escape was organized, because I was not interested in that."[12]

The interrogations of the half-dozen Commonwealth officers went on for three and a half hours. *Kriminalinspektor* Richard Max Hänsel*, who was in charge of the local Gestapo office at Görlitz, attended the interrogations. He recalled that interrogators questioned the prisoners one at a time. He said there was no torture, but that the questioning covered name, rank, place and date of birth, previous occupation, unit, targets bombed, where shot down, duration of captivity, organization of the escape, source of civilian clothing, origin of false papers, names of other escapees, and how each had been captured. Hänsel said the interrogation included the confiscation of the prisoners' watches and then a blanket threat from Scharpwinkel directed at everybody—prisoner and guard alike.

"Take care they don't get away," he said. "Otherwise something unpleasant will happen to you. Or something unpleasant will happen to them."[13]

The interrogations wrapped up at 12:30 in the afternoon, when the POWs were again pushed into the waiting cars. As there was insufficient room in the three cars for all the Commonwealth officers and the Gestapo men, Scharpwinkel told Hänsel he would have to drive a service vehicle with two of the POWs and the Gestapo chief to their next destination. The three cars and service truck travelled along the autobahn to a wooded area five miles past Halbau. Scharpwinkel ordered the column of vehicles to stop and the prisoners got out to stretch their legs. Hänsel said he led the two officers in his service truck to the head of the column where the others had gathered and returned to the truck to retrieve his lunch from a briefcase.

---

* *Kriminalinspektor* Richard Max Hänsel, in charge of the Gestapo sub-office at Görlitz, was in British custody by June 20, 1946, and four days later, the Royal Air Force War Crimes Interrogation Unit took a voluntary statement (quoted here) from him. A war crimes trial began in Hamburg on July 1, 1947, and lasted fifty days. The Judge Advocate General determined there was insufficient evidence to convict Hänsel; he was formally acquitted on November 6, 1948.

Two of Scharpwinkel's staff carried sub-machine guns as the Gestapo chief ordered the POWs deeper into the woods.

"The prisoners were placed in position," Scharpwinkel said, "and it was revealed to them that the sentence was about to be carried out. The prisoners showed considerable calm, which surprised me very much."

The six Commonwealth officers—several of them wearing their air force blue battledress, clearly military POWs—stood stationary, side by side in the woods. With a hand movement, *Kriminal Obersekretaer* Lux* gave the order to fire and the execution squad fired a burst into the unarmed prisoners of war. Lux shot the prisoners as well, and by the end of the second salvo, the officers were dead.

"While I was eating my slice of bread and butter," Hänsel said, "several shots were fired. I ran at once to the place in the wood, which was about 150 metres [500 feet] away and learnt . . . that the prisoners had attempted to escape and had been shot in the attempt. They lay sprawling in the wood about four or five metres [15 feet] from each other. . . . I myself do not suppose that the prisoners attempted to escape."[14]

After the shootings, Scharpwinkel ordered Hänsel to drive the service truck into Halbau to arrange for an undertaker to take away the corpses for cremation. When reports of the shootings leaked to the British Government via Switzerland, Hänsel was ordered to another conference, at which Scharpwinkel told him that they were to say that on March 30 their vehicles had broken down along the autobahn and that "the prisoners used this opportunity to attempt an escape."[15]

The great escape had ended in murder for these six Commonwealth air force officers. Mike Casey, the brilliant RAF Blenheim pilot who in the camp had managed to hide the priceless forgery tools from the earliest days of the North Compound, died at that roadside. Also killed there was Australian-born Spitfire pilot Al Hake,

---

* *Kriminal Obersekretaer* Lux was killed during fighting at Breslau in 1944.

who mastered technical drawing and metalwork so well that at Stalag Luft III he created the most sophisticated assembly line for the manufacture of compasses ever generated from thin air. Fellow Australian Tom Leigh was also murdered that afternoon. And New Zealand Flying Officer John Pohe, who had maintained a steadfast sense of humour throughout his imprisonment at Sagan by signing all official papers as a Maori tribesman named Porokoru Patapu.[16] British-born Squadron Leader Ian Cross had previously made an unsuccessful escape attempt, but this time paid with his life. As did Canadian George Wiley, who had no valuables for the Gestapo to confiscate that March 30 afternoon since he'd left his watch and a goodbye letter with his roommate back in North Compound the night of the escape. Somehow Wiley sensed it might end this way.

That night, Scharpwinkel's execution squad made its way back to the Görlitz prison. Through the same evening hours, the undertaker's vehicles arrived at the roadside where Casey, Hake, Leigh, Pohe, Cross, and Wiley had been shot, and the bodies were carried away to Görlitz to be cremated. Two days later, on April 1, the same group of henchmen, led by *Kriminal Obersekretaer* Lux, handcuffed ten more Commonwealth air force officers, drove them away from Görlitz, and killed them en route to Sagan in a similar fashion. This group of murdered officers included Flight Lieutenants Edgar Humphreys, Cyril Swain, Charles Hall, Brian Evans, and Flying Officers Wally Valenta, Wlod Kolanowski, and Bob Stewart.

Also killed in this execution were Canadian X Organization committee members George McGill, Pat Langford, and Hank Birkland. McGill was the RCAF navigator told to bail out of his burning Wellington in January 1942 only to learn later that the pilot had managed to get the bomber safely home to Britain; he'd spent twenty-six months behind wire, providing diversions for other escapers, and had co-led the team keeping all three tunnels secure night and day; he was dead at twenty-five. Also twenty-five, Alberta-born Pat Langford had survived severe burns bailing out of his Wellington in July 1942; a self-taught pianist and multi-faceted athlete, he'd served Canada as an air training instructor, a combat pilot, and at Stalag

Luft III was the man responsible for keeping tunnel "Harry's" trap entrance secret and safe for a year. But perhaps none had given as much of himself to the "operational function" of escaping than Manitoba's Hank Birkland; shot down in his Spitfire in 1941, Birkland had tunnelled at Dulag Luft, Stalag Luft I, and Stalag Luft III, and coped with claustrophobia in a hole, vomiting from lack of oxygen, and the challenge of tearing tons of earth from beneath his captives' feet to help his air force mates escape. At the end of three years underground, Big Train had tasted only a few hours of freedom for himself.

In total, Lux's shooters were responsible for murdering twenty-seven of the officers recaptured following the mass breakout on the morning of March 25. Simultaneously, another execution squad assembled at a police prison in Zlin, Moravia, where two more of the Commonwealth officers had been brought for interrogation. Despite being temporarily buried in sand during the cave-in the night of the escape, Tom Kirby-Green had emerged from "Harry" thirtieth on the escape list. Canadian Gordon Kidder came through the exit hole right behind him. The two were masquerading as migrant Spanish workers; both were fluent in German, French, and Spanish, so their linguistic abilities put them high on Nebe's hit list. They had managed to get through the air-raid blackout at the Sagan station and over the next three days travelled by train unnoticed as far south as Hodonin, in Moravia, where they were recaptured. Severe interrogation went on for twenty-four hours. Then, about 2 a.m. on March 29, under the direction of *Polizeiassistant* Erich Zacharias, Kidder and Kirby-Green were loaded into two cars, apparently for the trip back to Breslau. One of the two Gestapo drivers, Friedrich Kiowsky, recalled the prisoners being manacled with their hands in front of them.

"As I was driving, I asked [Erich] Zacharias what was going to happen to them," Kiowsky reported. "Zacharias sat beside me and said nothing, but turned his thumb downwards. . . . At the same time he told me to drive slower and looked around the countryside."[17]

About six miles from Moravska Ostrava, Zacharias ordered Kiowsky to stop his vehicle at the side of the road. Without realizing it, Gordon Kidder played into Zacharias's hands by asking if he could relieve himself. Zacharias directed Kidder and Kirby-Green (from the second vehicle) with their guard Adolf Knueppelberg to the curb. It was all going according to the Gestapo plan.

"Knueppelberg raised his right hand holding the pistol, with the barrel pointing in the direction of the back of [Kirby-Green's] head,"[18] Zacharias said. "I drew my service pistol, which was all ready for firing . . . and fired obliquely in the left side of my prisoner [Kidder] in order to hit his heart."*

To complete his action, Zacharias fired a second shot at Kidder's head, then crouched to check for a pulse and called to Knueppelberg** to make sure that Kirby-Green was also dead. When the first shots were fired, Kiowsky, then lighting the cigarette of the fellow driver, turned to see what had happened. First he saw blood all over the snow, then the two air force officers lying dead in the ditch, and finally the two senior Gestapo officials removing the handcuffs from Kidder and Kirby-Green. Half an hour later, a van from the Czech police force arrived to pick up the bodies. Gestapo higher ups told all those present to report that the two air force officers had been shot while attempting to escape.

"I saw nothing that gave me the impression that the officers had wished to escape or had made the attempt,"*** Kiowsky said. [19]

Among the other Commonwealth officers murdered outside Hirschberg by Lux, was James Wernham, the Winnipegger who had survived the first thousand-bomber raid on Cologne in May 1942

---

* In 1945, Gestapo officer Erich Zacharias managed to acquire papers from American occupation authorities in Germany identifying him as a Customs official with no Nazi record. He was eventually traced to a refrigeration plant in Wesermünde and arrested; he escaped and was recaptured April 1, 1946. His voluntary statement (quoted here) was taken April 12, 1946. He was found guilty of murder and hanged at Hameln jail on February 27, 1948.

** At the end of the war in Europe, Gestapo NCO Adolf Knueppelberg was in the (Soviet) Red Army Camp 33, near Brno, and prematurely released. He was never arrested.

*** In the fall of 1945, Gestapo driver Friedrich Kiowsky was arrested by the Czech police. His testimony and February 22, 1946, voluntary statement (quoted here) implicated Zacharais and Knueppelberg in the murders of Kidder and Kirby-Green, but he was found guilty and executed in Czechoslovakia in 1947.

and then the rigours of numerous productions in front of kriegies at the North Compound theatre. Meanwhile, Nils Fugelsang and fellow Norwegian officer Halldor Espelid, who'd been given Canadian pilot Dick Bartlett's escape number just before the breakout, together had attempted to make their way to Denmark; they were recaptured near Kiel on March 26 and then handed over to a hired Gestapo gunman, SS *Sturmbannführer* Johannes Post.* In a most macabre sequence of events, Post interrogated Espelid, Fugelsang, New Zealander Arnold Christensen, and James Catanach, the Australian bomber pilot decorated with the DFC and promoted to squadron leader in 1942 when he was only twenty.

Following his orders with particular zeal, Post had manacled the four air force officers with handcuffs behind their backs and loaded them into two cars—Espelid, Fugelsang, and Christensen into one vehicle, and Catanach into the other, Post's own staff car. En route through the city of Kiel, Post had directed his driver stop at a residence so that he could pass on a set of theatre tickets that (because of Post's orders to execute the prisoners that afternoon) he would not be able to use. Post even chatted to Catanach about the landmarks the vehicle passed, Catanach noting that he recognized them from previous combat operations over Kiel. Suddenly Post remarked, "I am going to shoot you."[20]

Catanach smiled at what he thought a tasteless joke and countered, "I have an appointment in the cooler at Stalag Luft III."

"Those are my orders," Post confirmed. At a field outside of Kiel, the destination Post had chosen to carry out the order, he ordered his prisoner out of the car and repeated his statement, "I have orders to shoot you." In the awkwardness of moving into the field on the premise of allowing the POW to relieve himself, Post's nervous assistant gunman accidentally fired a shot from his pistol. Afraid the man might botch the execution, Post pulled out his own pistol and shot Catanach through the heart. Moments later, when the second car arrived, Christensen, Espelid, and Fugelsang were quickly escorted

---

* SS *Sturmbannführer* Johannes Post was executed at Hameln jail on February 27, 1948.

to the same spot and shot at close range. Post later claimed proudly it was he who had killed "these terror-fliers. . . . For the glory of the Führer I have killed any number of sub-humans."[21]

While the Gestapo squads translated Nebe's paperwork to physical execution for some, those spared his death sentence were returned to do time in the cooler at Stalag Luft III. First, Bernard "Pop" Green and Doug Poynter arrived from Hirschberg. Alex Neely arrived from Berlin. Next, the first of the Canadians, Keith Ogilvie and Tommy Thompson, came back from Görlitz with Alistair McDonald and Paul Royle. Also transported from Görlitz back to Sagan were Shorty Armstrong, Tony Bethell, Les Brodrick, Dick Churchill, Johnny Marshall, Michael Shand, Bob Nelson* and Canadian Bill Cameron. The cooler at the North Compound was so busy following the mass escape, each cell contained four or five men. But the arithmetic quickly became obvious. Of the eighty kriegies who'd emerged from the tunnel the week before, only fifteen were back in the compound. And when the officers emerged from the cooler to share their individual stories, they tried to calculate what had happened to the scores of others they had seen recaptured.

It took nearly two weeks, but the ripple effect of the Sagan Order finally arrived at the North Compound on April 6, 1944. As George Sweanor remembered it, Hans Pieber came into the compound late that morning and summoned Group Captain Massey to a meeting with *Oberst* Braune at the *Kommandantur*. Leaning on his cane and accompanied by Squadron Leader Philip Murray, his personal interpreter, Massey accompanied Pieber out of the compound. The two Senior British Officers were inside the *Kommandantur* less than thirty minutes. Just after noon, word spread that a senior man from every room was expected in the theatre on the double. In minutes, three hundred kriegies occupied the Red Cross crate seats.

---

* When Bob Nelson and Dick Churchill considered their good fortune at being sent back to Stalag Luft III and not shot, the two men speculated that perhaps SS *Gruppenführer* Arthur Nebe recognized their surnames had historical significance to Britons and didn't want to tempt fate.

"As senior man in my room I left on the run," Sweanor wrote. "Massey limped onto the stage and came right out with, 'The new *Kommandant* has just informed me of the shocking, unbelievable news that forty-one of the escaping officers have been shot.'

"I was half expecting such an announcement. I raced back to my room to report. 'The bastards have shot forty-one!' I repeated the SBO's words."[22]

One of Sweanor's hut mates mocked him for being so gullible. He said the announcement was just a bluff to stop the remaining kriegies from attempting another escape. Sweanor hoped his fellow officer was right, but knew the news of the executions had to be true. Amplifying his certainty, Sweanor heard Hans Pieber imploring the kriegies not to blame the Luftwaffe. The shootings were committed by the Gestapo in response to the escape, he emphasized, not by his air force.

When Keith Ogilvie finished his term in the cooler, he immediately ran into Red Noble and got the latest news.

"They shot all those guys," Noble said, "trying to escape."

"That's not so, Red," Ogilvie retorted. "These guys were fine. I saw them. There's no way they could re-escape."[23] Until then, Ogilvie considered his brush with the Gestapo as little more than a fling away from the camp. All he and his mates wanted was to get back to the air force camp and wait for the end of the war.

A few days later, the Germans posted a comprehensive list of the officers shot. Someone counted the names. There were forty-seven names on it, not forty-one! Among the revised list of dead was Big X. Roger Bushell and Free-French officer Bernard Scheidhauer had been captured en route to France at Saarbrücken station and executed nearby on March 29. Also shot that day by the Danzig Gestapo were Gordon Brettell, who had escaped previously with Canadian Kingsley Brown in 1943, and Tim Walenn, the man who had directed many of the camp's printers, journalists, artists, cartoonists, photographers, and calligraphers in the production of official documents—all perfect forgeries—to ease the passage of his fellow escapers.

News of the shootings reached Britain in mid-May. Anthony Eden, the British secretary for foreign affairs, informed the House of Commons that word of the deaths had come from Switzerland. Then, in late June, he rose in Parliament to announce that official word had come from the German government about the deaths of fifty officers. The official German note claimed "the escapes were systematically prepared, partly by the General Staffs of the Allies, [with] both political and military objectives [that endangered] public security in Germany." Eden scoffed at Germany's contention the officers had met their deaths while escaping Stalag Luft III or resisting recapture. He accused Germany of "cold-blooded acts of butchery" and vowed His Majesty's Government would track down "these foul criminals . . . to the last man. When the war is over," Eden said finally, "they will be brought to exemplary justice."[24]

There were still Stalag Luft III prisoners of war who believed the trickle of information, the posted lists of dead officers, and even the Gestapo purge at the camp had all been a bluff to cow the remaining POWs into total compliance. The Germans couldn't have stooped to murdering all those air force officers, some kriegies insisted. Then, pieces of military kit, suitcases, and some personal effects the escapers had carried through the tunnel and into the Silesian countryside were delivered to huts in the North Compound. Belongings such as shoes, handkerchiefs, and even bloodstained personal photographs were brought to the SBO. Ultimately, all doubt about the finality of events following the breakout of March 24–25 were put to rest the day *Kommandant* Braune delivered urns of cremated ashes to Group Captain Wilson. And it didn't take the SBO to deduce why the fifty had been cremated. Ashes would offer no evidence of the cause of death.

"[It proved] that this had been a deliberate massacre,"[25] George Sweanor wrote. "I could not forget my old school chum, George McGill, nor the boyish face of Tom Leigh, nor my boss, a man with an envious war record, Tom Kirby-Green. . . . What a terrible loss to humanity."

McGill's ashes came from Leignitz, Sweanor remembered, Tom Leigh's from Görlitz, and Tim Walenn's from Danzig. He concluded from the locations of the crematoria engraved on the urns that many of the escapers had covered great distances before being recaptured and killed. Sweanor found some solace in knowing that the Germans had expended millions of man-hours away from the frontlines tracking down George McGill, his classmate from St. Clair Public School in Toronto. Eventually, as if reuniting the dead men with their wartime comrades, the remaining Commonwealth officers gathered and housed the fifty urns in a building inside the wire of the North Compound. One of the kriegies who had created so many of the theatre production sets, Wylton Todd, volunteered to design a permanent memorial and the new *Kommandant* provided stone for the masons among the POWs to build a crypt that would contain the urns.

"A committee was formed to collect the belongings of the fifty and to put all up for auction with the proceeds going to their families after the war,"[26] Sweanor wrote. "We gave promissory notes for payments and bid outrageous prices to show our sympathy: $200 for a pair of running shoes, $50 for a razor, and $15 for a handkerchief."

Even Staff Sergeant Hermann Glemnitz, still on duty at the North Compound, attended the highly publicized auction. He got swept up in the spirit of fundraising and could be heard urging the kriegies to bid higher for the benefit of the dead airmen's families. Among the auction items that drew particular attention, Tom Kirby-Green's wooden suitcase went for twenty-five pounds and some of the personal clothing of Canadian airman Pat Langford earned 104 pounds. To commemorate the fifty murdered air force officers, kriegies wore whatever black insignia they could find—black ties, black hats, black diamond cutouts sewn to their sleeves—to indicate they were in mourning. Though it was forbidden to sing it, at every opportunity in front of their captors, the kriegies sang "God Save the King," if only because, as Tony Pengelly put it, "we sang it and felt better."[27] The POWs considered every possible act of stubbornness, inaction, and passive resistance they could conceive as a protest to the killings.

George Sweanor didn't agree with the tactics, fearing their campaign of hatred might bring even more reprisals. He was right. The tit-for-tat psychological warfare inside the wire continued seemingly without end. *Kommandant* Braune responded to kriegie insolence by withholding incoming mail for six weeks. When Pieber conducted his roll calls, the prisoners made life miserable for him, ridiculing his *appell*, resisting his demands, and interfering wherever they could. One day, when the innocuous guard looked totally demoralized, George Sweanor took pity on him. They happened to be walking side by side across the compound.

"Cheer up, Pieber," Sweanor said. "We can't keep this up forever." Pieber flashed a quick smile, but that was all he could muster.

The spring and summer of 1944 brought a welcome rush of good news to the inmates of Stalag Luft III, news many of them wished had come six months earlier; it might have persuaded even diehard escapers such as Big X to wait out the war. Still, the BBC broadcasts received by the canary, Dick Bartlett's wireless radio receiver, gave officers in the North Compound a needed lift. Kriegies learned of the liberation of Rome on June 5, the Normandy landings on June 6, the main Soviet offensive in the Baltic region on June 22, the Chindits' victories in Burma on June 26, the attempt on Hitler's life on July 20, the liberation of Paris on August 25, the Canadian capture of Dieppe on September 1, and, on September 17, the bold airborne Operation Market Garden attempt to catapult the Allies to the enemy's side of the River Rhine. That same summer, letters addressed to Stalag Luft III prisoners from fictitious relatives informed kriegies around the North Compound that three Commonwealth air officers had actually completed Roger Bushell's so-called "home run." Per Bergsland and Jens Muller had made it back to Britain via Sweden within a week, while Bob van der Stok had reached his occupied homeland, the Netherlands, within thirty-six hours. He soon pushed on across the Pyrenees to Madrid and arrived back in Britain four months after emerging from tunnel "Harry."

A lot had changed at Stalag Luft III since the March 1944 escape. Von Lindeiner was gone; he would be court-martialled in October for allowing as many as 262 escape attempts during his command of POW camps and for defying the Sagan Order to hand over escapers directly to the Gestapo.* Von Lindeiner's nemesis Roger Bushell was also gone, executed under that same order. What remained, however, was X Organization, which both men had grappled with since April 1943. Bushell had determined and manipulated its objectives, its tactics, and its timing like a battle force pursuing an enemy. Von Lindeiner had fought back, trying to destroy its gains and blunt its resolve with unexpected appells, relentless surveillance by ferrets, and isolation punishment in the cooler. In some senses, both von Lindeiner and Bushell failed to control the fate of X Organization. True, the organization had delivered Bushell his greatest objective—a mass escape and a resulting nationwide manhunt—and ultimately von Lindeiner's Gestapo successors appeared to have buried its material gains by filling "Harry" with human waste and by exterminating X's ringleaders with the Sagan Order. And yet the Germans had never found tunnel "Dick," which still housed tunnelling tools, bed boards, and wire, and they had not annihilated all of X's brain trust—men such as Robert "Crump" Ker-Ramsey, Norman "Conk" Canton, and Tony Pengelly, who had given up his number on the escape list expressly so that the escape committee might carry on.

"Immediately after news of the executions reached England," Pengelly said, "Air Ministry told us over the BBC, via our smuggled radios, to stop escaping.... [But] with the incentive of escape work gone, many were losing the comparative peace of mind with which we had lived and endured the long years. Our morale was dangerously low."

The Normandy invasion in June and the attempt on Hitler's life in July re-inspired the kriegies and breathed new life into a dormant X Organization. Pengelly and what was left of his mapping and

---

* Colonel von Lindeiner was court-martialled and sentenced to eighteen months in prison. Reassigned to a mental hospital during the German capitulation, he was shot and wounded by Soviet troops, then handed over to the British. On July 1, 1947, the first of two trials in the Stalag Luft III murders began at the War Crimes Court in Hamburg. Testifying for the defence, Colonel von Lindeiner was asked if under the *Aktion Kugel* and *Stufe Römisch* III orders he would have shot the prisoners himself. "I should have put a bullet through my head," he said. He was exonerated, but remained in prison until November 1947.

document forgery team decided to reintroduce the war of wits to the education room of the North Compound library. They manufactured and posted a huge, detailed map of Europe on the library wall and began sticking in pins (thread strung between the pins graphically illustrated the front lines of the war). Based on the BBC reports, they updated the location of the pins and thread daily. That spring and summer of 1944, the thread lines showed Allied gains in mainland Italy, in Scandinavia, a toehold in France, and significant Soviet advances along the Eastern Front.

"On the Russian front there were two sets of thread lines, one red and one black,"[28] Don Edy recalled. "The one represented German news from the front . . . and the other based on the BBC news, which always showed the Allies closer than the German news. We often saw the German ferrets coming in to take a look at the map, then walking out shaking their heads."

"It gave us infinite satisfaction to show [the Germans] the ring drawing ever tighter,"[29] Pengelly said.

The war of the pins gave momentary satisfaction, perhaps, but the rapid westward advance of the red thread on the library wall map—representing victories for the Soviet armies over German armies along the Eastern Front—posed a number of new and potentially ominous threats to Stalag Luft III's imprisoned airmen, officers and NCOs alike. The first impact of the declining fortunes of the German Army in Lithuania, East Prussia, and eastern Poland arrived in the form of other prisoners of war that summer of 1944. Kriegies under guard began arriving from POW camps east of Sagan; they described their captors force-marching them ahead of the Soviet onslaught. With no new huts available for the newcomers, the Germans forced them into existing barracks. They supplied lumber and the loan of tools for the kriegies to convert double bunk beds to triple bunks in existing huts. Rations were halved. Sick parades ballooned. And Red Cross parcels for the original North Compound POWs became few and far between.

If the flight of POWs ahead of the Soviet advance didn't put the kriegies nerves on edge enough, the sudden arrival of a purge of

Commonwealth and American airmen from a place called Buchenwald certainly did. George Sweanor learned that in previous months German SS had had rounded up the 168 downed airmen, including twenty-six RCAF aircrew, stripped them of their identities, and shipped them off to the Buchenwald extermination camp. Starved, tortured, and bearing the scars of Nazi medical experiments, these latest additions to the North Compound shocked Sweanor and his roommates with their first question:

"How many do they shoot each day?"[30] they asked.

George Harsh discovered that such fears were based more in reality than in fiction. Shot down, interrogated, and sent to Stalag Luft III in October 1942, the American-born RCAF gunner had served X Organization inside the wire as a tunnel security boss. A sudden purge at the end of February 1944, just weeks before the planned mass escape, had then whisked Harsh and eighteen others away from the North Compound. He had learned about the March 24 breakout and the reprisals of the Sagan Order from their prisoner-of-war huts at Belaria, a satellite compound five miles from Stalag Luft III. Harsh had survived POW imprisonment for nearly two years, but he recognized that his experience on a chain gang in the 1930s had prepared him more than most to live one day at a time. Even so, he admitted that he still lay awake nights worried that Gestapo guards would suddenly descend, line them up, and shoot every tenth man unless the kriegies surrendered the radio the Germans knew was hidden.

"Toward the end of the war," Harsh wrote, "Count Folke Bernadotte of Sweden, as a representative of the International Red Cross, was allowed into the camp. [He] slipped word to us that Hitler had ordered Himmler to have every one of us shot rather than let us be liberated by the approaching Russians."[31]

Such rumours and fears sparked a reconstituted X Organization to a predictable response. In July, those comprising the core of the escape committee gathered at the now reopened North Compound theatre. Yes, there would be new productions that summer and fall, if the war went on that long. Airman John Casson would produce a version of J. B. Priestley's *I Have Been Here Before*, while airman David Porter would rehearse a musical comedy called *Palina Panic*. Since the Germans had never discovered the repository of all the tunnel sand excavated from "Harry"—in the space beneath the raked floor of theatre seats—the escape committee reopened the theatre's secret subterranean enterprise. This time, X Organization diggers began excavating tunnel "George" from beneath the theatre proscenium eastbound toward the North Compound exterior wire. It was a short distance from the new tunnel to the sand dispersal site, all under the same roof, and there was still plenty of room to store "George's" excavated sand under the same theatre floor.

*Kommandant Oberst* Braune may well have suspected that news passed along by new kriegies arriving in the North Compound, or indeed from BBC radio reports of Allied successes across Europe, would embolden his prisoners. In September, the new Stalag Luft III administration adorned the walls inside the camp huts with threatening posters. In broken English, the lengthy proclamations first accused Britain of instituting "illegal warfare in non-combat zones in the form of gangster commandos, terror bandits, and sabotage troops even up to the frontiers of Germany." The poster claimed that a captured British booklet, entitled "The Handbook of Modern Irregular Warfare,"[32] encouraged the English soldier to be "a potential gangster (with) the sphere of operations (to) include the enemy's own country . . . and neutral countries as a source of supply." The poster described the areas of Europe in which English soldiers might consider operating as a "death zone." Finally, if the message wasn't clear enough, the narrative concluded with a series of warnings to prisoners "against making future escapes. . . . All police and military guards have been given the most strict orders to shoot on sight all suspected persons. . . . Escaping from prison camps has ceased to be a sport!"

But the *Kommandant* hadn't finished his propaganda offensive. Soon after the death zone posters went up came another blizzard of proclamations with a provocative assessment of the war and a most peculiar invitation to "soldiers of the British Commonwealth and the United States of America."[33] The poster began with some apparent revisionist history, turning the retreat of German armies from occupied areas of the Soviet Union and Eastern Europe into "the great Bolshevik offensive [crossing] the frontiers of Germany. The men in the Moscow Kremlin believe the way is open for the conquest of the Western world. This will certainly be a decisive battle for us. But it will also be the decisive battle for England, for the United States, and for the maintenance of western civilization. Or whatever today remains of it."

The posters' rhetoric painted an even bleaker picture of Europe under Bolshevik domination than under Nazi occupation. Suddenly, German captors appealed to all POWs, "regardless of your rank or of your nationality," to recognize "the danger of Bolshevik-Communism" and (in bold type) to see "the consequences of the destruction of Europe—not just of Germany, but of Europe—[and what] it will mean to your own country." Unable to disguise its inherent racism, the document positioned its authors and readers not as captors and captives, but "as white men to other white men." Then it laid out a specific offer to the kriegies: "Whether you are willing to fight in the front-line or in the service corps, we make you this solemn promise: Whoever as a soldier of his own nation is willing to join the common front for the common cause, will be freed immediately after the victory of the present offensive and can return to his own country via Switzerland."

And finally, in bold-type exclamation, the poster completed its call-to-arms with, "Are you for the culture of the West or the barbaric Asiatic East? Make your decision now!"

George Sweanor remembered that the German press joined the propaganda initiative as well. Every time a *Völkischer Beobachter* or *Frankfurter Zeitung* arrived at the North Compound library, Sweanor devoured every detail, including the one-sided reports of "Soviet atrocities." Then, during one appell that autumn of 1944, representatives of *Kommandant* Braune called for volunteers to help the German war effort against the perceived Communist threat.

"We were surprised when one man volunteered,"[34] Sweanor said, "saying he would be glad to help. But we could not conceal our mirth when they asked him his civilian trade. He answered, 'Funeral director.'"

Bomb-aimer Sweanor had always considered the mass escape plan to be futile. He had served in the protection and completion of the tunnels from the moment he arrived at Stalag Luft III in 1943, but his highest priority was always survival. Consequently, he rejoined the X Organization service, assisting in the completion of tunnel "George" and preparing his fellow kriegies for the kind of chaos the propaganda posters had predicted . . . or worse.

"We knew that as the Soviets advanced there would be bedlam outside our compound. We would have no Red Cross food. The Germans would be evacuating and leaving weapons behind,"[35] Sweanor said. "I joined a group we were training as commandos. I had had some army training, artillery training, and so I was put in charge of a small platoon of people to find German weapons . . . so we could provide an armed united group. . . . We decided to use 'George' to store the equipment. The tunnel was considered to be our after-Soviet occupation outlet, our last survival exit."

As the snows of late November began to accumulate around Sagan, tunnellers under the North Compound at Stalag Luft III brought the face of "George" to a position just beyond the east perimeter wire and within feet of the surface. X Organization planners agreed the tunnel would not be used for another escape attempt, merely, as Sweanor had considered it, an emergency exit from the North Compound, a bolt-hole should either the retreating Germans or advancing Soviets decide to take out their frustrations on the kriegies. Meantime, under SBO Wilson's direction, the entire compound population was reorganized into sections, platoons, and companies of the commando self-defence force. The Klim Klub, as it was code-named, prepared for an expected final confrontation with either the camp guards or a hostile invading army.

As it turned out, however, there was a more lethal enemy than either the Germans or the Soviets in the final battle to survive Silesia: the natural elements, among the very reasons the creators of Stalag Luft III had located the prison there in the first place.

# LONG ROAD HOME

A RT CRIGHTON escaped Stalag Luft III for about an hour in late 1944. The twenty-five-year-old peacetime musician and wartime Wellington pilot was about to enter his third winter of captivity at the POW camp near Sagan. To occupy himself, during his first summer inside the wire, he had fashioned a left-handed five iron and golfed a nine-hole course inside the wire with his fellow krie-gies. Evenings he had played trumpet in the Commonwealth officers' band and eventually led the North Compound orchestra through every musical genre from Beethoven to big band music revues. He'd been dead against escape activity, conducting the orchestra on stage at the theatre even as sand dispersal teams packed tons of earth from tunnels "Harry" and "George" beneath his feet. But suddenly, on December 4, eight months after the mass breakout, word arrived that he was to retrieve his trumpet and report for a detail leaving the compound.

Crighton joined a group of about two dozen officers assigned to participate in an official ceremony commemorating the fifty dead escapers whose remains had been housed in an outdoor crypt just to the north of the North Compound wire. As both the leader of the orchestra and an accomplished trumpet player, F/L Crighton had been chosen to play "The Last Post" at the memorial. He gladly accepted the assignment, particularly since RAF pilot Les "Johnny"

Bull—the first down "Harry" the night of the escape and among the fifty murdered airmen—had been Crighton's roommate at the North Compound. And yet, as honoured as he felt to be asked to play at the memorial, Crighton recalled something even more indelible about his march to and from the service.

"[It was] my first walk out into the woods,"[1] he said. "I was excited as hell. A real tree. I could actually touch it."

Still surrounded by the pine forest, but beyond the wire, the members of the ceremonial party included the Senior British Officer, Group Captain D. E. L. Wilson, and fifteen other officers representing the home countries of the executed airmen. No Americans were permitted to be there. But seven officers from both the East Compound and the Belaria POW camp (including Wally Floody) were allowed to attend, as well as two representatives from the Swiss legation and an adjutant from *Kommandant* Braune's camp staff.

"The memorial is in the form of a large altar table with three scroll-like stones sweeping up at the back with the [censored] names on it," Floody wrote to his wife, Betty, that Christmas. "We all lined up around it while the R.C. and C. of E. padres read a burial service, then 'The Last Post,' after which the three group captains put wreaths on. . . . It was well done. Tell Betty McGill and others it was quite an impressive service."[2]

After he had performed his role on the trumpet and stood silent for the wreath-laying, Crighton and the other Commonwealth officers from North Compound were escorted down the dirt road and back through the main entrance.

A guard began shouting in German to his partner at the gate: "How many went by?"

"Twenty men," the guard replied.

"We're twenty officers," insisted one of the kriegies, who resented being downgraded by the compound guards. "Don't call us men. We're officers!"[3]

That same week, Flying Officer John Weir started his final letter of 1944 from Stalag Luft III to his fiancée, Frances McCormack, back home in Toronto. He began in very much the same way as he'd begun his first letter to her, soon after his Spitfire was shot down over Caen, France, in November 1941.

"Hi darling. I thought I'd end this day the best way possible, by writing you. I've had two-hundred-and-forty-six letters from you," he wrote. "This is my ninety-fifth epistle . . . so near and yet so far—the end of the war and you. I get more impatient every day . . . but it will be soon now."4

He wished Frances a Merry Christmas and Happy New Year and got her caught up on harmless news from around the camp, news that he expected the censors wouldn't blacken out on his letter paper. Several times in his letters sent during his hospitalization over the previous fall, he had reassured her that the surgery to graft new skin to his eyelids, burned away in the fire when his Spitfire went down, had gone reasonably well; however, he hinted any future portrait photographs wouldn't be particularly flattering. He kibitzed about his new roommates' names—Lorne, Pappy, Sam, Hank, and Pop, as well as his own, Scruffy—sounding "like something out of Snow White." But to his now savvy fiancée, he was also passing on valuable information about the state of affairs in the camp. First, he was alerting her to the whereabouts of the downed air officers now living in his hut, in case any of their families back in Canada didn't know. But he was also signalling something else, and Fran would certainly have spotted it.

"The members of our room have changed," he pointed out, meaning people were on the move. "Lorne Chamber (came in from the west) and Pappy Plant (also west), Sam Sangster, Hank Sprague, Pop Collette and Scruffy (that's me). Wally [Floody] is at Belaria now. All ye boys are hail and hearty. . . . If the optimism of this camp is right, I'll beat this [letter] home to you."5

Suddenly his barracks in the North Compound—previously offering its veteran kriegies fairly spacious sleeping, eating, and living quarters—were becoming overcrowded with newcomers, he was telling her indirectly. She would certainly have recognized, with five additional men in her fiancé's hut room, that living space at Stalag Luft III had become cramped, restful sleep less likely, and meagre rations stretched even more thinly than in previous months. His suggestion of beating the letter home offered more a hint of things being in flux at the camp than his honest belief that liberation was at hand. Then, in the same letter, which turned out to be his second last from Stalag Luft III, John Weir inadvertently acknowledged perhaps a greater threat to the well being of the kriegies than even he realized.

"Darling, it's so hard to write anything 'cause so little happens here of interest," he explained. He commented on an American movie called *The Spoilers* that had been screened in the theatre; it featured Marlene Dietrich and a lively bar room brawl. "I've been very lazy the last six or eight weeks, due mainly to bad weather, just reading and doing the occasional circuit [walk]."[6]

In other words, Scruffy Weir and the rest of the Stalag Luft III kriegies were leading a much more sedentary life without the exercise they had all experienced while digging, maintaining, and protecting the tunnels. Their idleness was reducing, if not eliminating, their higher physical fitness level, dulling their alertness, and certainly taking the edge off their preparedness for the unexpected. And if the officers weren't able to notice their fitness slipping, they certainly recognized that the quality of their nutrition was almost non-existent. George Sweanor, who had taken on the job of training the Klim Klub for potential commando action to the death, woke up one morning during the fall of 1944 and felt too weak to stand. Half rations, a leg infection, and several physical blows he'd sustained playing football were taking their toll on Sweanor's heart; his pulse was spiking inexplicably to 150 beats per minute. A South African Army doctor in the compound examined him and deduced that Sweanor was suffering from a severe case of malnutrition. His condition wasn't uncommon among the POW population.

Robert Buckham, the Toronto-born artist shot down about the same time as Sweanor in 1943, had served the Dean and Dawson forgery factory for a year during the lead up to the mass escape. However, because he had not drawn an escape number on March 24, he'd been forced to leave his bunk in Room 23 of Hut 104 as his fellow kriegies made their way down the shaft under the stove to freedom. After the breakout, with the need for forged documents gone, Buckham didn't stop drawing, but toward the end of 1944 he did begin to write and sketch in a diary. Some of his first entries noted they'd heard the population of Sagan had swollen from twenty thousand to one hundred thousand as civilians, fleeing westward, sought refuge from the fighting and the cold in the town. He noted in early 1945 that the Soviets were steadily advancing. But his more immediate diary subject matter focused on the basics of survival.

"A man's eyes betray his hunger,"7 he wrote as he surveyed the faces of his eight roommates. "Watch the eyes recede and narrow as they probe deeply for the taste of remembered meals. Watch them . . . comparing the size of portion, measuring the width of bread slice."

He described the typical daily menu among the Commonwealth officers that January of 1945. It consisted of one weak cup of Nescafé for breakfast, one cup of turnip soup containing well-boiled white maggots for lunch, perhaps a few slices of bread, and for dinner the boiled pulp of potatoes retrieved from a waste pile outside the huts. The tastiest parts of the ration, if they could salvage them, were the potato peelings salted and fried in margarine. If he and his hut mates could acquire a Red Cross parcel, the contents filled in the remaining ration gap. And though there were still a few evenings of deliciously distracting music or drama at the North Compound theatre that winter, Buckham noted that his mind ricocheted back to reality when his stomach rumbled with hunger during the performances.

"An empty belly is a very basic thing," he wrote.

Then, suddenly, on January 22, 1945, the bread ration stopped. The same day, Buckham described seeing a Soviet pilot—still clad in his helmet, boots, and other flying gear—wandering outside the *Vorlager* of the camp. This was followed by a large explosion just outside the wire. More and more, the approach of the Soviet armies became evident. Reports came to the camp that Breslau was brimming with evacuees from the east, and that both shelling and minus-eight-degree temperatures were taking a toll on civilians there. Some of the kriegies openly predicted the evacuation of Stalag Luft III and began preparing. Buckham described large crowds gathered at the cookhouse to read German news bulletins, but "equally large crowds were on the circuit, toughening feet and legs in case the threatened forced march becomes a reality."[8]

RCAF navigator John Colwell was as much a barometer of the compound's focus and tempo as anybody. The Tin Man, who had miraculously supplied the escape committee with so many of its working utensils the previous year, was busily supplying kriegies with homemade survival gear—items they would need during the next phase of their wartime experience. His diary entries became shorter and shorter, with simple references to the daily-life tools he was manufacturing or repairing from scraps of metal and wood—potato mashers, cooking pots, water jugs, cigarette containers, and slop pails. He also retrieved his Klim-tin suitcase from a hiding place in the wall of Hut 120.

"Half-soled my boots," Colwell wrote on January 25, 1945. "Everyone is sewing."[9]

That same day, the spearhead of the westbound Soviet armies reached the River Odra at Steinau, just forty miles east of Stalag Luft III. Though everyone inside the prison camp knew it, both the Germans and the POWs appeared to go about their daily routines ignoring the obvious. The Soviets were getting closer. In the Centre Compound, for instance, the guards carried out a barracks inspection. On January 26, teams of kriegies in both the North and West Compounds staged the first hockey games of 1945. Performances in the compound theatres went on as normal; in fact, that evening, the North Compound theatre troupe was in dress rehearsal for the first performances of *The Wind and the Rain*.[10] As late as Saturday morning, January 27, *Kommandant* Braune received orders from Berlin that the prisoners were not to be moved.

That night in Hut 119, Don Edy and his roommates—Joe Noble, Larry Somers, Ken Rees—had tidied up their room and were seated on stools at the group's wooden dining table. Fellow officers Barney Barnes and George Smith reclined in their bunks, and Jack Probert fussed with what little food the group had on hand. It was another bitter January night outside. Edy and company anticipated a visit from the Senior Canadian Officer Group Captain, Larry Wray. When he arrived, he joined them at their table for tea to ward off the nighttime chill. Wray initiated conversation by posing a few questions about the coming days: What did they think the Germans were up to? How soon before they reacted to the Soviet advance? For about an hour Wray listened to Edy and the others offer observations and opinions. Everybody had his say. Then Wray offered his view.

"Personally, I think the Germans have left it too late to move us," he said. "Their armies will be around and we could only clutter up the roads. I think they'll leave us here to be overrun by the Ruskies."

At about 8:30 that Saturday evening, Don Edy noted that Wray took a final swallow of tea and stood up to leave. Just then the door flew open and Bill Jennings, the group's liaison officer, rushed in.

"The camp has to be ready to move out in one hour's time!" Jennings roared.

Wray absorbed the shock of Jennings' announcement in momentary silence. The senior Canadian officer had come to the wrong conclusion. The Germans had in fact received orders to evacuate the entire prison camp almost immediately. And all the camp's officers would be force-marched away, it seemed, sixty minutes later. Group Captain Wray put down his empty tea cup, made his way to the door, and said, finally, "Good night, gentlemen, and good luck."

"I guess this is the beginning of the end," one of Edy's roommates said. "I wonder what's in store for us now?"[11]

Then, like every other hut and room inside Stalag Luft III, Edy's quarters were thrown into pandemonium. Edy admitted his first gut reaction wasn't to the forced march per se, but to the reality of being thrown out of his barracks. The last place he wanted to be on a late January night was outside in the elements. The thought sickened him, but fear propelled him. Edy had a tin suitcase (likely made by Colwell), so he began packing his blanket roll, extra socks, shirts, and a sweater inside. The room that had been cleaned up for Wray's visit became a shambles. Whatever rations of biscuits, cigarettes, and chocolate the men had saved were divided equally and thrown about as bunk mates in Hut 119 assembled their survival kits. A former RCMP officer in the barracks had shown some of the officers how to manufacture backpacks; another man gave out instructions for nailing bed-boards into a wooden box with skis and a tow rope to create a makeshift sleigh. And because their incarceration at Stalag Luft III had taught all kriegies the meaning of resourcefulness, an officer from each hut was dispatched to the library to tear pages of the thinnest paper he could find in the books to serve as toilet paper during the march.

When word of the exodus reached Colwell's hut, he and his room-mates—Bill Hoddinott, Jim Jamieson, Art Hawtin, and John Acheson—assembled their rations and all their worldly possessions and methodically went about preparing to leave. Hoddinott divided the so-called "iron rations," necessities, equally among the officers. Each man had pack boards for their backpacks. Colwell seemed to go into a trance, as if he had rehearsed his departure from the North Compound over and over in his mind. First, he changed into the clothes he was going to wear on the march. Next, he laid out two blankets on a couple of stools in the middle of the room and began piling his supplies on them. He laid out two shirts, six pairs of socks, six handkerchiefs, razor blades, a shaving set, toothbrushes, pyjamas, two pencils, shoelaces, his logbook, photographs, matches, and a towel. Then, the Tin Man gathered his portion of the food rations—raisins, biscuits, sugar, prunes, cheese, meat, and iron rations—that went into the centre of his pack. Finally, he retrieved a couple of pounds of chocolate, his sketches of camp life, and his daily diary, all hidden in his Klim clock. By 10 p.m., he was ready to go.[12]

But departure was delayed by a series of postponements to 10:30, then 11:30, then midnight. Rumours added to the confusion. Someone said the Allies had broken through on a one-hundred-mile front and the Germans were negotiating for an armistice. Another said POWs could hide in the bush and take their chances with the Soviets when they arrived. The suppressed panic and the prolonged delay were sapping the officers' strength. Colwell's group conferred and it was decided their colleague Bill Hoddinott was not well enough to travel. He left for the compound hospital in the *Vorlager* to be liberated, he hoped, by the approaching Soviets. Also during the delay, many of the kriegies tried to consume as much nutritional food as they could find, but couldn't pack. Remaining members of X Organization had last-minute loose ends to tie up, such as collecting the maps from the library walls in case they came in handy on the march. They also set bonfires to burn old clothes, furniture, and any leftover escape committee documents. In the rush to destroy anything the Germans might consider useful, Hut 104 caught fire[13] and the last of tunnel "Harry's" entrance went up in smoke.

At 1 a.m. on Sunday, January 28, the kriegies began moving through the main gate of the North Compound. Robert Buckham took a last look back and considered the significance of the moment. In addition to memories of imprisonment and lost comrades, the kriegies left behind thousands of books in the library; a theatre full of props, tools, and musical instruments; cupboards loaded with sports equipment; and 2.5 million cigarettes.[14] As they passed the stores buildings, each man received one last Red Cross parcel; the Germans had stockpiled as many as fifty thousand of them. But since the POWs had packed their kits to overflowing, most of the departing officers just tore open the boxes right there at the gate and hurriedly selected only items they didn't have, leaving thousands of partially opened and tossed parcels "bleeding their contents into the snow," Buckham wrote.

"I was outside the wire for the first time in twenty months," he went on. "Ahead the road disappeared into the darker mass of the forest, the trees soft in silhouette and taller than imagined from inside the camp."[15]

For the moment, Buckham had forgotten about his empty stomach, as Colwell had forgotten about the scores of utensils he'd bashed together—a veritable museum of inmate ingenuity in two years of imprisonment—ultimately left inside the wire. Don Edy had fond memories of his bit parts on stage at the North Compound theatre doing gymnastics in the *Six to the Bar* review and dressed up in a toga in the operetta *Messalina*. There were even photographs as evidence he had been featured on stage, but they never crossed his mind the night they left the prison camp. Art Crighton, the North Compound orchestra leader, said he had played countless solos during North Compound concerts on "a hell of a great instrument,"[16] a trumpet the YMCA had sent from Canada, but he somehow felt the trumpet ought to stay behind. He learned later someone had wrapped it around a tree in anger. But every memento, every memory faded at least temporarily as the kriegies marched away from Sagan. Even Hans Pieber was selective about what he carried out of the camp. The German duty officer, who'd been perhaps closest to the kriegies going back to their days at Barth in 1941, agreed to carry the canary—the illegal radio—since he too wanted to know the BBC's latest reports on the war.

"Although the sky was covered with clouds, it was quite light since the moon was up," John Colwell wrote in his diary. "Although my pack was heavy, I enjoyed the march, especially when we passed through small towns and villages where there were things to see besides barbed wire fences and Goon boxes."[17]

Kriegies completed their evacuation of the West Compound by 12:30 Sunday morning. The last of the North Compound prisoners passed through the main gate by 3:45 a.m. The Centre Compound was empty shortly afterward. By 6 a.m. Sunday, the final group of POWs from the East Compound was on the road. Stalag Luft III— once home to nearly ten thousand prisoners of war—was like a ghost town. Only those kriegies left behind in the compound infirmaries remained in the *Vorlagers*. They were under guard, attended by a doctor, and would wait for the Soviets to arrive to determine their fate. Because of his irregular heartbeat, for example, George Sweanor had been placed back on sick parade. He sat in the North Compound hospital as his fellow kriegies trekked out of the camp.

Later on Sunday, however, Sweanor, the one-time duty pilot inside the North Compound gate, got permission from the Germans guarding the hospitalized POWs to retrieve his personal belongings. As he dashed into the compound back to Hut 119, all he could think of were his letters from his wife Joan, his personal photographs, his books, and the food he'd stashed inside his palliasse. The food and some of his scribblers were gone, but the rest was intact. In fact, he

noticed that some optimistic kriegies had even bundled their belongings and inscribed them with some Russian words requesting their
personal effects be forwarded to home addresses later. The guards
then let Sweanor enter the parcel shed to gather rations for his imminent departure. From rations such as Berger's Food, condensed milk,
egg powder, dried fruit, and sugar, he cooked up a nutritious concoction and poured it into small tins, sealed the tops with tape, and
sewed the tins into the lining of his greatcoat. Much the way Colwell
had assembled his backpack, Sweanor prepared his. Then, on orders
from the infirmary doctor to vacate the compound and attend to two
other patients in the process, Sweanor too made his final exit from
Stalag Luft III.

"I glanced back for a last look at the compound that had been
my home and where I had met so many fine human beings,"[18] he
wrote.

But Sweanor didn't have much time to reflect on either his nearly
two years of imprisonment at the compound near Sagan, or the hundreds of men with whom he'd shared a prison camp bond. He suddenly faced different responsibilities on the road to survival. He was
a patient tending other patients. He had to keep a USAAF officer
with pneumonia comfortable as they marched. And he regularly had
to apply a calamine-like lotion to the oozing sores of a Rhodesian
airman in his care. And when the elderly German assigned to guard
the sickly patients en route to a train siding a full night's march away
could no longer carry his heavy rifle, Sweanor agreed to carry it part
of the way. Dick Bartlett carried more than his fair share too. The
Canadian Skua dive-bomber pilot shot down over Norway in 1940,
and the custodian of the secret radio, had befriended fellow Fleet Air
Arm pilot John Nicholson at Stalag Luft III. Sub Lieutenant Nicholson had been shot down at Dunkirk the same year, but a bullet had
remained lodged in his chest near his heart throughout his time in
German prison camps. On the march from Sagan, Nicholson kept
asking Bartlett if he could just stop and lie down in the snow.

"Hang on and keep moving,"[19] Bartlett encouraged his friend as
he half dragged and half carried the still wounded Dunkirk veteran.

When they did stop, Bartlett would loosen his bootlaces to relieve pain and swelling in his feet. After the short rest, when Bartlett's hands were too numb to retie his own boots, Nicholson was able to reciprocate his friend's care and concern during the forced march that winter.

Similarly, Edward Nurse and Mac Reilley—two officers who'd crewed up together in 1943, flown ops together with 405 Squadron, bailed out together from the same doomed Halifax bomber,[20] and vouched for each other upon arrival at Stalag Luft III—turned to each other for support in the exodus from prison camp a year and a half later. In moments when they felt too frozen to continue, too hungry to find that extra burst of energy, and too exhausted to keep moving, both Nurse, the pilot, and Reilley, the navigator, leaned on each other to keep going.

It was Sunday evening by the time the Germans emptied the satellite prison camp at Belaria, a few miles from Sagan. Since February 1944, just a month before the mass escape, the Belaria camp had been home to three members of the original Stalag Luft III X Organization—tunnel architect Wally Floody, intelligence specialist Kingsley Brown, and security boss George Harsh. It hadn't taken the three RCAF men long to realize that Colonel von Lindeiner's purge of officers to Belaria had likely spared them the wrath of the Sagan Order and murder at the hands of the Gestapo. Now it was up to them to fend for themselves as their German guards rounded up kriegies by the thousands to "save us from the Bolshevist terror," Kingsley Brown remembered a camp officer saying. Brown added that "we found it difficult to appreciate their solicitude,"[21] and concluded that their German captors actually hoped to buy their way out of the war using the kriegies as human bargaining chips.

George Harsh imagined the future outside the Belaria prison and immediately drew several conclusions. Though he had endured twelve years on a chain gang in the United States prison system back in the 1930s, and nearly three more as a POW during the war, when the evacuation order came Harsh recognized his best shot at survival depended on his two resourceful roommates. Floody told Harsh to line the insides of his jacket with newspapers[22] for warmth, and to fill his pockets with chocolate for quick energy. Brown told him to stash cigarettes as barter for food along the way. Each man tied a Klim tin to his belt with a loop of string so that anything liquid, hot, and edible could be contained in it for a meal. Together, the three men tore apart a table and stool, and with bed-boards for skis and belts and blankets for harnesses, fashioned a crude sleigh for transporting their clothing, bedding, and survival food supplies.

"As Wally, Brownie, and I marched out the gate our pockets were bulging, but our hands were free," Harsh wrote, "except for the tins of bully beef we were wolfing."[23]

During his pre-war civilian days, Kingsley Brown had enjoyed his life as a journalist gathering and publishing stories for newspapers in Toronto and Halifax. When the X Organization at Stalag Luft III learned of his researching and writing talents, it immediately dispatched Brown to gather intelligence information from library newspapers and magazines for the Dean and Dawson forgery section. By his own admission, Brown did most of his gathering for the escape committee, not for himself. In the mad dash at Belaria to assemble his own survival gear before he marched out the gate, however, he allowed himself the luxury of salvaging one keepsake: a German beer stein with a delicate silver top. But the first hours of marching through drifting snow and penetrating cold imposed a sudden reality among the prisoners. Out in the elements and in the POWs' weakened state, the supply sleighs became heavier by the hour. The kriegies began to unburden themselves of extra tins of food, packs of cigarettes, and blocks of chocolate—all but the absolute minimum luggage needed to survive.

"The beer stein . . . was my one souvenir of my prison years,"[24] Brown wrote. "But I tossed it into the ditch. The ditch was strewn with violins and guitars, books, trumpets, framed family pictures—precious items in a prisoner's 'life savings.'"

Though his colleagues often called him a loner, Wally Floody left Belaria in close company with his two tunnel co-conspirators,

Harsh and Brown. Aside from survival supplies, however, the only mementoes he took with him were a small journal and a photograph of his wife, Betty, whom he hadn't seen in almost four years. Leaving Belaria prompted mixed emotions for the Tunnel King. Still bitter about the way German authorities had hauled him away from the North Compound and potential escape through the tunnel he had designed, excavated, and protected, Floody recognized that the twist of fate had likely extended his life. And as costly as the Gestapo reprisals had been, he continued to insist the escape had achieved its ultimate objective. When news of the mass escape reached the German population, Floody continued to point out, it was the first time since the war began in 1939 that every German in uniform had been called back from leave. Every fifteen minutes on German radio authorities broadcast the latest on the escape of the *Terrorflieger* (terror flyers).

"The slowdown of the German economy caused by the tunnel and the breakout had been the equivalent of dropping a couple of divisions of paratroopers into German-occupied Europe," Floody reminded his comrades. "I think the cost was worth it."[25]

Only outside the wire did Commonwealth air officers come face to face with the other realities of the war. Most of the east-west highways had become the exclusive domain of Germany military traffic, moving troops and weapons to and from the rapidly approaching Eastern Front. So the kriegies and their guards made their way along secondary dirt roads, where they were soon caught in the backwash of the war. Roads were clogged with slave labourers from occupied countries, starving civilians pushing carts of their moveable possessions, homeless women and children huddling from the cold, nuns and priests uprooted from their parishes, and domesticated animals wandering beside the traffic. The kriegies told the civilians where they could find thousands of Red Cross boxes of provisions abandoned in the Sagan pine forest. For at least the moment, the former inmates of Stalag Luft III had the advantage of provisions they had packed in their pockets and packs, but as one kriegie noted, on the road "we were just people now, all members of the human race . . .

sharing common levelers of cold, lice, misery, and despair. . . . This was truly *Götterdämmerung.*"²⁶

The first night outside the wire, the aircrew officers and their guards coped with temperatures well below freezing. Few prisoners had the kind of winter gear the conditions demanded. Greatcoats proved too thin. Summer boots cracked and leaked in the cold and snow. Mitts and scarves were in short supply. In addition, though the moon had originally cast some light en route, before long the weather closed in and the men were marching through falling snow that deteriorated into nearly white-out conditions. Marching into the teeth of a blizzard slowed everybody down, and within a few hours the columns of POWs stretched over twenty miles of road.²⁷ Stragglers feared they would be shot. Even as the kriegies marched from the Stalag Luft III camps, the BBC was broadcasting an order each afternoon that the officers and men should not risk escape attempts, and further, that they should try to stay together for safety in numbers and better identification.²⁸ But the German guards fared no better. Most were older men who grumbled about having to escort *Luftgangsters* across the frozen countryside. It appeared the guards were constantly in search of shelter for themselves and their prisoners.

Sometimes, survival on what kriegies soon dubbed "the Death March" came down to the individual strength of fellow air officers rising to the occasion. Musician Art Crighton said the cold wasn't nearly as penetrating when he was walking; when his body was moving, his circulation seemed to fend off the freezing temperatures, the winds, and the driving snow. But when the columns had to stop and he had to stand for hours out in the open waiting for congestion to ease or an order to be issued, he could feel himself going numb at the extremities. That's when Crighton remembered Scruffy Weir coming to the rescue.

"Wave your arms!"²⁹ Weir shouted as he ran up and down the columns of men. Then he'd cuss and add to his call to action: "Wave your legs!"

Later in the march, Crighton said his German guards occasionally found shelter for their prisoners in empty or nearly empty barns.

Hungry, exhausted, and sick, the kriegies were jammed like sardines into stalls, troughs, and lofts of straw for the night. At one end of the barn, the guards placed a rain barrel full of water. They were fearful of the possibility of fire ignited by careless prisoners sneaking a smoke during the night. Next to the rain barrel was also the spot where prisoners could relieve themselves in an emergency. One night in just such a setting, Crighton got an attack of "squitters," prompting him to dash from his straw bed through the dark to the relieving spot next to the rain barrel.

"In pitch black, I stumbled . . . down the hall and crashed into the rain barrel. I fell head first into two feet of icy water. Then I collapsed on the floor. Losing control, disaster followed," he said. "I remember nothing more [except] my comrades wiped me clean and dry and laid me on my straw bed."[30]

Over the next few days, all of the prisoners from the various Stalag Luft III compounds—as many as ten thousand airmen of the Allied air forces—made their way via back roads south from Sagan and west about fifty miles to the German rail centre at Spremberg. Men from the South Compound, finding ample shelter at a brick factory along the way, arrived first on January 29. Two days later, the kriegies from the West Compound made their way into the town. A group of five hundred Americans from the Centre Compound had joined up with POWs from the East Compound by the time they reached Spremberg on February 4. Of the larger groups, the last to arrive at the railway yards were the North Compound air officers. At Spremberg, German authorities divided the prisoners into new groups, loaded them into boxcars, and sent them in different directions—the Americans to Stalag XIII-D outside Nürnberg; those from Centre and South Compounds to Stalag VII-A near Moosburg; the POWs from the Belaria Compound were transported to Luckenwalde, a prison camp southwest of Berlin; and prisoners from the North Compound (including most of the six hundred Canadian kriegies) travelled to Marlag-Milag, a naval facility in northwestern Germany.

In that first week of February 1945, the ancient locomotives and boxcars—the infamous "forty-and-eights"—threaded their way from

Spremberg westward across Germany, away from Soviet armies advancing from the east and toward Allied armies advancing from the west. Apparently dodging higher priority military trains and both daylight and nighttime air raids, the POW trains chugged from one marshalling yard to the next. The lack of food and water were bad enough, but darkness and confinement compounded everybody's anxiety and ailments. Occasionally, when the trains pulled into sidings, guards unlocked the doors and allowed the prisoners to exit, stretch, and relieve themselves. John R. Harris was positioned at a boxcar door when it was suddenly thrust open.

"I had no sooner alighted from the car than I promptly fainted,"[31] he said. "The others picked me up, but . . . I keeled over once again. This time, I was carried back to the [box]car. Someone brought me a cup of water. I don't know where it came from. . . . It was full of rust particles, so it could have come from the train's engine."

In his boxcar, Robert Buckham's group also had to do without water, artificial light, or straw for bedding, but they found a margarine lamp and lit it. The kriegies tried to make the best use of the lack of space. They hung bags and sundry gear on the walls and from the ceiling of the car. Any available blankets were spread on the floor so they could take turns resting in a prone position. Others slept sitting. The rest stood, attempting the same. When his train got to Hanover, Buckham and his group could see water being rationed to the two cars ahead of theirs. The Canadians began shouting and banging on their boxcar door to get a water ration too. Through a crack in the door, they could see a guard approaching with a bucketful of water. He unbolted the door and slid it back a few inches. But before the kriegies could reach the water, the train lurched forward. The door slid shut. The guard re-bolted the door and tossed the water away. To add to his discomfort, Buckham ended up beside an Australian airman who screamed and groaned through the night and banged his fists on the boxcar door during the day.

"We could do little for him. Dysentery," Buckham said. "A Red Cross box served as his toilet, barely ten inches from my head. Endurance was our only resource."[32]

The trio of Canadian kriegies from the Belaria compound had stuck together all the way to Spremberg, and even as the Germans divided the prisoners into groups for train transit, Kingsley Brown, George Harsh, and Wally Floody managed to get aboard the same boxcar. That was about the only redeeming aspect of the trip. Fifty men were crammed into their railway car and struggled to get comfortable in the shared space. There was a bit of straw on the floor and a single wooden box in the middle of the car to serve as its latrine. There was no food and no light except what entered through cracks between the wallboards. A determined group of card players enlarged a crack in the wall with a penknife so that they could carry on their game. And when night came, so did the endless struggle to organize arms, legs, and heads into any degree of comfort to sleep. The odour of fifty unwashed bodies mixed with the stench of the "thunderbox." And when the train stopped on a siding to wait out a Bomber Command attack some distance away, the assault on the senses heightened the claustrophobia, fatigue, and fear. Several nights into their trip west, men awoke to cries in the darkness of the boxcar.

"I want my mother,"33 a man called out. When he heard the plea again, George Harsh knew it came from one of the youngest airmen among the prisoners. Just twenty, with several kills in the Fighter Command books, the fighter pilot had been shot down over France in 1942. Otherwise a dynamic and bright young warrior, this night he called out like small child for his mother.

"Okay, boy, okay," a voice answered from across the boxcar. The consoling response came from a man making his way through the tangle of arms and legs and bodies. "It's all right now."

"I want my mother," the first man repeated, nearly weeping.

"We'll get you to your mother," came the assurance. It was Wally Floody. The big former Spitfire pilot and X Organization leader had reached the younger man in the dark and was rocking him gently in his arms. "There now. Get some rest."

In the three years George Harsh had known the hard-driving tunneller with nine lives, he had never seen this caring side of Wally Floody. Like John Weir shouting encouragement up and down the columns of men in the cold, George Sweanor nursing two fellow patients' medical needs while trying to stay alive himself on the forced march, and those who had cared for Art Crighton during his dehumanizing bout of dysentery, Floody playing mother to a distressed young pilot on a prison train in the middle of Germany illustrated the brotherhood that bound these longtime prisoners of war together. If one were going to make it safely to the end of this long road, each man would somehow try to ensure that everybody else did as well. Harsh witnessed further proof of such loyalty even as the numbers of the POWs trekking west from Belaria dwindled to less than one hundred. One morning, weeks into their overland marching and gruelling boxcar transit to an unknown destination, Harsh and Floody found themselves "sleepwalking, silently lost in our own personal miseries"[34] as a twosome. It slowly dawned on them that their number three, Kingsley Brown, was missing. For as long as they could muster the strength and not drawing unnecessary attention from their guards, the two kriegies searched high and low for their absent comrade. They had all but held a requiem for their missing friend when he suddenly reappeared.

"Where in the hell . . . ?" Floody started in on him.

"Never mind," Brown laughed. "There's a group of Frenchmen back there . . . and they've got a small cart with 'em loaded with bread."[35] And with that he opened a blanket he'd been wearing like a shawl to reveal three loaves of German black bread. He informed his buddies he'd swapped his wristwatch for food.

"A Rolex watch for three loaves of bread," Harsh protested.

"They promised for the next watch to throw in a bottle of *Schnaps* too," Brown quipped.

"That's different," Harsh grinned.

"Jesus," Floody sighed. "What a set of values!"

After several days cooped up in their boxcars bound for Marlag-Milag, northeast of Bremen, the kriegies from Spremberg arrived in the marshalling yard at Tarmstedt. Peering through cracks in the boxcar walls, they could see a changing of the guard out in the pouring rain. Since

Marlag-Milag—a naval prison—was to become their new home, their Luftwaffe guards now handed the Commonwealth air officers over to German marines. It was a two-hour walk from the railway yard to the gates of Marlag-Milag. There, outside the barbed-wire fencing, along a cinder roadway, the kriegies chain smoked cigarettes and stood "like cattle [with] our backs to the wind and rain,"[36] waiting to experience a naval guard search of their belongings, one man at a time. The marine *Kommandant* seemed determined to conduct as thorough a search as any the prisoners had received from the German air force. But John R. Harris discovered that the marine guards detailed to do the inspection were just as frustrated as the kriegies; a judicious bribe to the guards resulted in a perfunctory search, and the Canadians were admitted to the compound. It still took six hours.

As best they could, Harris and some of his former roommates from the North Compound searched out a barracks block where they could sleep comfortably. In the following days, they discovered how well off they had been at Stalag Luft III. They now had to live— fifteen or twenty to a room—in huts lit by a couple of naked light bulbs, with no furniture and no bunks, but plenty of rats. All they had to sleep on were bags of damp wood shavings. There were very few stoves and even less firewood to burn in them. So the kriegies began stripping the floors and walls—not to procure shoring for an escape tunnel, like the old days, but to fuel fires to heat their rooms and cook their meagre rations. Despite the Spartan surroundings, John Colwell seemed perfectly at home. The morning after he'd arrived and settled into a room in the Marlag-Milag barracks, the Tin Man had managed to visit all the dumps in the camp to collect any discarded tin. On that first day, he manufactured a soldering lamp with a blowpipe and bashed together a two-gallon water pail and stew pot.[37] By the second day, his fellow kriegies from Hut 120 at Stalag Luft III had cooked a small meal for themselves and a dozen roommates. Meanwhile, Don Edy's first edible intake at Marlag came from the dregs of his kit bag and some boiled water.

"My powdered milk was gone,"[38] he wrote. "And there was only a tablespoon of Nescafé left. So I put it all together with all the sugar

I could find and poured in the hot water. It was a good brew all right, but it was too strong for my poor old stomach. Seconds after it went down, I was up and outside, sicker than a dog."

The infirmary at Marlag-Milag rarely had fewer than a hundred patients. The sick bay seemed continuously crammed to the four walls with patients on cots or lying on the floor under any available greatcoats and blankets. There was one shower in the entire camp. It was located in the ablution shed and consisted of one wall, a tin roof, a cement floor, and a cold-water shower with a pretty much unobscured view of the great outdoors. And the north Germany dampness seemed to seep into everything. Robert Buckham said the rain in Tarmstedt would "take first prize in density;[39]" it could penetrate broken windows, roofs, floors, and walls, as well as socks and shoes, no matter how dried out they seemed. The continuous rain even forced cancellation of numerous appells—remarkable in a naval prison. The Commonwealth aircrew kriegies, mostly Canadians, would spend the next ten weeks at Marlag-Milag. At least half their stay occurred under oppressive grey skies that pelted them with rain and snow from the nearby North Sea. The kriegies at Marlag-Milag didn't see sunshine until March 8.

Clear skies brought a clear view of things other than the farthest reaches of their prison compound, however. Most of the kriegies who'd been imprisoned at Stalag Luft III hadn't been close to an Allied bomber since the day or night they were shot down—often months or even years ago. But suddenly, in those first days of March, they found themselves in front-row seats for some of the final airborne operations of the war. On March 8, the kriegies at Marlag-Milag were witness to a massive nighttime bombing attack on Hamburg. Robert Buckham watched the stream of hundreds of bombers almost circle the camp overhead en route to the target (U-boat construction pens in the harbour). When the visual show seemed over, Buckham went to bed to get warm, but was thrown back out of bed when the ground began to shake with the bomb explosions at Hamburg that continued for ninety minutes. The air battle that followed left quite an impression on fighter pilot Don Edy.

"The bomber stream headed home directly over the camp,"[40] he wrote. "We were thrilled at the sight and felt very close to those friends of ours just overhead. Suddenly, we heard the [German] night fighters on the attack. We followed the course of the battle . . .

"We would see a pattern of twinkling lights . . . cannon shells from the fighters. . . . Then all of a sudden an orange ball of flame as a bomber caught fire . . . then dropped towards the earth in a heart-breaking arc. I saw ten planes shot down that night in as many minutes. I don't think any other incident of the war shook me quite so deeply."

In contrast, John Colwell was again busily grinding out pots and pans and stools and bunk beds. And because he sensed both the winter and the war were nearing an end, he fashioned a pair of shorts for sitting outside in the sunshine and tore apart his flying boots to make a pair of bedroom slippers.

"The spring is sprung. The grass is riz. I wonder where the armistice is,"[41] he wrote in his diary on the first day of spring.

Then, just a few days later, the *Kommandant* called an unscheduled afternoon appell, ordering all the prisoners to pack for a 6:30 p.m. evacuation of the compound. That night, April 9, Colwell reported in his diary that Group Captain Larry Wray instructed the kriegies to break into the compound kitchen, steal as much white soap powder as possible, and write "R.A.F." and "P.O.W." in block letters on the sand of the parade ground,[42] indicating with a huge arrow their likely march route out of the camp, so that Allied fighters wouldn't fire on the kriegies in transit. Wray also attempted to delay departure. He'd learned that British ground forces were just seven miles from Bremen. One day's delay might allow the Desert Rats (British 7th Armoured Division) to overtake the evacuation march and hasten the kriegies' liberation. But it didn't happen. The next day, all of the prisoners from Stalag Luft III were on the march again, heading northeast from Tarmstedt and bound for Lübeck.

The first deadly strafing of kriegies happened on the road near the town of Zeven the next day, April 10. Several marines were killed when a flight of RAF Tempest fighter aircraft attacked one of the marching columns. They didn't realize they were shooting at POWs. Other strafings occurred near Harsefeld over the next few days; two kriegies were killed and seven were wounded. A few days earlier, the group of kriegies that included RCAF officer George Sweanor, housed at Stalag XIII-D near Nürnberg, were ordered to evacuate. Depending upon which rumour he believed, Sweanor's group was either en route to Hitler's mountain retreat at Berchtesgaden to become his personal hostages or toward Dachau, the Nazi death camp just outside Munich. In southeastern Germany too, however, Allied aircraft supporting General George Patton and the US Third Army had virtual air supremacy. In fact, Allied bombing of the bridge over the Danube had stopped Sweanor's train at Ingolstadt for several hours.

"Kriegies, who still had some cigarettes, bartered them for red and white paint," Sweanor said, "and we painted large red crosses on white backgrounds on the roofs and sides of our boxcars."[43]

But the POW train had barely left Ingolstadt when the kriegies aboard heard sirens warning of an imminent air attack. Their guards flung open the doors of the boxcars and the prisoners in the railway cars watched the last waves of Flying Fortresses and Liberators bombing Ingolstadt. A flight of P47 Thunderbolts flew low over the prisoner train, but then climbed steeply, banked, and lined up the train for a strafing run. Sweanor and his kriegie comrades instinctively knew the boxcar was the least safe place to be under these circumstances and dashed toward ditches about three hundred feet away. The Thunderbolts were gaining too quickly, so Sweanor went to ground and felt their strafing bullets cut a deep furrow a few feet from his prone body. When he tried again to make it to the ditch, more Thunderbolts began strafing from the other direction. Kriegies by the hundred were scattering in every direction, Americans among them.

"You God-damn trigger-happy idiots," one US pilot yelled up at them. "You can see our Red Crosses."[44]

Several other kriegies on the periphery of the attack stood and waved their arms wildly as the fighters swooped in for their final attacks at treetop level. One of the Thunderbolt pilots apparently spotted the Allied uniforms on the people scattering before him and ceased firing. He climbed to rejoin the rest of his flight, likely shared his discovery, and the flight raced away before any of the kriegies lying on the ground could record their squadron markings. An American pilot taking fire on the ground had flown with the same squadron over Italy.

"I know those bastards," he swore out loud. "I'll have them all crucified!"

But the damage was done. A South African air officer near Sweanor had most of his wrist shot away. A doctor in the group supplied a tourniquet to stop the bleeding and a cigarette to calm the man, while the surviving German train guards raced around herding the non-wounded kriegies back into the boxcars. It turned out the locomotive hauling their boxcars was mortally wounded by the strafing and barely managed another dozen miles before dying right there on the tracks. Meanwhile, inside the boxcars the kriegies experienced a new ambiance as a result of the air attack.

"At least we could thank the Yanks for the ventilation,"[45] Sweanor wrote.

The American Thunderbolt pilots weren't the only "trigger-happy" airmen in the final days of the European war. On April 19, 1945, RCAF pilots flying Typhoons had inadvertently strafed and killed twenty-nine kriegies[46] as they marched under German guard near Gresse, on the road to Lübeck. Among the five Canadians killed in the attack was Sergeant Robert Douglas, one of Sweanor's 419 Squadron comrades. During a bombing operation against St. Nazaire in March 1943, Douglas's aircraft was thrown on its back and into an inverted spin. Bomb-aimer Douglas managed to bail out, but the pilot got the Halifax out of the spin and flew the aircraft home; a month later, the same crew (minus Douglas, who was then in a German POW camp) was shot down over the Skagerrak; all crew were killed. Douglas had survived the near crash, and made it through the rest of the war imprisoned, but he died at the hands of Allied fighter pilots just twenty days short of German capitulation in Europe, May 8, 1945.[47]

There were too many close calls for Commonwealth air officers who had come so far, but had not yet been liberated. On April 20, John Colwell's group heading north from Marlag-Milag managed to get makeshift tents erected just before the heavens opened on their campsite near Elmenhorst. Then, during the night, Mosquito night fighters from Bomber Command shot up the town. Colwell and the others watched cannon tracer bullets coming out of the sky during the attack. With the rain continuing into the next day, Colwell's group— about thirty-five kriegies—sought shelter in a barn near Neritz, until two SS army officers showed up to move the POWs along.

"*Aus! Aussteigen!*" came the order from the Germans. They wanted everybody out of the barn in ten seconds or they would start shooting.

The kriegies realized how serious the SS officers were and scrambled out through windows and doors as fast as they could. One man missed the top rung of a ladder coming from the loft and slid to the bottom in a heap. Then, the SS men lined up Colwell and the others.

"*Terrorflieger,*" they shouted at the air officers, criticizing them for bombing women and children. And the more they shouted, the more they flashed their guns.

"I really thought it was the end,"[48] Colwell told himself. The POWs turned to a pastor who had been trekking with them, but the religious man was frightened to the point of being speechless. Finally, somebody made it clear the air officers were not fugitives, but that they were billeted in barns and sheds in the area under instructions from their guards. They were supposed to be there.

"We didn't stir from the barn for the rest of the day. We ate cold meals," Colwell wrote in his diary. Nor did it make any sense to enter Lübeck. A Red Cross medical officer, the SBO, and a German *Kommandant* had inspected what were to be the kriegies' final quarters, but pronounced them medically unfit. In his final war diary entry, on May 2, Colwell wrote, "Goons deserting. Tanks arrived at noon. FREE!"[49]

Don Edy, John R. Harris and the kriegies in their group were liberated nearby, on the Trenthorst Estate, about the same time. They had occupied a two-storey barn sturdy, stately, and well stocked with dry straw. Edy had set up a kitchen for cooking in the barnyard. Bags of flour from Red Cross parcels arrived and some of Edy's buddies found a bakery in a village and began baking. The resulting white bread was the first he'd tasted since he'd been shot down in North Africa in February 1942, three years before. On the night of May 1, 1945, Edy heard the British guns booming closer, saw Spitfires overhead, and awaited release. By daybreak the German guards had disappeared.

"We lined the road west of the estate like children waiting for the Santa Claus parade,"[50] he said. "Sure enough, about four o'clock in the afternoon, an armoured car came careening down the road.... We cheered like mad and swamped the car trying to shake the hands of the men in it. The demonstration was one of exuberance and relief."

Frank Sorensen rushed those same tanks that afternoon. Earlier in the day, May 2, a German guard had handed him a Luger as a sign of surrender. But that paled in comparison to seeing the convoy of Scottish armoured vehicles arrive at Wulmenau farm near Trenthorst.

"If I hadn't been so keen to get back to England in a hurry, I would have jumped on the tanks . . . and gone with them through Denmark," he later wrote his family. "They were some of the happiest moments in my life when I climbed up on the first tank and had my picture taken by the tank commander together with a whole tank-load of yelling and crying kriegies."[51]

Robert Buckham, Ley Kenyon, both artists and forgers inside the wire, and Les Brodrick, the former *trapführer* for tunnel "Dick," experienced liberation somewhat differently. With no accommodation available for them in any of the barns outside Lübeck, the three air force officers were taken at gunpoint to another prison, this one holding several thousand French officers. In the final days of April they burned straw in a chip heater to cook food, slept in cellars with double bunks, and scrounged for food around the barracks. On May 3, 1945, tanks from Bernard Montgomery's Second Army clattered out of cloud of smoke and dust. Then a khaki-clad commander emerged from the lead tank and waved at the POWs gathered on the parapet of the prison. Buckham made his last diary entries.

"A roar of cheers; crudely made flags waving; laughter and tears mingling; the guards running off, weaponless; men climbing the wire to run to the tanks; men embracing each other, shouting incoherently; men kneeling to pray; men staring vacantly, bewildered; thousands of men in a state of hysterical, blessed release. It continued for minutes,"[52] he wrote.

The first Allied officer dispatched to enter the prison near Lübeck to liberate the thousands of Allied POWs, including hundreds of Commonwealth air officers, arrived after 6 p.m. that day. The kriegies watched with some sense of irony as finally the tables turned. All German troops captured there were paraded in the square, without gear, and marched off. The liberators found a German general hiding in the basement and took him away too. But the kriegies were told they would have to stay in the prison ten more days, until arrangements for flights to Britain could be arranged.

"We have been liberated," Buckham wrote, "but we are not free."

Liberation proved equally bittersweet for George Harsh, Kingsley Brown, and Wally Floody, who had trekked and trained across Germany from the satellite prison camp at Belaria to one of the worst Wehrmacht prison camps in Germany, at Luckenwalde, south of Berlin. When the three RCAF officers were incarcerated there at Stalag III-A, in February, they were already hungry, filthy, and in a generally weakened state.[53] And conditions at the prison didn't help. For most of the winter they had survived on a ration of a cup of soup and a few slices of bread a day. They had slept in bug-infested bunks and had heated their quarters by burning twigs and bed shavings in a tin can. Then, on April 22, 1945, two days after Adolf Hitler's birthday, Soviet Army troops pushed the Germans out of Luckenwalde and the prison camp. However, the Canadians (along with other Allied air force officers) were separated from civilian prisoners at Stalag III-A, and kept for another six weeks while the Soviets negotiated with the Americans on the west side of the River Elbe to be traded for an equal number of Soviet prisoners the US Army had liberated.[54]

Finally, at the end of May 1945, the three Canadians arrived at the pontoon bridge over the Elbe where they would be exchanged for three Soviets. Harsh led the trio, followed by Brown and Floody.

When they reached free soil at the west end of the bridge, an American infantry colonel greeted them.

"Here you are, chaps," the American said in an exaggerated British accent. "Right this way to Tokyo!" And he waited a moment for their reactions.

"Fuck you, Jack," retorted the American-born George Harsh. "And the same . . . for any friends you may have in California."

Brown just leapt down from the bridge and shook his head in disbelief. Then Floody, with greater reverence for the significance of the moment, joined his two ex-kriegies on the ground and said, "By God, we made it."[55]

Meanwhile, Tony Pengelly's liberators nearly killed him with their kindness and efficiency. Once in the hands of the British Army, north of Marlag-Milag, Pengelly and the rest of his group of Commonwealth officers became just another lot of freight that had to be dealt with. When army drivers arrived at the frontlines, they simply unloaded ammunition and other battle supplies; then with equal dispatch they loaded POWs into the empty space and made the return trip. Similarly, once inside an Allied military base, British officials were convinced the Commonwealth air officers had typhus and had them deloused.

"They assumed we were totally contaminated,"[56] Pengelly said. "So they took all our clothes, burned them . . . and we took hot showers using special lice soap."

The next day, the kriegies were moved to a new location. They were stripped again and their new battledress from the day before was also burned, while their bodies were deloused with hot showers and lice soap yet again. On May 7, the day before V-E Day, the Commonwealth officers, who hadn't been airborne in several years, boarded Lancaster bombers and were flown back to England.

"We landed at a big reception field," he said. "And they assumed we were all lousy and they did the same routine. Took our army battledress, burned it, and gave us air force battledress."

Then, the British reception centre greeters led the former kriegies into aircraft hangars filled with card tables and chairs for an afternoon social. Local community ladies, Red Cross women, and nurses soon descended to entertain the officers over tea and gin rummy.

"From seeing no women for four years to being swamped—hundreds of them—and here we were with teacups and scones. It was the most absurd scene."[57]

Now ex-kriegies, the air force officers of the Commonwealth who had somehow succeeded in surviving to this first week of May 1945 marked the achievement in personal ways. George Sweanor, penned up in a barracks in Moosburg, Germany, remembered his best friend Pat Porter[58], who had kept their Halifax aloft long enough for the crew to bail out two years before. When Don Edy arrived at the rehabilitation centre in Bournemouth, England, he took the small tin suitcase in which he had carried his belongings for more than three years—from the first POW camps in Italy, to Sagan at Stalag Luft III, and throughout the forced march across Germany—and chucked it under his bed for good; he was shipping out to Canada and the tin case "looked silly and rather childish."[59] Art Hawtin, who credited his dedication to staying physically fit for his survival, salvaged one souvenir of his POW experience—a photograph of the Canadian All-Star Baseball Team that had routed the Americans in that summer tournament of 1943.[60] Darrell Larlee saved a photo too, one depicting the POW roommates for whom he had cooked; the picture hung on a wall at the family home in Campbellton, New Brunswick, as a constant reminder to be thankful and frugal—to the point that his son, Peter, said, "nothing would get thrown out. Everything got put back in the fridge. . . . We'd eat Sunday dinner until Thursday."[61] Alan Righetti, an Australian air force officer, carried a piece of Canada with him almost all the way home. On the night of the breakout, his roommate, RCAF fighter pilot George Wiley, had entrusted Righetti with his watch in the event he didn't make it. En route home to Australia in 1946, Righetti stopped in Windsor, Ontario, to fulfill the promise and delivered the watch to Wiley's parents and sister.

The memento snapshots, the jettisoned belongings, the lost comrades, the legacy of the murdered fifty, and the recollection of a thousand other experiences in airborne combat or inside the compound wire stayed with the ex-kriegies—sometimes by design, often not. Most former POWs returning to Canada chose to leave any tangible evidence of being shot down or being imprisoned tucked inside flight logs, shoeboxes, or basement cupboards. Best forgotten, they thought. Phil Marchildon returned to Penetanguishene, Ontario, walked the familiar streets of home, and noted that everything looked exactly the way he remembered, "as if the war had never happened."[62] As with other returning vets, the former air force POWs tried to get their lives back on track—retooling in school, returning to jobs that had been held for them, and restoring relationships with families and friends. For many ex-kriegies, there were understanding spouses who learned to tolerate their nighttime outbursts, idiosyncratic eating habits, or their need to sleep in a single bed. Often there was little or no other post-trauma help. When enough time had passed, there were air force reunions they might join, Remembrance Day observances they might brave, and special POW gatherings they might attend. During a memorial service held in London, England, several months after the spring breakout and Gestapo murders in 1944, a chaplain offered an assessment of the kriegies' plight: "Their sacrifice was touched by the finger of God," he said. "Their freedom in a measure lost, they fought on, doing their duty twice over."[63]

Volunteers, they had trained for war, served in aerial combat, been blown out of the sky, withstood interrogation for secret intelligence, and been imprisoned for the duration. Prisoners of war, some had joined The Great Escape to spite their captors or stave off boredom, others out of a sense of duty. Still others viewed the plot to dig to freedom as simply futile. But all faced its brutal aftermath. Ultimately, as hostages to a dying regime, the air force officers faced one last test of their fortitude and sense of duty, trekking toward a liberation that always seemed just one more day away. Theirs was service *many* times over.

# "A PROUD, SPECTACULAR DISTRACTION"

T HE IRONY of his May 8th experience took a while to sink in. RAF pilot Philip Gray had spent most of the previous four years preparing for, enduring, and feeling grateful for surviving the nightly combat operations of Bomber Command. He flew his sixteenth and final bombing raid against a marshalling yard between Bremen and Hamburg, Germany. It was not a piece of cake. En route home, Gray's Lancaster had to evade heavy anti-aircraft fire. The crew discovered one five-hundred-pound bomb still hung up in the bomb bay, but safely released it over the North Sea. Then, on final approach to his home airfield, Gray grappled with falling pressure in the landing-gear brakes. But when he brought the Lanc to a dead stop halfway down the runway, it dawned on him. His war was over. The tension of living life on the edge was gone. Any anxiety about surviving evaporated. One day, Bomber Command's strategists led an all-out bombing campaign, dispatching hundreds of aircrews and their four-engine bombers from aerodromes all over the country. The next—May 8, 1945—with all those airmen and their aircraft on hand, there was nothing for them to do.

Suddenly, Gray received a briefing on Operation Exodus, an overnight solution to a problem he and his RAF bomber crew hadn't even

known existed. Air officers and men by the thousands* had been cut
loose from prison camps all over the Reich. They were holed up in
former prisons, fenced compounds, hospital wards, warehouses, and
makeshift tent cities next to recaptured aerodromes waiting for a ride
home. Learning of their plight, Prime Minister Winston Churchill
gave their repatriation the highest priority. The luxury of commanding such a well-organized machine as Bomber Command, its ready
aircrews, and now all its available aircraft, seemed too good to ignore.
Nearly five hundred round trips of Lancasters, Halifaxes, and other
heavy bombers would do the job.

"[We were] ideal magic carpets to whisk the ex-POWs back to
freedom in a hurry,"[1] Gray wrote.

Not unlike each of his bombing runs over Europe, Gray's first
flight bringing kriegies home to Britain proved instructive, if a bit
unsettling. Serving in the war as "Lords of the Air" and never having
experienced the daily task of survival in a POW camp, Gray admitted
that he was ignorant of the trauma the former prisoners of war had
known. Only when he loaded twenty-four passengers that first day
of Operation Exodus did he learn that some of them had been four,
five, and six years in enemy stalags, mostly cut off from the Allied war
effort, and all of them entirely reliant on their own resourcefulness to
make it through the war. To learn that freedom and home were less
than an hour's flight away proved overwhelming for the physically
weakened and emotionally drained ex-kriegies.

"The sun was shining during that first Exodus touchdown," Gray
wrote as he watched the POWs step from his Lancaster onto the tarmac at Westcott Airfield in Buckinghamshire. "Some got down on
their hands and knees and kissed the concrete. Others simply burst
into tears where they stood, while others lay on the grass and sobbed.
I was thunderstruck . . ."[2]

---

* The official Bomber Command records show that Operation Exodus aircrews from 1,
5, 6, and 8 Groups carried out 469 flights, principally from Brussels to the UK, and repatriated approximately seventy-five thousand officers and airmen. Aircrews completed the
operation without a single mishap.

With an awakened recognition that these former prisoners of war needed time and space—even aboard their flights back to Britain—Gray had a greater sense of empathy at the controls during his second Exodus sortie. He dropped his jovial "we'll-get-you-home" act. He simply nodded and smiled as they climbed aboard. He let them be by themselves. He made sure that he and his crew delivered as smooth and uneventful a ride home as possible. He merely wondered about "the stories that lay behind the eyes, the docile manner, the resigned, rather sad, expressions that [came] back at me from these men, stories which would possibly never be told in full."[3] Never, indeed.

The pilot of the Lancaster bomber with ex-kriegie Kingsley Brown aboard that first week of May embellished passage to England slightly more. And the former Nova Scotia journalist soaked up the trip like a kid on a carnival ride. For his flight back to the UK, Brown got a front-row view, seated in the bomb-aimer's bay. Leaving the Belgian coast, the Lanc pilot brought the bomber down to a few hundred feet off the North Sea as he followed the coastline and flew right over the French port of Dunkirk. Brown recognized the burned out vehicles and the sunken hulls as the sight of the British Expeditionary Force retreat in 1940. Then, on the opposite side of the Channel, the Lanc made an equally dramatic flypast over the white cliffs of Dover.

"To me they seemed a little blurred,"[4] Brown wrote, "but actually they hadn't changed a bit."

Later stationed at Bournemouth, on the south coast of England, Brown and his forced-march comrade George Harsh waited for the RCAF repatriation system to process them home to Canada. Not surprisingly, the bureaucracy didn't move quickly enough for either of them. So Brown, the former intelligence expert for X Organization, and Harsh, the former security boss for tunnels "Tom," "Dick," and "Harry," hatched a plan to solve their immediate problem. They decided to liberate a local rowboat and paddle out to a four-engine RAF Sunderland flying boat[5] moored in the harbour at Poole. The fact that Brown had only piloted twin-engine Hampdens and Harsh had served as a tail-gunner didn't seem to faze them. They crept aboard the Sunderland and had gotten one engine started when the military police arrived. It took the pull of two decorated wing commanders to spring Harsh and Brown from jail, and a week or so later the two veterans had been booked aboard *Île de France* for their trans-Atlantic passage.

Back home and back in civilian life, George Harsh chose big city publishing while Kingsley Brown appeared to avoid contact with a lot of people in a confined space. He took over his great uncle's general store in the community of West Jeddore (population two hundred) on the south shore of Nova Scotia. By 1950, he had returned to life as a professional communicator—in public relations, then reporting and editing, and eventually the civil service as a special assistant to Ellen Fairclough, Canada's first woman cabinet minister in the John Diefenbaker government.

Perhaps because he'd been a journalist first, Brown eventually put his memories of Stalag Luft III to paper—from harnessing bumblebees with propaganda on onion skin paper, through several escape attempts, to his role in stockpiling intelligence for the forged documents, and eventually the forced march across Germany with Wally Floody and George Harsh. When he finished his account of the experience he titled *Officers Travel First Class*, he sent the manuscript to publishers, but kept receiving rejection letters. In the late 1980s, Brown had given up. "I never expected to see a book of mine make the light of day. And this proves it,"[6] Brown told his wife, Marion. "Nobody is going to buy this manuscript. Nobody."

"That's not true," Marion interrupted. "Be patient. Someone will buy it."

"Who?"

"I will," Marion said. "I'll buy it."

"And just how much are you prepared to pay for the manuscript, Angel?"

"Five hundred dollars," she said without hesitation.

"Then consider it sold to Marion, the highest bidder."

Kingsley signed over the work to Marion, and in February 1989, his story of life at Stalag Luft III, renamed *Bonds of Wire*, was published by Collins in Toronto. His daughter Ethel recalled watching Kingsley flip through books at home as if he were speed reading. When she asked him what he'd read, he illustrated chapter and verse how well and how much he had digested, perhaps a skill developed in the North Compound library, skimming German newspapers for information that could be used in forged documents for the escapers.

"He had the intellect of an encyclopedia,"[7] Ethel (Brown) Alle said.

In one of his last letters home in January 1945, just before the Germans marched their prisoners out of Stalag Luft III, John "Scruffy" Weir remembered he'd better wish his fiancée, Frances, a happy birthday for the upcoming April, just in case the vagaries of the mail system delayed his best wishes until after the fact.

"Perhaps I'll be there in time to give you a birthday kiss,"[8] Weir wrote. "I find it impossible to visualize what our reunion is going to be like. But I still dream of it."

Almost five months later to the day—June 1945—Hugh Godefroy, Weir's former squadron mate, got word that Scruffy had been shipped home to Canada and would arrive in Lachine, Quebec, for a formal repatriation ceremony. By the time the RCAF officers arrived at Lachine to be marched into an assembly hall and officially released to their families, Weir's father and fiancée, Frances McCormack, had travelled up from Toronto. First the repatriation was set for 9 p.m. But thanks to air force protocol, it was postponed and then postponed again.

"Finally, at two in the morning,"[9] Frances remembered, "John and his crew marched in. John was in the front line, about dead centre and he spotted his father. And I was beside his father. Well, John just walked out of the lineup and came to us. Broke up the whole ceremony."

But John Weir's triumphant return to civilian life in Canada still had a few bumps to endure. After the ceremony, they all hopped into Colonel Weir's automobile and began the drive to the Godefroy home. Minutes into their trip, they got a flat tire; so while Frances sat in the backseat of the car, John and his father jacked up the car, removed the flat, and replaced it with the spare. It was the middle of the night when the trio reached its destination. And while the rest of the household went to bed, John and Frances sat in the household sunroom and talked the night away. "We never drew a breath all the way home," Frances said of the train ride back to Toronto. "It was like we were [in Toronto] in a minute."

Weir had warned his fiancée he didn't look the same with his eyelids gone, burned in the descent when his Spitfire was shot down four years before.

"But it didn't change him as far as I was concerned," she said. "He never came to terms with it. I didn't see what he was talking about. We got married October 2, 1945. Love is blind."[10]

There were only a few important women in Don McKim's life. The youngest of three children, Don had grown up on a farm near Lynedoch, in southern Ontario. At age sixteen, Don was told by his father he would be leaving the farm for a job at the Canadian Bank of Commerce. Just before he joined the RCAF late in 1940, he was working at a branch of the bank in Sault Ste. Marie, Ontario. There he had enjoyed an acquaintance with Doreen Olson, a telephone company employee, but bank employees were not allowed to marry or else they would have to forfeit their jobs. Still, McKim found creative ways to enjoy Olson's company. On each day she came to the bank to deposit the cash receipts of her telephone company, he always found a way to be the teller who counted her cash.

"Did you bounce?"[11] McKim always asked her, meaning was the cash amount different from the total on the deposit slip.

"Yes," she would generally reply.

"I'll count it again after we close," he'd say. While he confirmed that the cash and deposit slip balanced, they could have a conversation about anything but money.

After McKim was shot down in December 1942 and introduced to German air force prison camps, he depended on any supplies his mother would send from home. Agnes McKim was a lifeline for her son, sending clothing, dry goods, and letters. Following his liberation and repatriation to England, McKim finally got passage back to Canada aboard a troopship, where he ran into a Canadian Army corporal named Sid Olson. It was Doreen's brother, who had also been captured during the war and liberated about the same time Don was. And though McKim's air force officer comrades frowned on it for a while, throughout the trans-Atlantic voyage home when meals were served, Don would always retrieve Sid from his Spartan third-class accommodations onboard the ship and bring him up to the first-class officers' dining area to eat.

Home in Ontario again, Don returned to civilian life and to his teller's wicket at the Canadian Bank of Commerce. He left Doreen Olson behind, as the bank reassigned him to a branch in Binbrook, Ontario (near Hamilton). There, he connected with a previous acquaintance, Grace Crozier. Soon after they began to see each other, she told him the grim coincidence that had occurred during the war.

"Grace's husband was in the air force like I was,"[12] McKim said. "When she heard that I was missing in action [in December 1942], she sat down to write a letter to tell her husband Dave [Crozier] who was also overseas. The very moment she was writing that letter, a knock came at her door. A man had arrived to inform her that her husband was also missing. [She learned later] he'd been killed . . .

"When I got back, I went to see Grace . . . and I married her," McKim said.

Former RAF Spitfire pilot and scrounger at Stalag Luft III Keith Ogilvie finished his war near Bremen, where his forced march had ended in March 1945. Like so many air officers during the trek, he'd survived thanks to employing a buddy system with fellow officer Samuel Pepys. Perhaps what had contributed equally to his survival was that a year earlier, on the morning of March 25, 1944, F/L Ogilvie had been the last officer out of tunnel "Harry" to get away from the North Compound. He was probably the hard-arser who'd covered the greatest distance on foot—about forty miles—before being recaptured by German Home Guards near Halbau, Germany.

Back in England after VE Day, Ogilvie was hospitalized in Glouces-ter, as much to ensure that fractures in his arm, sustained in July 1941 when his Spitfire was shot down, had healed, as to aid his recovery from the forced march. Nevertheless, during his convalescence, Ogil-vie made up for lost time on a number of fronts. He reconnected with a Canadian friend who had worked with the British Ministry of Infor-mation censoring the letters of Canadian servicemen, Irene Lock-wood.

As well, Ogilvie filled out the forms to transfer from the RAF to the RCAF. And finally, he met with British Intelligence officers of MI9 to recount his experiences at Görlitz prison following his recap-ture from the breakout on March 24–25, 1944. In question was the German assertion that the Commonwealth air officers had been shot while attempting to escape custody and that, at the time, they had been disguised as civilians.

During the debrief, a British Intelligence official asked Ogilvie to describe what he witnessed on March 29–30, 1944, from his Görlitz cell.

"I saw [F/L Mike] Casey, [S/L Ian] Cross, [F/L George] Wiley, [F/L Cyril] Swain, and maybe two others [F/O John Pohe and F/O Al Hake] leave handcuffed under the control of civilians," Ogilvie said. "After this, other parties also left at night usually in fours or sixes."[13]

"What clothes were the officers wearing?" the MI9 man asked.

"They were almost entirely dressed in Air Force uniform. [F/O Denys] Street for instance, had an RAF officer's tunic with wings, rank, and buttons."

"As far as you [are concerned] had they committed any criminal offences?"

"Absolutely none!"

F/L Ogilvie returned home to Canada in July 1945 and married Irene Lockwood in the summer of 1946. He dedicated much of his early return to active service in the RCAF, officially welcoming those aircrew members who returned to Canada through the ports of New York, Montreal, and Halifax. He served in the RCAF another eigh-teen years. He died in Ottawa in May 1998.

Ogilvie is remembered largely for his DFC, his eight damaged or destroyed victories as a fighter pilot, and his nearly quarter century of service in the air force. Equally important in the story of the Great Escape, however, was that account given to MI9. Based, in part, on Ogilvie's specific recounting of events on March 30 at Görlitz prison, *Oberregierungsrat* Wilhelm Scharpwinkel of the Gestapo and *Kriminal Obersekretaer* Lux were found to be complicit in the murders of the Commonwealth officers at Halbau and found guilty (in absentia) during the war crimes trials in 1947–48. Scharpwinkel was traced to a prison in the Soviet Union in 1946, and interviewed by Capt. M. F. Cornish of British Intelligence. The Gestapo chief at Breslau never faced trial at Hamburg, but died in a Moscow prison in 1947. Lux died during the advance of the Soviet Army at Breslau in 1944. Ogilvie had at least helped to deliver the promise that the British Foreign Minister had made in June 1944.

"These foul criminals," Anthony Eden had said, "will be brought to exemplary justice."[14]


The fifty murdered air force officers weighed heavily on Wally Floody's mind for a long time afterward. Perhaps the impact of those bad memories took away Floody's impulse to speak about the escape and its aftermath for many years. Unlike other kriegies, Floody the Tunnel King wasn't liberated until the end of May 1945, when the Soviets exchanged him for Russian POWs the Americans had liberated. Floody had spent his twenty-seventh birthday, April 28, awaiting his freedom. He missed VE Day in England. He was just as glad to get home and leave the war and its experiences behind. Indeed, a year later, when his first son was born, Wally learned he was to receive the Order of the British Empire.

"Flight Lieutenant Floody . . . became one of the leading organizers and most indefatigable workers in the tunnels themselves," the OBE citation read. "Time and time again, projects were started and discovered by the Germans, but despite all dangers and difficulties, Floody persisted, showing a marked degree of courage and devotion to duty."[15]

The announcement put Floody in the spotlight. Reporters wanted his story again and again. Buckingham Palace wanted him to come to London for the OBE investiture. As far as he was concerned, however, he didn't deserve the fuss. He never considered his tunnel designing and digging heroic. He turned the invitation down and attended to his chartered air service based on the islands along the Toronto waterfront instead. Eventually, Floody abandoned the flying business altogether.

"I can still see their faces,"[16] Floody told reporters years later, "especially the six Canadians. The Gestapo and SS took the fifty out, two by two and . . . dispatched them with shots in the back of the head."

During the time of the trials of those complicit in the murders of the fifty officers, Floody happened to be employed as a marketing manager and living in Britain. There he reconnected with Wings Day, who, after the Great Escape, had been recaptured and thrown into the Sachenhausen concentration camp. The two ex-POW comrades watched with fascination as the work of S/L F. P. McKenna and the RAF Special Investigation Branch yielded convictions of the Gestapo gunmen during trials at Hamburg in 1947 and 1948. Floody steadfastly refused to talk about his memories, even when Paul Brickhill's book, *The Great Escape*, was published in 1951. It took another decade before Floody felt comfortable enough to openly reflect on events at Stalag Luft III.

A phone call from moviemaker John Sturges came when Floody was in the right frame of mind. The Hollywood director requested Floody's expertise as a technical advisor during the shooting of his $4-million feature film, *The Great Escape*, in the spring and summer of 1962. Then in his mid-forties, Floody visited the set at Geiselgasteig, in Bavaria near Munich. Initially for two weeks, he offered his impressions and suggestions on many aspects of the production— the way the Commonwealth officers' uniforms should look, how the underground air pump worked, and in particular the way set designers had reconstructed the tunnel "Harry" for the digging and escaping scenes. At one point, before the filming began, Floody was asked to crawl into the tunnel replica. He noted it had a little too much room, so the production designer lowered the tunnel ceiling to make it believably claustrophobic. Just before Wally and Betty Floody left the film location, they enjoyed a dinner with some members of the production crew, who wondered about the production's authenticity.

"I know you're getting everything right," Floody said, "because I had terrible nightmares last night."[17]

*The Great Escape* opened in the summer of 1963. Its Canadian premiere in Toronto on July 3 featured a march past by an RCAF band, and attendance by the Ontario lieutenant governor and as many former kriegies as Wally Floody could contact. As well as initiating a successful summer of box office receipts in Canada, the opening netted $10,000 for the RCAF Ex-Prisoner of War Association. Wally Floody regularly participated in POW reunions and memorials in Canada and abroad. One in Toronto in 1970 reunited not only ex-kriegies, but also Hermann Glemnitz, the former staff sergeant at Stalag Luft III. As Floody posed for a *Globe and Mail* photographer with Glemnitz, the two men offered an exchange for reporter Arthur Moses.

"I didn't know anything about any tunnels,"[18] Floody grinned.

"Come on, Floody," the former German guard said, "I won't put you in the cooler now."

George Sweanor never fully endorsed the tunnel escape plan. Nor did he feel comfortable with Roger Bushell's confrontational strategy when dealing with the Luftwaffe guards at Stalag Luft III. Nevertheless, he co-operated fully with every demand the escape committee made of him. Almost from the day the North Compound became home to two thousand Commonwealth flyers, in April 1943, Sweanor had committed to serving X Organization as a duty pilot, making note of everyone who entered or exited the main gate. In addition to those security duties, he had also served as a penguin, dispersing his share of excavated sand, and as a stooge, spying on the ferrets who were spying on the prisoners. As much as anybody else inside the wire, Sweanor felt motivated to get home, where his wife, Joan, and the daughter he'd never seen awaited his return. However, when it came time to draw numbers for the order of escape down tunnel "Harry," George Sweanor had refused to enter his name.

"I was all for it initially," he said. "You were a member of the military. You were expected to carry on degrading the enemy's ability to make war, and escaping would be . . . degrading their manpower."[19]

But somewhere between his drive for survival and his conception of trekking through hundreds of miles of enemy-occupied territory back to England, Sweanor discovered a reality that shaped his days of captivity and the rest of his life. Aside from the obvious confinement, surveillance, and deprivation he experienced at the Luftwaffe prison camp near Sagan, Poland, he came to believe that his existence inside the wire had had a lasting intellectual impact on him too.

"I consider Stalag Luft III my alma mater,"[20] Sweanor said. "With years to discuss life with intelligent aircrew from well over a score of countries, and with interaction with the enemy, it was evident that people are people—good, bad, and indifferent—in every culture."[21]

With the help of textbooks that were specially imported from Canadian universities, Sweanor upgraded his education with a political science course. In the library he read newspapers the Luftwaffe regularly supplied because their content endorsed the German position in the war. Together with the BBC broadcast content passed along by the kriegies operating the wireless radio hidden inside the compound, the library books and magazines helped fill in gaps that his wartime imprisonment had created.

"We knew much more about the war than the people who were still fighting it," he wrote.

And while it was a chore, he dutifully attended German language class, in part to be conversationally capable should the need arise, but mostly for the discipline of attending and learning. He participated as actively in sports in the prison compound as he would have at a Canadian university; he realized, if nothing else, that the physical exertion maintained fitness and health when the lack of adequate nutrition sometimes did not. And while he only assisted in the functioning of the North Compound theatre peripherally, helping out with set construction once in a while, Sweanor felt the regular weekly drama and musical productions constantly boosted the kriegies' morale.

George Sweanor also took up the pencil and paper while imprisoned at Stalag Luft III. As with so many other rituals developed inside the wire, writing became a daily habit he has continued throughout his life. When the first edition of his memoirs, *It's All Pensionable Time: Twenty-five Years in the Royal Canadian Air Force*, was published in 1967, fully two-thirds of the book's content was drawn from notes on his experience at Stalag Luft III. And in the years following the war, when he continued to serve in the RCAF—in Interim Force, the Arctic, the Korean Airlift, the Distant Early Warning (DEW) line, and NORAD at Colorado Springs—he never stopped writing his observations and thoughts. Preparing his journal for publication, assembling articles for periodicals, and composing notes for speeches, he downplayed as "verbal diarrhea," but as of 2013, George Sweanor, age ninety-three, continues to prepare the monthly newsletter of 971 Air Marshal Slemon Wing of the RCAF Association, in Colorado Springs, Colorado. His sign-off is a regular feature of the publication: "Ye Olde Scribe."

Richard Bartlett's landing back in England proved nearly as bumpy as his crash landing in Trondheim, five years before, during the Allied defeat in Norway. After hiding "the canary," the radio that brought BBC broadcasts to the POWs, Bartlett then survived the forced march to Lübeck and was liberated that first week of May 1945. But as had become the routine on arrival in the UK, ex-kriegie Bartlett had his uniform virtually stripped from him and his body subjected to repeated delousing showers. When Sub Lieutenant Bartlett emerged from the final medical and debugging sessions, he did not receive the appropriate Fleet Air Arm uniform he required, but a British Army uniform instead. Nevertheless, the RAF put him on a plane with three other Royal Navy personnel and sent ahead a message to Portsmouth to the effect that four naval POWs were en route and transport had to be arranged. The Portsmouth officer in charge misinterpreted the note and sent a paddy wagon to meet "the prisoners." To add to the insult, Bartlett soon learned British authorities had shipped all his uniforms and kit to his family's Canadian home in Fort Qu'Appelle, Saskatchewan.

Bartlett arrived at the Royal Navy air station at Lea-On-Solent in southern England on the eve of VE Day with no uniform, no back pay, and no access to the victory celebrations about to begin all over the UK. Not unaccustomed to scrounging and making do, however, Bartlett liberated a white shirt, collar, and tie that substituted for his navy whites and he joined the party suitably dressed anyway. Next, Bartlett wondered if he might be allowed to get to Canada. He learned he was entitled to three months leave, but the rules blocked his way home.

"Royal Navy personnel are not allowed to take foreign leave in wartime," the regulations stipulated.

As it turned out, there was a way around that barrier too. Bartlett's commanding officer simply arranged to have him posted to Northern Ireland. With Royal Canadian Navy ships regularly passing through the port of Londonderry, his CO surmised that with his "on the job training in escape and evasion," Bartlett would have no trouble getting aboard a westbound ship. Indeed, he hitched a ride with a North Atlantic convoy corvette and several days later landed in Halifax. He was nearly stopped with insufficient domestic currency in his pocket, did a quick exchange with a stranger, and bought train fare to Regina en route to being reunited with his family in Fort Qu'Appelle.

But that ended Richard Bartlett's career path of dipping and dodging, since by summer's end he was back on station in the UK, ready for his next assignment with Fleet Air Arm. The Allies had secured victory in Europe and it would soon be theirs in the Pacific as well. Bartlett received his full lieutenant commission in addition to a transfer to the Royal Canadian Navy, and in early 1946 he joined the squadron serving aboard carrier HMCS *Warrior*. By 1947, he had married Margaret Falconer and assumed peacetime command of the Firefly squadron. It didn't seem to matter. In spite of his exemplary career in the RCN—from 1946 to 1964—he couldn't seem to shake his kriegie past nor the interest from family and friends about his imprisonment at Stalag Luft III. In 1992, Dick and Margaret Bartlett attended the Remembrance Day assembly where their grandson, Nick Dumonceaux, attended elementary school. During the observance, the students were asked if their grandparents had fought in the Second World War. Seven-year-old Nick gladly went to the microphone.

"My grandfather spent the war in jail,"[22] he announced proudly.

Both the assembly and his grandparents got quite a chuckle out of Nick's perception of Dick Bartlett's POW time from 1940 to 1945. But the youngster grew up to understand his grandfather's war and, in a world that offered more than a microphone to express himself, in 2011, after his grandfather had died, a twenty-six-year-old Nick Dumonceaux posted a tribute on his Facebook page.

"You are the reason I am here today," the post said. "You gave so much and never asked anything in return. You were a part of what made this country great and we will never forget."

It took just as long for Frank Sorensen's three children to understand his Stalag Luft III experience. They were all at least young adults before the real story of their father's Second World War air force record—his training in the BCATP, his propaganda speech from England to the Danish Resistance on Radio Free Europe in 1942, his posting with RAF 232 Squadron to North Africa, his victories over the Tunisian desert, then being shot down in 1943, and his eventual participation as a language specialist in the Great Escape—all came to light. The three Sorensen children were born within a dozen years of the end of the war: Glenn in 1948, Stephen in 1950, and Vicki in 1957. All they knew was that their dad was a successful dentist married to Betty Bodley, a former schoolteacher. But that was the Frank Sorensen whom most knew outside his Kingston, Ontario, home.

Inside their home, the three Sorensen kids never went without, but they came to know a father who had a short fuse (sometimes sparked by his weekend drinking) and who seemed haunted by something or someone. At night Glenn, Stephen, and Vicki all recalled their parents suddenly shouting—their father screaming at demons of some sort, their mother trying to wake him with the assurance he was safely in bed in his own home. The three children were specifically told never to stand in a doorway where their father slept because he might suddenly attack the silhouette by kicking the door closed without realizing a family member was standing there.

"Things got worse as we all grew up,"[23] Stephen said. "Glenn and I [had bedrooms] in the basement. We could hear all the fighting and bickering through the basement wall. Vicki was literally across the narrow hallway next to my parents' bedroom."

"I asked my mom, 'Why did you stay [with him]?'"[24] Vicki said. "And she told me with the veterans returning from the war . . . all the women knew they would be traumatized, but they had a sort of unspoken pact, that they were going to stand by them no matter what."

"When I was a teen,"[25] Glenn said, "to suggest that [my dad] get psychiatric help would be admitting he had problems. . . . It was never really addressed throughout his lifetime."

In school in the late 1950s, Stephen read Eric Williams' *The Wooden Horse*, the fictionalized version of his own escape, with Michael Codner and Oliver Philpot, from Stalag Luft III in 1943. Then, when *The Great Escape* Hollywood movie was released, Frank Sorensen took Stephen to see it at the Grand Theatre in Kingston, just the two of them. Little by little, Frank began to share some of his own Great Escape remembrances with his two sons—the food he ate, his work as a penguin dispersing sand, teaching Roger Bushell conversational Danish on the circuit, even the horrors of the forced march in the winter of 1945. The boys eventually learned about their father's extraordinary athleticism at Stalag Luft III, such that he could throw a golf ball farther than almost every other kriegie in the North Compound.

"[Dad] was very thin at the end of the war," Stephen said. "When he got out [of the service,] he started lifting weights, building his body back. There are pictures in which he looked nicely chiselled and cut. But my mother never had any interest . . . in his physique. He would say, 'I married the wrong woman. She didn't appreciate it when I started putting muscles back on.'"

In some respects it took a discovery after Vicki's father died to put him, his wartime past, and his postwar life of torment into focus for her. Like her brothers, Vicki had absorbed the passed-down stories about her father's career as a fighter pilot and a prisoner of war, but she said it was all a bit like watching a sub-title without any detail. Then, late in 2010, she gained access to some photographs of her father in the air force and the letters exchanged between her father and family members while he was a POW at Stalag Luft III.

"[From his letters] I learned . . . he was keen. He wanted to serve his country. . . . One of his greatest fears was not being posted overseas. He never complained about doing what was asked of him. He was fearless."

Since reading the correspondence and viewing the photos, Vicki Sorensen has willingly dedicated countless hours on the phone, on the internet, and on her own time to discovering as much about her father's role in the Great Escape as she can. She methodically contacts other former kriegies or their families all over the world in pursuit of any details about her father's time in the prison camp. Perhaps what motivates her most is a drive to understand Frank Sorensen's decision to trade his position on the escape list; since she surmises her father gave his spot to either James Catanach or Arnold Christensen (both shot by the Gestapo), she believes that the demons he experienced came from knowing he survived and they did not.

"My father never let go of the guilt, saying, 'That should have been me,'" she said. "My father never got over the execution of the fifty. . . . A good friend of his told me when he was visiting, my father showed him the Tunnel Martyrs memorial picture and said, 'These were my buddies. They're all gone.'"

Family correspondence continues to shed light on the silent battle that Frank Sorensen waged as his wife and children struggled to understand him. Among the passages Vicki Sorensen turns to for explanation and comfort is her grandfather's assessment of Frank at an early reunion as the war was ending.

"There he was tall and smiling," her grandfather noted in his diary. "He was in his battledress with a kitbag under his arm, thin and tanned. We had lunch and got out for the table some of the things we have been saving up just for this occasion. His appetite is not great, but it is growing. He needs building up. His spirits are rising and he has improved much . . ."

A final observation from Vicki's Uncle Ben about his brother concluded that "after the war Frank was . . . without his former zest for life. He suffered [from] post-traumatic stress syndrome, which in my opinion affected the change in Frank from his youthful exuberance to essentially an unhappy life and old age."

As she grew up in London, Ontario, in the 1960s, Barbara Edy recognized her father Don Edy had two careers. She knew he was involved in business, earning a living, paying the bills, and raising a family. But her dad had also devoted plenty of time to an equally important avocation—getting his wartime memories off his chest and down on paper. The resulting book, called *Goon in the Block*, was published in 1961 and it recounted Don's experiences inside Stalag Luft III from his arrival there in November 1943 until the kriegies were marched out of the compound and across Germany in the winter of 1945. When *The Great Escape* movie hit the theatres in 1963, for the first time in her life, Barbara could see (even if distorted by Hollywood fabrication) "a visual perspective"[26] of her father's war inside German prison wire.

Unlike the children of other kriegies, who wouldn't (or couldn't) talk about their POW experiences, Barbara and her four older siblings grew up hearing about Stalag Luft III as told and written by their father. Not only did he record the events with precision, Barbara noted that he told the stories with the flair of a raconteur. What's more, word of *Goon in the Block* had spread and more than just Don Edy's family members wanted to read it; but there weren't any more copies of the book around and Don had no interest in a reprint. That's when Barbara sensed he was passing the torch. She felt compelled to help her father stay in touch with his wartime comrades at the same time she wanted and keep his stories in circulation among historians and journalists. She became Don's "information gal." More than that, her work became a personal crusade.

"The families and offspring of the kriegies all express the same sentiment," Barbara said, "to carry on the memory of not only the fifty [escapers] whom Hitler ordered murdered, but, as well, the two hundred, huddled in Hut 104 waiting their turn to escape, the hundreds [of others] who assisted, and all the men of Stalag Luft III and its famous, proud, spectacular distraction to create havoc in the midst of Germany's war effort."[27]

Via correspondence and personal contact, Barbara has built a rapport with ex-kriegies and their children in Australia, New Zealand, the UK, the US, and Canada. In 2012 she and her sister Jane Hughes helped to recover and restore a collection of published photographs originally compiled in a book of remembrances and reflections, called *Wire Bound World*, to redistribute to other survivors of Stalag Luft III. Then, through a series of emails, she initiated an internet exchange of information called *The Beginning of List 200*, designed to pool stories, images, biographies, and communications about the two hundred men on the original escape list.

Along the way, like other kriegie offspring, Barbara believes she has learned how that "proud, spectacular distraction" succeeded in binding her dad and the rest of the Commonwealth flyers together, and why that common bond made the events leading up to March 24–25, 1944, so significant. Just as bomber pilot and Stalag Luft III forger Tony Pengelly had deduced when he was first imprisoned at Barth in 1940, that "we would have to organize to be successful,"[28] Barbara Edy concluded that none of the kriegies' accomplishments at Stalag Luft III would have been possible without that large group of captives working together as one.

"The Great Escape would not have been possible," she said, "save for the absolute co-operation from over a thousand POWs' non-stop secrecy, vigilance, persuasion, distraction, cunning, bravery, spirit, and talent."[29]

David Pengelly was three years old in 1938 when his older brother left the family home in Weston, Ontario. At eighteen, Tony Pengelly couldn't vacate the household fast enough. He had not enjoyed a close relationship with his father, besides which, he had his heart set on a career in the Royal Air Force whether his father endorsed his decision or not. A few weeks later, the older Pengelly son stepped off a cattle boat in the UK and was quickly accepted into RAF training, which had him flying combat operations in Bomber Command from the first week of the war in September 1939. Periodically, Tony sent mementos to his little brother, the first being a picture postcard depicting a Fairey Battle bomber. Tony had addressed the card "To Liney," since Lionel was David's middle name. He cherished the card. On David's fifth birthday, just a few months before F/L Tony Pengelly and his Whitley bomber crew were shot down over Germany, David received a Dinky toy model of a Whitley in the mail.

"From the time I was five," David Pengelly said, "I adored the thought of my brother. Spitfire and bomber pilots were like rock stars or astronauts flying these wonderful machines."[30]

In July 1945, Tony Pengelly, former flight lieutenant and forgery chief at Stalag Luft III, came home to Canada. The family made plans to help Tony decompress on Pengelly Island, a one-acre rock outcropping on Sawyer Lake in the Haliburton Highlands of Ontario. There was no electricity on the island, nor indoor plumbing, just a family cottage accessible only by boat. With limited accommodation inside the cottage, David and Tony were encouraged to camp outside in a tent. The first night alone together, older brother regaled younger brother with some of his wartime yarns. Then, the boys' mother prepared a meal with all of Tony's favourites—roast beef, corn-on-the-cob, and fruit pies—and watched the former kriegie dig into his first home-cooked meal since he'd left Weston in 1938.

"Do you have a little more?"[31] Tony asked when he'd finished his first portion.

"Sure! Sure!" his family all said. And he dove into a second portion and a third until he couldn't eat another mouthful.

"There's two or three cobs of corn left," Tony noticed. "What's going to happen to those?"

"Oh well, they'll be cold," his mother said. "We'll just throw them out."

"Don't do that. I'll have them for breakfast," Tony insisted. And he promised he'd do the same with the beef and the pies.

Mementos that prisoners of war brought home were few and far between. Any personal items Tony Pengelly may have carried with him when he was shot down on November 14, 1940, were destroyed in the crash of his Whitley bomber or confiscated during questioning by Luftwaffe interrogators as they processed him for imprisonment in Germany and later Poland. And since he became one of X Organization's principal forgers, Pengelly would have shown or shared very few of his possessions publicly inside the compound either. In other words, despite helping to win the war, Pengelly had little to show for it outside of service medals and replenished air force insignia. Consequently, when he married and had his own children, Tony came to his younger brother David for a favour.

"Do you still have that Whitley [Dinky toy] I sent you?" he asked.

"Of course," David told him. It was the favourite memento from his big brother's service overseas as a bomber pilot during the war.

"Can I have it for a while? I'd like my kids to see it," Tony said.

David agreed to loan it, but then never saw it again. Some of the other keepsakes that Tony did manage to salvage from his time at Stalag Luft III ended up in a small briefcase passed down to his son, Chris Pengelly. A few RAF certificates, diagrams, letters, newspaper clippings, and photographs of Tony posing in a group in front of barracks huts or on stage at the North Compound theatre survived in the leather case. Of his father's role in the Great Escape, Chris Pengelly knew just a little. His father had shared more with his Uncle David than with him. Chris was a teenager in 1963 when *The Great Escape* was released; his mother Pauline reported the movie disrupted Tony's sleep with recurring nightmares. In contrast, when the sitcom *Hogan's Heroes*—depicting life in a mythical German POW camp—appeared on television between 1965 and 1971, Chris recalled that his parents loved the series.

"They watched it all the time,"[32] Chris Pengelly emphasized. "He laughed so hard each time [the farcical German Sergeant Schultz] said, 'I see nothing. I hear nothing.' He considered it very funny, but quite realistic. You don't get shot down and say, 'Oh, I'll just take my digital camera with me.' He knew they had to make things from scratch and bribe the guards for things like the camera . . .

"*The Great Escape* movie gave him nightmares," Chris said finally. "The TV show let him laugh about it."

Very little of the North Compound that the six hundred Canadians knew from 1943 to 1945 exists intact today. On the actual site, just outside the town of Zagan (the Polish spelling of Sagan), the double fencing is gone. So are the watchtowers, the *Vorlager*, and any above-ground evidence of the cook house, the theatre, or the fifteen barracks huts. All gone. Only concrete pads and some masonry walls remain the way they were when the Commonwealth kriegies were transferred there from the East Compound in the middle of the war. The rest of the former prison camp, the forest and weeds have pretty much reclaimed. Periodically, Polish groundskeepers chop back the brush that pokes through the bricks of the fire pool or the theatre foundation so that visitors passing through each summer can get an idea of what they once looked like.

At the northern edge of the property, a walkway of crushed stone with wooden borders, twenty inches wide, runs 336 feet north-south the full length that tunnel "Harry" did—from the concrete pad where Hut 104 stood to the approximate exit hole just shy of the woods. At the edge of that same pine forest (that stands very much as it did during the war) are sun-faded commemorative plaques. Near the end of the walkway nearest Hut 104 rests a series of flat stone markers with the names of the fifty executed air force officers engraved on them. The markers include the names of Hank Birkland, Gordon Kidder, Pat Langford, George McGill, James Wernham, and George Wiley—the Canadians murdered after the breakout.

To their credit, the volunteers at the Museum of Allied Forces Prisoners of War Martyrdom periodically welcome groups of tourists, school children, and some of the kriegie offspring who occasionally stop to explore and imagine on their own. West of the former prison compound, at the museum site, a replica of Hut 104 gives visitors an approximation of the Commonwealth air officers' barracks experience. There's a stove (like the original that covered the trap to tunnel "Harry") sitting in the appropriate corner of Room 23, as well as bunk beds, a dining area, and the "To All Prisoners of War! The escape from prison camps is no longer a sport!" propaganda poster tacked on the hut wall after the Great Escape. A nearby pavilion contains a small library and an exhibit room. Out in front of the pavilion, a reproduced watchtower lords over a stretch of tunnel containing replica bed boards, trolley, and tracks. This is a facsimile of about fifty feet of "Harry" constructed a few feet down and covered in a see-through plastic ceiling. The replica gives a false sense of accessibility and ease of passage.

Nowhere on the old compound property nor among the museum exhibits can visitors experience the claustrophobia that tunnel designer Wally Floody and diggers John Weir and Hank Birkland knew underground . . . or realize the audacity and skill of scroungers Barry Davidson, Joe Noble, and Keith Ogilvie . . . or recognize the volume of intelligence Kingsley Brown amassed for Dean and Dawson . . . or appreciate the precision of Tony Pengelly's work forging documents and performing female roles on the theatre stage . . . or witness the speed with which *trapführer* Pat Langford opened and closed the entrance to "Harry" each day it moved the kriegies closer to a shot at freedom . . . or hear the conversation basics that language trainers Gordon Kidder and Frank Sorensen gave potential escapers . . . or comprehend the nerve that security men George McGill, George Sweanor, and Dick Bartlett exhibited to protect the escape committee's greatest secrets . . . or understand the efficiency of the penguins, stooges, and duty pilots all running interference at the camp their German captors described as "escape proof" . . . or feel the helplessness the six Canadians murdered by the Gestapo must have known in their last moments.

Proof of their contribution to the Great Escape is recorded in these pages and in the stories yet to be gathered and verified by historians, the families of ex-kriegies, and an apparently ever-growing community that refuses to let this story die.

# Notes

---

INTRODUCTION: "HEROES RESURFACE"

1. "has created a classic": *Time* magazine, July 1963.
2. "take notice and find inspiration": Arthur A. Durand, quoted in *The Making of the Great Escape* documentary, produced by Prometheus Entertainment in association with Van Ness Films, Foxstar Productions, Fox TV Studios, and A&E TV Network (Metro Goldwyn Mayer, Home Entertainment Inc.).

CHAPTER ONE: THE KING'S REGULATIONS

1. "a way through": Winston Churchill quoted in Charles Messenger, *"Bomber" Harris and the Strategic Bombing Offensive, 1939–1945* (London Arms and Armour Press, 1984), p. 39.
2. "dropping leaflets": Tony Pengelly, diary notes, courtesy of Chris Pengelly collection.
3. strategic bombing campaign: Martin Middlebrook and Chris Everitt, *The Bomber Command War Diaries, An Operational Reference Book: 1939–1945* (Penguin, London, 1985) p. 92.
4. Fairey Battles: Ibid., p. 93.
5. apprehension: Russell Braddon, *Cheshire V.C., A Study of War and Peace* (Evans Brothers Limited, London, 1954), p. 60.
6. "remarkable breed of men": Leonard Cheshire quoted in ibid., p. 69.
7. "chute off and buried it": Daniel G. Dancocks, *In Enemy Hands, Canadian Prisoners of War 1939–1945* (Hurtig Publishers, Edmonton, 1983), p. 8.
8. "protect the Security": "The Responsibilities of a Prisoner of War" (RAF Air Publication 1548, RAF Command of the Air Council, March 1936).

9. "name, rank and number": Ibid.

10. "give him in return": Ibid.

11. "you chaps down": Dancocks, p. 10.

12. "succeed in escaping": "The Responsibilities of a Prisoner of War"

13. "private flying machines": Certificate of Competency and Licence to fly Private Machines, C.A. Form 64, issued by Great Britain and Northern Ireland.

14. first mass escape: Sydney Smith, *Wings Day: The Man Who Led the RAF's Battle in German Captivity* (William Collins, London, 1968), p. 77.

15. "prison camp life": Tony Pengelly, "X For Escape," by Flt.-Lieut. Tony Pengelly, as told to Scott Young, with permission from *Maclean's* magazine, November 1 and 15, 1945.

16. "organize to be successful": Ibid.

## CHAPTER TWO: BOND OF WIRE

1. "anything about this": John Weir, note to Frances McCormack, 1940, with permission.

2. "bomber pilot": Frances Weir (née McCormack) interview, June 19, 2012, Toronto.

3. "scruffy looking individual": Sandra Martin, "He played a role in The (real) Great Escape," *Globe and Mail*, November 11, 2009.

4. war work herself: Frances Weir interview, June 19, 2012.

5. "in the least": Ibid.

6. "first ever sweep": Hugh Godefroy, *Lucky Thirteen* (Canada's Wings Inc., Stittsville, Ontario, 1983), p. 100.

7. "Weir and Gardiner are missing": Ibid., p. 107.

8. "a perpetual clown": Ibid., p. 107

9. "an important prisoner": Robert Stanford Tuck, quoted in Larry Forrester, *Fly For Your Life: The Story of R. R. Stanford Tuck* (Nelson Doubleday, New York, 1956), p. 275.

10. seventy yards wide: Arthur A. Durand, *Stalag Luft III: The Secret Story* (Patrick Stephens Ltd., UK, 1989), p. 79.

11. "safe and sound in Germany": John Weir, letter to Frances McCormack, December 13, 1941, with permission.

12. "back to you soon": John Weir, letter to Frances McCormack, December 22, 1941, with permission.

13. door-to-door salesman: Jonathan Vance, *A Gallant Company: The Men of the Great Escape* (Pacifica Military History, Pacifica, California, 2000), p. 120.

14. mining companies' sports teams: Barbara Hehner, *The Tunnel King, The True Story of Wally Floody and The Great Escape* (HarperCollins, Toronto, 2004), pp. 3, 7.

15. *Luftgau*: Durand, p. 134.

16. "how many, four": John Weir, letter to Frances McCormack, February 26, 1942, with permission.

17. "no similarity between the two": Wally Floody, interviewed by the National Air Force Museum, CFB Trenton, c. 1970.

18. "a total success either": Wally Floody, interviewed by the National Air Force Museum, CFB Trenton, 1989.

19. collapse tunnels: Durand, p. 81.

20. "I got claustrophobic": Barry Davidson, "Barry Davidson—Prisoner of War," Bomber Command Museum of Canada, courtesy of Barry Davidson Jr., 2000.

21. "pound bombs": Ibid.

22. "for the duration": Ibid.

23. cutting or digging tool: Jean Morrison McBride, quoted in Patricia Burns *They Were So Young: Montrealers Remember World War II* (Véhicule Press, 2002), p. 239.

24. plastic surgery: Eric Howald, "Mac Jarrell Remembers: Spent 45 months as prisoner of war," *The Kincardine Independent*, November 11, 1979.

25. "the prisoners hated it": Ibid.

26. "kick from a mule": Dick Bartlett, quoted Stuart E. Soward's *One Man's War: Sub Lieutenant R. E. Bartlett, RN Fleet Air Arm Pilot* (Neptune, 2005), p. 53.

27. "into the camp": Ibid., p. 90.

28. "news and intelligence": Ibid., p. 90.

29. "be home again": John Weir, letter to Frances McCormack, January 21, 1942, with permission.

30. "escape campaign": Vance, p. 32.

31. "operational function": Smith, pp. 58–60.

32. "slippers, gloves, and cap": John Weir, letter to Frances McCormack, April 29, 1942, with permission.

33. "lots of fresh air": Ibid.

34. "is fatten me up": Ibid.

CHAPTER THREE: "SPINE-TINGLING SPORT"

1. "fenced-in feeling": John Hartnell-Beavis, *Final Flight* (Merlin Books, Braunton, Devon, UK, 1985), p. 31.

2. *Kommandantur*: Durand, p. 103.

3. both his artificial legs: Paul Brickhill, *Reach for the Sky, The Story of Douglas Bader* (Collins, London, UK, 1954), p. 335.

4. months to accomplish: Les Allison, *Canadians in the Royal Air Force* (self-published, Roland, Manitoba, 1978), p. 177.

5. "flown over Berlin": Andrew Thompson, quoted in documentary "The Great Escape: The Canadian Story," 2004, courtesy of producer Don Young.

6. "courtesy and consideration": Tommy Thompson, quoted in Ibid.

7. back to England: Vance, p. 39.

8. Focke-Wulf 190: correspondence, Stephen Sprague, Bracebridge, Ontario, September 11, 2014.

9. "escape proof": Floody interview, 1970.

10. Göring's luxury camp: Paul Brickhill, *The Great Escape* (Faber and Faber Ltd., London, UK, 1951), p. 24.

11. thousand-foot area: Durand, p. 258.

12. cutting through the soil: Brickhill, *The Great Escape*, p. 28.

13. "noses of the Germans": Floody interview, 1970.

14. "expert at it": Ibid.

15. "a minor one": George Harsh, *Lonesome Road* (W. W. Norton & Co., New York, 1971), p. 176.

16. "flamboyant *beau geste*": Ibid., p. 132.

17. 4.3 per cent loss rate: Middlebrook and Everitt, p. 297.

18. "you're an American": Harsh, p. 187.

19. "secure all this": Ibid., p. 191.

20. "he's an ex-convict": Ibid., p. 192.

21. "the black hole": Kingsley Brown, *Bonds of Wire, A Memoir* (Collins, Toronto, 1989), p. 50.

22. "propaganda job": Ibid., p. 57.

23. "Hitler kaput": Ibid., p. 58.

24. "free side of the wire": Ibid., p. 65.

25. Red Cross parcels: A. K. Ogilvie, "Tigers in the Tunnel," Air Intelligence Training Bulletin, Vol. XIV, No. 1, January 1962.

26. wallet on the floor: Ian Darling, *Amazing Airmen: Canadian Flyers in the Second World War* (Dundurn, Toronto, 2009), p. 27.

27. "my mittens. Everything": Don McKim, interview Simcoe, Ontario, January 2, 2011.

28. Germans guarding them: Durand, p. 159.

29. five-foot-two: Lyn Tremblay, "Veteran prisoner of war took part in the Great Escape," *Simcoe Reformer*, December 3, 2009.

30. "doing anything else": McKim interview, 2011.

31. "a little longer": Bob McBride, quoted by Jean Morrison McBride in Burns, p. 239.
32. "burned forever": Ibid., p. 240.
33. hidden him in Prague: Brickhill, *The Great Escape*, p. 32.

CHAPTER FOUR: ESCAPE SEASON

1. Goleb Plasov: Brown, p. 63.
2. North Compound: Brickhill, *The Great Escape*, p. 34.
3. "the enemy has ears": Kingsley Brown, "The Good Grey Days of Stalag III," *The Globe Magazine*, May 18, 1957, p. 10.
4. "a sense of danger": Ibid., p. 10.
5. "better luck next time": Kingsley Brown quoting arresting police officer, *Bonds of Wire*, p. 75.
6. war was forgotten: Op cit, p. 11.
7. Hut 101: John S. Acheson, *A World War II Tale of Stalag Luft III and of The Great Escape* (unpublished manuscript housed at the Kitchener Public Library, 2002, with permission). p. 9.
8. half a minute or less: Soward, p. 114.
9. "swing a stunted cat": Brickhill, *The Great Escape*, p. 42.
10. "or we'll start shooting": Gordon King, interviewed by Byron Christopher, Edmonton, October. 20, 2011.
11. "just something to do": Ibid.
12. "German shepherd dog": Floody interview, 1970.
13. "three major tunnels": Brickhill, *The Great Escape*, p. 34.
14. "a lot more troops": Floody interview, 1970.
15. "vertical shaft to Harry": Henry Sprague, interviewed by the National Air Force Museum, CFB Trenton, 1989.
16. "complete surveillance": Floody interview, 1970.
17. "twenty to thirty seconds": Floody interview, 1989.
18. "toward the showers": Pengelly, "X For Escape."
19. Bob van der Stok: Vance, p. 138.
20. cardboard holster: Larry Forrester, *Fly For Your Life: The Story of R. R. Stanford Tuck* (Nelson Doubleday, New York, 1956), p. 282.
21. "dressed as German soldiers": Pengelly, "X For Escape."
22. "our cheapest commodity": Ibid.
23. "rolled around the pebble": Arthur Crighton, *Memories of a Prisoner of War* (privately published memoirs, 3rd edition, February 2012), p. 21.

24. "whole of Kriegiedom": Ibid., p. 22.

25. "weren't digging tunnels": Arthur Crighton, interviewed by Byron Christopher, Edmonton, Alberta, March 18, 2012.

26. tunnel projects: Durand, p.116.

27. "it's foolproof": Michael Codner, quoted in Eric Williams, *The Wooden Horse* (Collins, London, UK, 1955), p. 38.

28. weary of inspecting the horse: Edward Patrick Nurse, *The Last Glorious Flight of Halifax Bomber Lima Quebec Papa 741: A chronicle of the wartime experiences of Edward Patrick Nurse* (unpublished manuscript, 2012, with permission), p. 48.

29. "heavens beyond the wire": Williams, p. 122.

30. had been killed in action: Ian Crofton, *Great Escapes* (Quercus, London, UK, 2009), p.145.

CHAPTER FIVE: SERVANT TO A HOLE IN THE GROUND

1. Eastern Townships of Quebec: Betty Sorensen, family wartime letters transcription, 1939, courtesy of Vicki Sorensen.

2. "Roskilde boys": Frank Sorensen address to Denmark via BBC Radio Free Europe, October 15, 1942, courtesy of Vicki Sorensen.

3. "driven out of Denmark": Ibid.

4. thirteen operational sorties: Mikkel Plannthin, "Fra Roskilde Katedral Til Stalag Luft III—Og Den Store Flugt"/"From Roskilde Cathedral School to Stalag Luft III—and the Great Escape," published in *Flyvehistorisk Tidsskrift/ Journal of Aviation History*, Dansk Flyvehistorisk Forening/Danish Aviation Historical Society, Forening, December 2011.

5. "Bay of Tunis": Frank Sorensen letter to brother Eric Sorensen, July 23, 1945, courtesy of Vicki Sorensen.

6. "home on the deck": Ibid.

7. "Hands up": Ibid.

8. "is reported missing": letter to Mrs. M. B. Sorensen, from F/L W. R. Gunn, RCAF Casualties Officer, Department of National Defence, Ottawa, April 17, 1943, courtesy of Vicki Sorensen.

9. "a prisoner of war": letter to Mr. M. B. Sorensen, from S/L A. B. Matthews, Air Officer Commanding-in-Chief, RCAF Overseas, London, May 11, 1943, courtesy of Vicki Sorensen.

10. "one of them": Frank Sorensen letter to parents, April 19, 1943, courtesy of Vicki Sorensen.

11. "'round the perimeter": Frank Sorensen letter to parents, May 8, 1943, courtesy of Vicki Sorensen.

12. "taught a horse": Frank Sorensen letter to parents, July 21, 1944, courtesy of Vicki Sorensen.

13. "thesaurus dictionary": Frank Sorensen letter to parents, May 18, 1943, courtesy of Vicki Sorensen.

14. insurance company: Vance, p. 172.

15. advance his studies: Linda Tweddell, correspondence with Vicki Sorensen, February 13, 2012.

16. in political science: George Sweanor, interview Colorado Springs, Colorado, July 6, 2011.

17. westerns and biographies: Durand, p. 227.

18. "studying it though": Frank Sorensen letter to parents, August 11, 1943, courtesy of Vicki Sorensen.

19. "wood for shoring": Floody interview, 1970.

20. rusty gas cans: Brickhill, *The Great Escape*, p. 57.

21. "tunnel as it was dug": Bob Nelson, "Tom, Dick and Harry of Stalag Luft III" (unpublished manuscript, 1948, with permission).

22. from the Germans: Vance, p. 125.

23. "thirty feet underground": Bob Nelson monologue on Great Escape, recorded by family, 1987.

24. "a bit more cautious": Floody interview, 1970.

25. "trouser bags": Peter Fanshawe quoted in Brickhill, *The Great Escape*, p. 52.

26. hole in the ground: Brickhill, *The Great Escape*, p. 56.

27. "repairs themselves": Harold Johnstone, preface to unpublished diary of John Colwell, 2001, with permission, p. 2.

28. "jump at 11 p.m.": John Colwell, unpublished diary, April 3, 1943, with permission.

29. "Room 14, Block 120": Ibid., April 17, 1943.

30. "they lost": Ibid., June 17, 1943.

31. "hair all cut off": Ibid., June 20, 1943.

32. "as a penguin": Ibid., June 22, 1943.

33. "what was going on": John Colwell, quoted in Lynn Welburn, "A witness to the Great Escape," *Harbour City Star*, May 17, 2001.

34. "deaden the sound": King interview, 2011.

35. "a matter of minutes": John Weir, quoted in "The Making of the Great Escape," Prometheus Entertainment, 2007.

36. "with us separated": John Weir letter to Frances McCormack, April 30, 1943, with permission.

37. any excess wiring: Brickhill, *The Great Escape*, p. 94.

38. "South Compound is ready": Alan Burgess, *The Longest Tunnel: The True Story of World War II's Great Escape* (Grove Weidenfeld, New York, 1990), p. 45.

39. "suspicions were aroused": Nelson, unpublished manuscript, 1948.

40. "very imperceptible": Nelson monologue, 1987.

41. "British are coming": George Sweanor, notes on "The Great Escape—24 March 1944," with permission.

42. "huts with a band": Colwell diary, July 1, 1943, with permission.

43. "1 and 4 a.m.": Ibid., July 13, 1943.

44. "in turn and searched": Ibid., July 15, 1943.

45. "barbed wire used": Ibid., July 24, 1943.

46. "know fuck all": Brickhill, *The Great Escape*, records the exchange with the expletive "damn," p. 106; several kriegies, including Pengelly, Wallace, and Sweanor, report Pieber used the word "fuck," making the exchange all the more ridiculous.

47. "in Hut 101": Colwell diary, August 21, 1943.

48. "my soldering outfit": Ibid., August 31. 1943.

49. "to inspect it": Nelson, 1948.

50. "late Tom's trap": Ibid.

51. "with the appendix": Frank Sorensen, quoted in Plannthin.

52. "the winter after this": Frank Sorensen, letter to family, September 17, 1943, courtesy of Vicki Sorensen.

CHAPTER SIX: "SHYSTERS AND CROOKS AND CON MEN"

1. "an only child": Joan Sweanor interview, Colorado Springs, Colorado, July 5, 2011.

2. "Who Wants War": George Sweanor interview, July 5–7, 2011.

3. "could walk her home": George Sweanor, correspondence, February 6, 2013.

4. "looks, poise, and figure": Sweanor, *It's All Pensionable Time: 25 Years in the Royal Canadian Air Force* (self-published, 1967, with permission), p. 36.

5. "life is so temporary": Ibid.

6. "the office at eight": Joan Sweanor interview, 2011.

7. "letter for me": Arthur Morlidge, quoted in George Sweanor, p. 58.

8. "delightfully foul weather": Ibid., p. 75.

9. "only military targets": Ibid., p. 103.

10. "get out of here": George Sweanor interview, 2011.

11. "last ticket home": Ibid.

12. "not coming home": Joan Sweanor interview, 2011.

13. "E for Edward": Sweanor, *It's All Pensionable Time*, p. 120.

14. "nerves could relax": George Sweanor, notes on "The Great Escape—24 March 1944," with permission.

15. German-English dictionary: Ibid., p. 107.

16. "years of our wives": Shag Rees, quoted by George Sweanor in *It's All Pensionable Time*, p. 121.

17. "worthy of his sacrifice": Sweanor, p. 112.

18. "mark me down": Hermann Glemnitz, quoted by George Sweanor in *It's All Pensionable Time*, p. 133.

19. "the workman's tools": Nelson.

20. inside tunnel Harry: Brickhill, *The Great Escape*, p. 135.

21. "Luftwaffe ferrets": Nelson.

22. "by the prisoners": von Lindeiner, reference in "Sagan," Royal Air Force Special Investigation Branch report, Report No: WCIU/LDC/1460, JAG Ref: MD/JAG/FS/22/2(2a) War Crimes Interrogation Unit, London, December 1946, p. 17.

23. "impression in the camp": Ibid., p. 17.

24. "very severe penalties": von Lindeiner, quoted by John E. (Willy) Williams in Ibid., p. 21.

25. appropriate documentation: Durand, p. 291.

26. Group of Seven: Ken MacQueen, "A Brutal March: Wartime diaries record a trek of 10,000 POWs," *Maclean's*, January 13, 2003, p. 48.

27. "and I did": Robert Buckham, quoted in Ibid.

28. the library Bibles: Durand, p. 291.

29. "morning to night": Frank Sorensen, letter home, June 26, 1943, courtesy of Vicki Sorensen.

30. "an empty belly": Robert Buckham, diary excerpt quoted in Op cit.

31. the violin case: Brickhill, *The Great Escape*, p. 122.

32. "some coffee home": Pengelly, "X for Escape."

33. "he believed necessary": Ibid.

34. "than in a prison camp": Don MacDonald, quoted in Dancocks, p. 112.

35. "orders I don't like": Sweanor, p. 142.

36. panel for stage lighting: H. P. Clark, *Wire Bound World* (self-published, 1946), p. 13.

37. "announcing the play": Don Edy interview, London, Ontario, March 6, 2012.

38. Mena House resort hotel: Don Edy, *Goon in the Block* (self-published, 1948, with permission), p. 52.

39. garter snake in its place: Ibid., p. 14–15.

40. "Padula boys, Hey, Hey.": Ibid., p. 95.

41. "an immediate depression": Ibid., p. 57.

42. "got to him first": Ibid., p. 130.

43. a coffee percolator: Ibid., p. 140.

44. "to see the shows": Ibid., p. 136

45. recorded for posterity: George McKiel, quoted in Doug Pricer, "Survivor of the Great Escape," *Military History*, May 2005, p. 30.

46. "out of kriegieland": Sweanor, *It's All Pensionable Time*, p. 141.

47. grease-paint makeup: Durand, p. 243.

48. "create feminine characters": Edy, Op cit., p. 161.

49. "people doing everything": King interview, 2011.

50. "walk and talk like a woman": McKiel, quoted in Pricer, p. 30.

51. "Second World War in drag": Rick Cluff interview, Vancouver, B.C., May 25, 2012.

52. Red Cross parcels: Durand, p. 77.

53. "organization could use": Pengelly, "X for Escape."

54. "along the same route": Ibid.

## CHAPTER SEVEN: THE PLAY'S THE THING

1. "couple of years ago": Art Ross, quoted in Brian McFarlane, *Stanley Cup Fever: 100 Years of Hockey Greatness* (Toronto, Stoddart, 1992), p. 97.

2. men left to play: Kenesaw Mountain Landis, quoted in *Time Capsule* (Time-Life, 1943), p. 138.

3. "their team over": Art Hawtin interview, Beaverton, Ontario, January 8, 2011.

4. "landed safely": Ibid.

5. married men against bachelors: John E. Dreifort, "Anything but Ordinary: POW Sports in a Barbed Wire World," *Journal of Sport History*, Vol. 34, No. 3, Fall 2007, p. 420.

6. "struck out sixteen batters": Hawtin interview, 2011.

7. "fourteen to one": Ibid.

8. "let them hit, Bill": Harold Garland, quoted in Dancock, p. 101.

9. leather boot enthusiastically: Durand, p. 248.

10. "panes are broken": Art Hawtin, "Grandpa's Wartime Album: Memories Surrounding the Great Escape" (unpublished diary prepared by Janet Hawtin, with permission).

11. "shot him dead": Phil Marchildon with Brian Kendall, *Ace Phil Marchildon, Canada's Pitching Sensation and Wartime Hero* (New York, Viking, 1993), p. 138.

12. "over the wire": Frank Sorensen, letter home, June 15, 1944, courtesy of Vicki Sorensen.

13. author Kaj Munk: family letter to Frank Sorensen, March 10, 1944, courtesy of Vicki Sorensen.

14. "the Tin Man": Hawtin interview, 2011.

15. "a master tinker": Ibid.

16. "two fire bricks": John Colwell diary diagrams, September 26, 1944, with permission.

17. "and cooking utensils": card contained in John Colwell's diary, with permission.

18. "in Stalag Luft III": Brickhill, *The Great Escape*, p. 129.

19. "itching to be home": John Weir, letter to Frances McCormack, October 31, 1943, with permission.

20. "a friendless room": Albert Wallace, correspondence, March 15, 2013.

21. "didn't realize": Albert Wallace, interview, Toronto, January 5, 2011.

22. "extremely security conscious": Ibid.

23. "our new chimney": Ibid.

24. "Your brother, Wally": Wally Floody, postcard to Catherine Floody, January 26, 1944, with permission.

25. "before roll call": Hawtin diary.

26. "and out went the sand": Wallace interview, 2011.

27. theatre's crawl space: Harold Johnstone, "More Memories of Stalag III Days," additional notes to John Colwell's diary, 2001, with permission.

28. "twelve tons of sand": Pengelly, "X for Escape."

29. "a severe shock": Hartnell-Beavis, p. 36.

30. disappear in seconds: Brickhill, *The Great Escape*, p. 140.

31. "all kinds of weather": John R. Harris, *Serving and Surviving: An Airman's Memoirs*, self-published, 2004, with permission, p. 117.

32. "Germans blitzing England": John R. Harris, interview, London, Ontario, March 6, 2012.

33. "out of the kite": Harris, *Serving and Surviving*, p. 71.

34. RCAF Blues tunic: John Crozier, memoir in *Aircrew Memories: The Collected World War II and later memories of members of the Aircrew Association, Vancouver Island Branch, Victoria, B.C.* (Victoria Publishing Co., 1999), p. 88.

35. "where he'd come from": Harris interview, March 6, 2012.

36. "and he apologized": Ibid.

37. "I was shot down": Ibid.

38. bottoms of their boots: Dreifort, p. 425.

39. "a lot of work": Davidson.

40. sticks simply ran out: Dreifort, p. 426.

41. him and his crew: Vance, p. 47.

42. "sooner than expected": George Wiley, quoted in Vance, p. 210.

43. "before he got back": Floody interview, 1989.

44. camp at Belaria: Sweanor, p. 156.

45. "a tunnel digger": Floody interview, 1989.

46. gassed or shot: "Sagan," Royal Air Force Special Investigation Branch report, Report No: WCIU/LDC/1460, JAG Ref: MD/JAG/FS/22/2(2a) War Crimes Interrogation Unit, London, December 1946, p. 67.

47. and 69 lamps: Johnstone.

48. and Tony Pengelly: H. P. Clark, *Wire Bound World*, self-published, 1946, p. 32.

49. "in it, or who": Pengelly, "X for Escape."

50. about two hundred: Alan Burgess, *The Longest Tunnel: The True Story of World War II's Great Escape* (Grove Weidenfeld, New York, 1990), p. 124.

51. "number ninety-three": Pengelly, "X for Escape."

CHAPTER EIGHT: "THROUGH ADVERSITY TO THE STARS"

1. "prisoner of war": Pengelly, "X for Escape."

2. "chance at freedom": Ibid.

3. a sure thing either: Sweanor, *It's All Pensionable Time*, pp. 156–57.

4. "name was not drawn": Sweanor interview, July 5–7, 2011.

5. into the tunnel: Jacek Jakubiak, names and escape numbers are published in *Guide to the Site of the Former POW Camps in Zagan* (Museum of Allied Forces Prisoners of War Martyrdom, Zagan, Poland, 2008) pp. 42–43.

6. though not fatally: Brickhill, *The Great Escape*, p. 133 (the Canadian's name was Probert).

7. the other at Luft III: Barry Davidson, *A Wartime Log: A Remembrance from Home Through the Canadian YMCA*, unpublished, with permission of Barry Davidson Jr.

8. "miracle to get back": Wallace interview, 2011.

9. "time go any faster": Frank Sorensen, letter to parents, March 20, 1944, courtesy of Vicki Sorensen.

10. through the tunnel: Vicki Sorensen, Frank's daughter, has searched for his exact number on the escape list and has anecdotal information to support that he drew a number in the high teens, but forfeited the spot to either James Catanach or Arnold Christensen.

11. Fugelsang and stay behind: Margaret Davidson, interview Victoria, BC, August 13, 2012.

12. "and not go out": Davidson.

13. "how do I look": Bob van der Stok, quoted in King interview, 2011.

14. Wiley's final wish: Vance, p. 214.

15. "the set of maps": Harris interview, 2012.

16. "just waiting my turn": King interview, 2011.

17. to the next three: Brickhill, *The Great Escape*, p. 185.

18. "rope to shelter": Ibid., p.179.

19. station and boarding platforms: Mirek Walczak, guide, Museum of Allied Forces Prisoners of War Martyrdom, Zagan, Poland, June 22, 2011.

20. "sand that fell in": Nelson monologue, 1987.

21. "cold and frosty": Keith Ogilvie, quoted in Dancocks, p. 130.

22. "when it all ended": Mac Reilley, "Another Perspective of the Great Escape from Luft III," *The Kriegie Eagle* newsletter, January 1995, the National Air Force Museum, CFB Trenton.

23. bed and listened: Edy, p. 158–59.

24. food in his pockets: Sweanor interview, July 5–7, 2011.

25. soon stopped: Sweanor, p. 161.

26. "shot doing it": King interview, 2011.

27. "Sax's bum blocking the way": Rees, Ken, "Stalag Luft 3—The Great Escape: The Wartime Experiences of Wg. Cdr. H.K. Rees," at Rob Davis website, www.elsham.pwp.blueyonder.co.uk

28. "half the camp down": Harris, *Serving and Surviving*, p. 119.

29. "get rid of the lot of you": Friedrich von Lindeiner, quoted in Sweanor, p. 161.

30. "burn the maps": Harris, p. 120.

31. "Johnny or me again": Ibid., p. 120.

32. "provoke them further": Edy, p. 159.

33. "done that to him": Hans Pieber, quoted in Sweanor, p. 162.

34. some 70,000 Germans: Thomas Fleming, "The Great Escape," *Boy's Life*, March 1997, p. 46.

35. "broomstick for a cane": Gordon Venables, from interview by (granddaughter) Katie Bendell, c. 1990, with permission.

36. entry shaft to Harry: Sweanor, p. 162.

CHAPTER NINE: THE HATE CAMPAIGN

1. run in another direction: Darling, Ian, *Amazing Airmen: Canadian Flyers in the Second World War* (Dundurn, Toronto, 2009), p. 30.

2. "bloody miserable": Keith Ogilvie, quoted in Dancocks, p. 133.

3. in his pockets: Darling, p. 31.

4. and pressed on: Vance, p. 240.

5. "whilst trying to escape": Kriminal Kommissar Peter Mohr, quoted in "Sagan," Royal Air Force Special Investigation Branch report, Report No: WCIU/LDC/1460, JAG Ref: MD/JAG/FS/22/2(2a), War Crimes Interrogation Unit, London, December 1946, Appendix 'C' p. 57.

6. "linguist": Hugh A. Halliday, "Flyboys in the Great Escape," *Legion* magazine, July 1, 2007.

7. "from the Dominions": Ibid., p.19.

8. "my duty to escape": Ogilvie, quoted in Dancocks, p. 134.

9. "will not be so lucky": transcripts entitled "Testimonies of Prisoners of War who escaped on March 25th from Stalag Luft III," courtesy Don Young.

10. "back to your camp": Ibid.

11. "morning you'll go": Ogilvie, quoted in Dancocks, p. 134.

12. "interested in that": Wilhelm Scharpwinkel, quoted in "Sagan," Royal Air Force Special Investigation Branch report, Report No: WCIU/LDC/1327(a), JAG Ref: MD/JAG/FS/22/2(2a) War Crimes Interrogation Unit, London, December 1946, p. 1.

13. "will happen to them": Richard Max Hänsel, quoting Scharpwinkel, in "Sagan," Royal Air Force Special Investigation Branch report, Report No: WCIU/LDC/1221, JAG Ref: MD/JAG/FS/22/2(2a) War Crimes Interrogation Unit, London, December 1946, p. 2.

14. "attempted to escape": Ibid., p. 2.

15. "attempt an escape": Ibid., p.3.

16. Porokoru Patapu: Allen Andrews, *Exemplary Justice* (Harrap & Co., London, 1976), p.49.

17. "around the countryside": Friedrich Kiowsky, quoted in Ibid., Report No: WCIU/LDC/1450 MFC/GEP, JAG Ref: MD/JAG/FS/22/2(2a), p. 2.

18. "back of [Kirby-Green's] head": Erich Zacharias, quoted in Ibid., Report No: WCIU/LDC/1133(a) MFC/LH, JAG Ref: MD/JAG/FS/22/2(2a), p. 2.

19. "made the attempt": Kiowsky quoted in Op cit.

20. "to shoot you": quoted in "Sagan," Royal Air Force Special Investigation Branch report, Report No: WCIU/LDC/1460, JAG Ref: MD/JAG/FS/22/2(2a), War Crimes Interrogation Unit, London, December 1946.

21. "number of sub-humans": Johannes Post, quoted in Allen Andrews, *Exemplary Justice*, p. 10.

22. "the SBO's words": Sweanor, *It's All Pensionable Time*, p. 163.

23. "they could re-escape": Keith Ogilvie, quoted in Dancocks, p. 135.

24. "to exemplary justice": Anthony Eden, in House of Commons Hansard, May 19 and June 23, 1944, quoted in Andrews, p. 211–13.

25. "a deliberate massacre": Sweanor, p. 166.

26. "families after the war": Sweanor, p. 167.

27. "we sang it and felt better": Pengelly, "X for Escape."
28. "one red and one black": Edy interview, 2012.
29. "ring drawing ever tighter": Pengelly, "X for Escape."
30. "they shoot each day": Sweanor, p. 172.
31. "the approaching Russians": Harsh, p. 177.
32. "The Handbook of Modern Irregular Warfare": poster quoted in Sweanor, p. 174.
33. "the United States of America": poster quoted in Sweanor, p. 175.
34. "one man volunteered": Sweanor, p. 173.
35. "leaving weapons behind": George Sweanor interview, 2011.

CHAPTER TEN: LONG ROAD HOME

1. "out into the woods": Crighton interview, 2012.
2. "quite an impressive service": Wally Floody, letter to his wife, Betty Floody, December 6, 1944, with permission.
3. "we're officers": Crighton interview, 2012.
4. "it will be soon now": John Weir, letter to Frances McCormack, December 5, 1944, with permission.
5. "this letter home to you": Ibid., June 28, 1944.
6. "the occasional circuit": Op cit., December 5, 1944.
7. "eyes betray his hunger": Robert Buckham, *Forced March to Freedom* (Canada's Wings Inc., 1984), p. 10.
8. "becomes a reality": Ibid., p. 12.
9. "everyone is sewing": John Colwell, unpublished diary, January 25, 1945, with permission.
10. The Wind and the Rain: Harris, p. 127.
11. "for us now,": conversation recorded in Edy, p. 166.
12. he was ready to go: Colwell.
13. Hut 104 caught fire: Durand, p. 328.
14. 2.5 million cigarettes: Ibid., p. 329.
15. "from inside the camp": Buckham, p. 18.
16. "a great instrument": Crighton interview, 2012.
17. "wire fences and Goon boxes": Colwell.
18. "many fine human beings": Sweanor, p. 180.
19. "and keep moving": Bartlett, quoted in Soward, p. 136.
20. same doomed Halifax bomber: Nurse, p. 31.
21. "appreciate their solicitude": Brown, p. 195.

22. his jacket with newspapers: Hehner, p. 99.

23. "beef we were wolfing": Harsh, p. 214.

24. "souvenir of my prison years": Brown, p. 196.

25. "I think the cost was worth it": Floody interview, 1970.

26. "truly Götterdämmerung": Harsh, p. 216.

27. over twenty miles of road: Stuart Gardner Hunt, Stuart Gardner, *Twice Surreal: A Memoir of World War II and Korea* (self published, 2005), p. 123 (author reports the column as 20 miles long).

28. safety in numbers and better identification: Durand, p. 330.

29. "wave your arms": John Weir, quoted in Crighton interview, 2012.

30. "on my straw bed": Crighton, p. 19.

31. "when I promptly fainted": Harris, p. 133.

32. "endurance was our only resource": Buckham, p. 37.

33. "I want my mother": officer quoted in Brown, p. 208.

34. "own personal miseries": Harsh, p. 219.

35. "loaded with bread": Brown, quoted in Harsh, p. 220.

36. "to the wind and rain": Buckham, p. 40.

37. water pail and stew pot: Colwell, diary, February 5–6, 1945, with permission.

38. "powdered milk was gone": Edy, p. 173.

39. "take first prize in density": Buckham, p. 43.

40. "directly over the camp": Edy, p. 177.

41. "where the armistice is": Colwell, diary, March 21, 1945, with permission.

42. "R.A.F. and P.O.W.": Ibid., April 9, 1945.

43. "sides of our boxcars": Sweanor, p. 195.

44. "see our Red Crosses": USAAF pilot, quoted in Sweanor, p. 196.

45. "Yanks for the ventilation": Sweanor, p. 196.

46. twenty-nine kriegies: Hugh Halliday, correspondence, November 2007, with permission.

47. May 8, 1945: Sweanor, footnote p. 134.

48. "it was the end": Colwell, diary, April 21, 1945, with permission.

49. "arrived at noon. FREE!": Colwell, diary, May 2, 1945, with permission.

50. "Santa Claus parade": Edy, p. 184.

51. "yelling and crying kriegies": Frank Sorensen letter to family, May 15, 1945, courtesy of Vicki Sorensen.

52. "It continued for minutes": Buckham, p. 92.

53. generally weakened state: Floody, journal February 8, 1945, quoted in Hehner, p. 104.

54. US Army had liberated: Harsh, p. 221.

55. "By God, we made it": Ibid., p. 222.

56. "we were totally contaminated": Pengelly, quoted in Dancocks, p. 207.

57. "most absurd scene": Ibid., p. 209.

58. best friend Pat Porter: Sweanor, p. 200.

59. "and rather childish": Edy, p. 186.

60. summer of 1943: Hawtin, unpublished diary prepared by Janet Hawtin, with permission.

61. "Sunday dinner until Thursday": Peter Larlee, quoted in "Son recalls his father's fight for freedom," *Vancouver Sun*, c. 1995.

62. "war had never happened": Marchildon, p. 152.

63. "their duty twice over": quoted in documentary *The Great Escape: The Canadian Story*, 2004, courtesy of producer Don Young.

CHAPTER ELEVEN: "A PROUD, SPECTACULAR DISTRACTION"

1. "freedom in a hurry": Philip Gray, *Ghosts of Targets Past: The Lives and Losses of a Lancaster Crew in 1944–45* (MPG Books, England, 2005), p. 166.

2. "I was thunderstruck": Ibid., p. 167.

3. "never be told in full": Ibid., p. 168.

4. "a little blurred": Brown, p. 262.

5. RAF Sunderland flying boat: Vern White, "The Sunderland Caper," RCAF 427 Squadron Association website, 2007.

6. "and this proves it": Kingsley Brown, quoted in correspondence from Ethel (Brown) Alle, Barrie, Ontario, March 19, 2013.

7. "an encyclopedia": Ibid.

8. "a birthday kiss": John Weir, letter to Frances McCormack, January 21, 1945, with permission.

9. "two in the morning": Frances Weir (née McCormack) interview, June 19, 2012, Toronto.

10. "love is blind": Ibid.

11. "did you bounce": McKim interview, 2011.

12. "air force like I was": Ibid.

13. "in fours and sixes": transcripts entitled "Testimonies of Prisoners of War who escaped on March 25th from Stalag Luft III," courtesy of Don Young.

14. "exemplary justice": Anthony Eden, House of Commons, Hansard, May 19 and June 23, 1944, quoted in Allen Andrews, *Exemplary Justice* (George H. Harrap, London, 1976), p. 211–13.

15. "courage and devotion to duty": Member of the British Empire citation, October 1946.

16. "see their faces": Wally Floody, quoted by Ron Lowman, "Airmen still see the faces of comrades slain by Nazis," *Toronto Star*, March 25, 1984.

17. "terrible nightmares last night": Hehner, p. 122.

18. "about the tunnels": Wally Floody, quoted in Arthur Moses, "Prisoners and guard from Stalag Luft III reminisce about war and the Great Escape," *Globe and Mail*, August 1970.

19. "degrading their manpower": George Sweanor interview, July 5–7, 2011.

20. "my alma mater": Ibid.

21. "in every culture": George Sweanor, "Bomber Command, 1939–1945," 971 Air Marshal Slemon Wing, RCAF Association Newsletter, November 2011.

22. "the war in jail": Nick Dumonceaux, quoted in email correspondence with his mother, Anne Dumonceaux, Port McNeill, BC, September 12, 2012.

23. "as we all grew up": Stephen Sorensen, interview, Howe Island, Ontario, August 13, 2011.

24. "why did you stay": Vicki Sorensen, interview, Howe Island, Ontario, August 13, 2011.

25. "when I was a teen": Glenn Sorensen, interview, Howe Island, Ontario, August 13, 2011.

26. "a visual perspective": Barbara Edy, correspondence from Calgary, Alberta, April 6, 2013.

27. "Germany's war effort": Ibid.

28. "organize to be successful": Pengelly, "X for Escape."

29. "bravery, spirit, and talent": Op cit.

30. "these wonderful machines": David Pengelly, interview, Dundas, Ontario, June 19, 2012.

31. "do you have a little more": Ibid.

32. "watched it all the time": Chris Pengelly, interview, Milford, Ontario, May 8, 2011.

# Photograph Credits

1. Whitley interior and barracks room, Tony Pengelly collection; four POWs, Imperial War Museums HU-1604; Roger Bushell, US Air Force Academy, McDermott Library, Stalag Luft III Collections.

2. East Compound, Imperial War Museums HU-21013; Sentry tower interior, Barry Davidson collection; North Compound, US Air Force Academy, McDermott Library, Stalag Luft III Collections.

3. Barry Davidson, Barry Davidson collection; Dick Bartlett, courtesy Anne Dumonceaux; Keith Ogilvie, courtesy Keith Ogilvie Jr. and Jean Ogilvie; Kingsley Brown, 1945 sketch by Lieut. John Lundquist, USAAF, courtesy Ethel Alle.

4. Sketches of digger, workshop, and trap entrance to tunnel, sketches by Ley Kenyon, Royal Air Force Museum, Hendon, UK.

5. German guard and prisoner assembly at Stalag Luft III, Imperial War Museums HU-21043; Biewer and Lindeiner, Imperial War Museums HU-21052; German "ferret" guards, Imperial War Museums HU-21190.

6. John Colwell POW card, courtesy Harold Johnstone; Frank Sorensen, courtesy Vicki Sorensen; Canadians at North Compound, Tony Pengelly collection.

7. Aerial intelligence photo of Stalag Luft III 1944, Don McKim collection.

8. George Sweanor and Joan Saunders, courtesy Sweanor family; Don Edy in desert, courtesy Barb Edy and Jane Hughes; George Harsh, courtesy W. W. Norton & Co., New York.

*page*

1. Theatre sketch by Ley Kenyon, courtesy Barry Davidson Jr.; Tony Pengelly in female role and theatre interior seating area, Tony Pengelly collection; Arthur Crighton conductor from *Wire Bound World* by H. P. Clark.

2. Baseball team "Clare's Cards," courtesy Art Hawtin; hockey game, Barry Davidson collection; boxing match, Imperial War Museums HU-21164.

3. Don McKim, courtesy Al McKim and Wendy Johnson; Albert Wallace, Albert Wallace collection; Red Cross parcel, *Wire Bound World* by H. P. Clark; wireless radio, photographer Harold Kious, US Air Force Academy, McDermott Library, Stalag Luft III Collections.

4. Sketches of February purge to Belaria and March escape from tunnel "Harry," sketches by Ley Kenyon, Royal Air Force Museum, Hendon, UK.

5. Guards show off trolley, Imperial War Museums HU-21219; guards and ventilating pump, Imperial War Museums HU-21215; guard with sand-dispersal sacks, Imperial War Museums.

6. Massey and Pieber, Imperial War Museums HU-1603; Arthur Nebe, courtesy documentarian/filmmaker Don Young.

7. *The Great Escape* 1962 movie publicity stills, Catherine (Floody) Heron collection.

8. POWs marching from Sagan, Poland, courtesy Marilyn Walton, US Air Force Academy, McDermott Library, Stalag Luft III Collections; British POWs sign, *Wire Bound World* by H. P. Clark; Ley Kenyon sketch, Frank Sorensen collection, courtesy Vicki Sorensen.

# Index